The

WINNER'S

BIBLE

REWIRE YOUR BRAIN
FOR PERMANENT CHANGE

**WINNER'S
INSTITUTE**

The WINNER'S BIBLE

REWIRE YOUR BRAIN
FOR PERMANENT CHANGE

DR KERRY SPACKMAN

ACKNOWLEDGMENTS

The most important thing I'd like to acknowledge up front is how enjoyable it has been working with the people I'm about to mention. They've all combined exceptional professionalism with excitement and fun. It's been a thoroughly enjoyable journey.

Marcel Boekhoorn believed in the *Winner's Bible* series of books from the very beginning and genuinely wanted to help make the world a better place. Marcel funded the entire Winner's Institute and even started his own publishing company to ensure we got the very best result and reached the most people. Without Marcel's vision, none of this would be possible.

Sir Jackie Stewart, because he was the person who first showed me what a true *winner* is. I learnt more lessons about life, business and winning from him than from anyone else. A true living legend.

My grandpa, Sir Trevor Henry, who as you will soon see, has a large role in this book because of his deep wisdom and insight.

The key members of the Winner's Institute Team, Gijs J. Rooijens and Sabine Tyrvainen, who have been with me every step of the way as my business partners and who have helped make this project better than I could have imagined.

My editor Martin Roach – or *Shakespeare* as I like to call him – because he helped me learn the tricky art of writing. A consummate professional who was always great fun to work with. And Phil Gambrill my typesetter, who turned my words into attractive flowing pages.

To each of you I owe more than words could ever say.

Kerry

CONTENTS

■ CHAPTER 1
WHY OTHER BOOKS DIDN'T CHANGE YOU – AND THIS ONE WILL 13
    The Gap Between Theory And Practice 14
    Your Designer Program And Your *Personal Winner's Bible* 15
    You Are Not A Computer 17
    The Kayak Analogy 19
    Nature Isn't Best 21
    A Comprehensive Tool Box 22
    Rules v Tools 23
    Balance And Counter-Rules 24
    Images And Allegories 24
    What Is A Winner? 25

■ CHAPTER 2 STARTING YOUR OWN *PERSONAL WINNER'S BIBLE* 26
    Getting Underway 27
    Creating Your Front Cover 28
    Your Goals And Images 29
    Visualization Techniques 29
    Construct Stories 31
    What Makes Good Images? 31
    Finding Your Images 33
    Images For Goals That Aren't Material Goals 33
    Heroes And Mentors 34
    Your Family And Friends 35
    Why Goals Are Important 36
    Winner's Goals Are Different 36
    Visualization Influences Your Whole Day 38
    Visualization Gives Your Brain An Upgrade 39
    This Is Not 'The Secret' 40
    How To Use Your *Winner's Bible* Every Day 40

■ CHAPTER 3
YOUR STRENGTHS, WEAKNESSES AND REPEATED MISTAKES 42
Assessing Your Resources 42
The Distorted Mirror 43
The Anonymous Online Independent Audit 44
The Lonely Woman 45
Choose Carefully 47
Self-Evaluation 48
Repeated Mistakes 48
Your Skills 48
Ali's Perfect Mirror 50
The Unexamined Life 52

■ CHAPTER 4 THE FOUR PILLARS 53
My Technique With Elite Athletes 53
The Interaction Of The Four Pillars 56
Using The Four Pillars 58

■ CHAPTER 5 AN INTRODUCTION TO YOUR PHYSIOLOGY PILLAR 59
Your Limbic System – Emotions 59
Your Frontal Lobes 63
Your Split Personality 65
Sports Modules 67
Inverting Goggles And Rewiring Your Brain 68

■ CHAPTER 6 INTRODUCTION TO YOUR HISTORY PILLAR 70
Accidental Hypnosis 70
Knots In Your Mind 74
Overcoming Your History 76
Your Early History Is Disproportionately Powerful 76
The Other Two Pillars 80

■ CHAPTER 7 EMOTIONAL TRANSFORMATION 82
The Dog And Bone 82
The Cocaine Girlfriend 85
A Quick Recap 88

■ CHAPTER 8 THE WHEEL OF LIFE 89
    Vibrations 89
    Your Unique Balance 89
    Dynamic Balance 90
    Your Central Axle 90
    The Wise Person 91
    Other People 92
    Action Items: Checking Your Wheel 93

■ CHAPTER 9 EMOTIONALLY SUPERCHARGED CDs 95
    The Tough Old Coach 95
    Finding His Intrinsic Satisfaction 96
    The CD Recording 98
    Having 'Sensitive Radar' 102
    The Coach's Second CD 103
    Options For Making Your Own CDs 105
    The Three Stages Of A 'Supercharging CD' 105
    Suzie Q And Why The CDs Work 106
    Bringing The Four Pillars Together – The Fijian Chief 108

■ CHAPTER 10 POMEGRANATES 113

■ CHAPTER 11 GONZALES' HAPPY DAY 115
    How *The Winner's Bible* Got Started 115
    Winning And Happiness 115
    The Blank Sheet of Paper .116
    Miss Universe 117
    Daily Devotions 118
    Being The Captain 118
    The Happy Section In Your *Winner's Bible* 119
    Kerry's Happy Section 120
    Savoring Happiness 121
    Custom-Made 'Happy CDs' 122

■ CHAPTER 12 AN UNSHAKEABLE BELIEF IN YOURSELF 123
    Arnold Schwarzenegger 123
    Adolf Hitler 126
    The Emotional Connection With Your Belief 127
    Loretta's Story 128
    Your *Winner's Bible* And Your Unshakeable Belief 131
    Step 1: Believing In Belief .132
    Step 2: Write Down Your Own Optimal Path 133
    Step 3: The Clear Plan 133
    Optimism v Unshakeable Belief 135
    Poems 135
    It's All In The State Of The Mind 136

■ CHAPTER 13 'CARPE DIEM' 137
    The Dead Poets Society 137
    Your Own 'Carpe Diem' Page .139
    If 140

■ CHAPTER 14 YOUR INTRINSIC DRIVERS 141
    Driven By Passion 142
    Accidental Careers 143
    The Surgeon And The Banker .144
    The Oracle Of Delphi 145
    The Difference Between Mike And John 147
    Uncovering Your Intrinsic Drivers 149
    Consolidating Your Drivers .153
    Putting Your Intrinsic Drivers To Work – Knowing Yourself 154
    Unexpected Benefits – Sports And Business 155
    Transcending Your Nature 156
    Ongoing Revision 156

■ CHAPTER 15 FINDING AND FEEDING YOUR PASSIONS 158
    Constructing Passions Out Of Thin Air 158
    Growing A Passion 160
    Passions Are Contagious 161
    Passions Change 161

■ CHAPTER 16 THE HIGHWAY OF LIFE .162

■ CHAPTER 17 OVERCOMING DISAPPOINTMENT AND DISASTER 165
    The Fugitive 165
    Vaccination Against Tragedy 166
    Lessons From Happy 100-year-olds 167
    Disappointment Is Inevitable 168
    Consequences Get More Serious As You Get Older 168
    The Four Stages of Disaster 169
    Stage 1: Comprehension: Your Brain's Model In Conflict 169
    Stage 2: Emotion – Your Initial Response 172
    Stage 3: Reason 175
    Stage 4: Progress .178
    Inoculation: Starving Your Tragedy Of Oxygen 178
    The Philosophy Of Disaster – Life Is Not Fair 179
    Becoming A Victim And Taking Things Personally 181
    The Parable Of The Sailor 182
    The Hidden Benefit Of Tragedy 182
    The Seasons Of Life 184

■ CHAPTER 18 'YOU.INC' 185
    Your Business Mind Map 186
    Your Life Mind Map .187
    Constructing Your Life Mind Map 188
    How To Use Your Mind Maps Each Morning 189

■ CHAPTER 19 PUTTING YOUR *WINNER'S BIBLE* INTO ACTION 190
    An Unsolicited E-mail 190
    How did you Score? .193

■ CHAPTER 20 THE END OF THE BEGINNING 195
    The Billionaire Team Owner 195
    Outer Success 197
    Porphyrius 197
    Inner Beauty 199
    A Very Large Man 199
    Lessons From A Funeral 200
    Ozymandias 201

■ CHAPTER 21
   PEOPLE ARE THE MOST IMPORTANT THINGS IN YOUR LIFE 203
        Choosing People 204

■ CHAPTER 22 GRANDPA'S LITTLE STORIES .206
        Little Stories Without Words 208
        Your Own 'Little Stories' .210
        Detective Work 211
        Show Me Your Friends 212
        The Mangere Matau 213

■ CHAPTER 23 WEATHER FORECASTING 216
        The Importance Of Knowing The Future 216
        Weather Forecast Competition 217
        Angela And The Parking Warden 217
        The Weather Can Change 218

■ CHAPTER 24 ALBERT'S COMPASS 220

■ CHAPTER 25 THE WORLD'S HAPPIEST PERSON 222
        The Guinness Book Of World Records 222
        What Is Happiness? 222
        Happy Genes 223
        No Brain – No Pain! 224
        Choosing The Harder Path 225
        The Worst Case Scenario 225
        Meeting The World's Happiest Person 226

■ CHAPTER 26 EFFICIENCY 228
        The Percent That Lasts 228
        Do Your Homework Well .229
        Resources: The Rule Of Two 230
        Reasons Why Not To Do The Project 230
        Special Documents On Your PC 230
        Organization 233
        Imposing A Hierarchy 233
        Re-organizing And Restructuring As You Grow 234

■ **CHAPTER 27 THE 'LIMBIC MASTER'** 235
    A Bit Of A Dilemma 235
    The 'Wise Person' and the 'Limbic Master' 236
    Moccasins And The Golden Rule .237
    Egocentricity, Selfishness And The Limbic Master 237
    Forgiveness And The Limbic Master 238
    Romance And The Limbic Master 238
    The Intellect And The Limbic Master 239
    The Lotus And The Limbic Master 240

■ **CHAPTER 28 GRANDPA'S COTTAGE** 241
    Central Otago 241
    My Father 243
    My Childhood 245
    Albert Town Holiday 247
    Grandpa's Cottage Revisited 250
    My 'Second Dad' 253

■ **FORTHCOMING *WINNER'S BIBLE* BOOKS** 256
    The Winner's Bible For Society 256
    The Winner's Bible of Philosophy .258
    The Winner's Bible For Elite Sport 261

CHAPTER 1
WHY OTHER BOOKS DIDN'T CHANGE YOU – AND THIS ONE WILL

You've probably read plenty of books which promised to turn you into a happy, rich and successful person. Books filled with brilliant ideas that were *finally* going to transform your life. As you turned each page you no doubt ticked off all your mistakes and rehearsed the clever phrases that were going to change your life. *This* time you were *definitely* going to improve.

However, if you're like most people, you'll find a year later not much has actually changed in your life. After all, how many people who read books about how to make millions of dollars actually become millionaires overnight? Sure, each new book teaches you fresh ideas and you *do* make incremental improvements in your life, but somehow it's never quite enough. You've improved a bit but you haven't been transformed into a Winner or a champion. And so you continue to muddle by until one day you see another book with a catchy title and the cycle is repeated again. Sound familiar?

Well, the good news is the problem isn't with you – it's with the books! Those books weren't good enough for the long list of motor racing champions, Olympic champions, world champions and business people I've coached and so it's not surprising they're not enough for you either. Those elite athletes and business people had also tried psychologists, psychotherapists and read hundreds of self-help and psychology books without any real benefit. They didn't want any more empty theory. What they desperately needed was something that actually worked in the heat of competition *and* in their daily lives. Something that not only helped them become better performers, but more importantly, helped them to become better people and to enjoy their life more. This book grew out of that need.

I didn't wake up with a clever idea and set out to write *The Winner's Bible.*™ I only started writing it because my clients kept telling me they wanted a single book which contained ALL the Tools they'd ever need in one place. They wanted practical, worked examples to use in their lives rather than just a book full of good ideas. They wanted techniques that had been tested and proven to work in the real world. The end result has been so successful that one racing driver proudly told me he'd used his *Winner's Bible* every single day for a whole year. Even though he had a shelf full of 'self-improvement' books by his bed, the only book he reached for each morning was his *Winner's Bible.*

THE GAP BETWEEN THEORY AND PRACTICE

To see why other books failed to change your life let's imagine someone has written a book with the catchy title: *The 7 Steps To Beating Federer And Winning Wimbledon.*

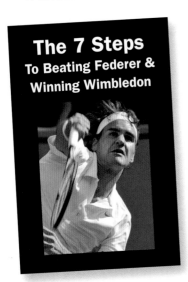

The first problem with a title like this is the inevitable gap between the ideas in the book and your ability to put those ideas into practice. For example, suppose Rule 1 says:

'Always hit the ball where Federer can't reach it.'

This is certainly a great rule and you'd definitely win Wimbledon if you were able to do that. Unfortunately knowing *what* to do and being *able* to do it are two entirely different things. The chances are, if you played Federer you wouldn't even get close to his serve, let alone be able to place your own return out of his reach. And that's the problem!

Most books tell you *what* you should do but not *how* you can acquire the mental and emotional Skills necessary to make it all happen in your daily life. For example, they might tell you to 'be positive' and list all the benefits of being positive. But what are the step-by-step actions that will actually give you a positive approach to life even after you have been dealt a bad hand?

Going back to our tennis analogy, if you want to place the ball where Federer can't reach it you need to have a cracking return. And this means a lot of work. Your coach will video your swing and analyze it in great detail. He'll tell you how to alter your stance, your grip and your action. Then you'll have to practice his suggestions thousands of times until they become automatic. You'll need to master a huge amount of *detail* before you can hit the ball out of Federer's reach. This mastery is only achieved by combining the correct techniques and rules with plenty of discipline and effort. And the same is true in your life. You're going to have to do a lot more than just wake up each day and recite seven phrases as if they are some magic mantras that will transform your life. If you think otherwise, then you might as well put this book down now.

Fortunately, *The Winner's Bible*™ contains step-by-step instructions rather than just Goals that are forever out of your reach. Each instruction has practical things for you to do. These instructions have been proven in the cut and thrust of international competition and in everyday life. They're only in this book because they work. You will find you take personal responsibility for each item and *you will make them happen*.

YOUR DESIGNER PROGRAM AND YOUR *PERSONAL WINNER'S BIBLE*

The second problem is that no matter how good the rules are, you're never going to win Wimbledon unless you have the right physical attributes. No 65-year-old has ever won Wimbledon and neither has anyone who was only five-feet-tall ever won the gold medal in the Olympic high-jump. Put simply, any manual which is going to turn you into a Winner must take into account the cold hard facts of who you are.

It is absolutely vital you understand at the outset how *unique* you are.

Let's start with your brain. Because your brain is wired differently to everyone else's, you literally see and smell the world in your own unique way. No two people see and smell a rose in exactly the same way because how your brain processes information from your eyes and nose is different to every other person. Similarly, your genes affect how food tastes which explains why I can't stand beetroot but my friend loves it. Even which foods are good for us and which foods are bad for us is unique to each person. An extreme example would be bananas – they are a great source of potassium for some people, but are so toxic to others that they will die if they eat a single mouthful. On top of all this there are also differences in your History, experiences, emotions, dreams, fears and thoughts.

You are so much more different to anyone else than you think. And so any program worth following ought to be custom-designed with *your* unique factors in mind. Winning is not a 'one size fits all' business. Athletes have programs that are tailored to their unique make-up and so it is not surprising that in the much more complex game of life you'll need a personally tailored program too. Just because a famous and successful person used a particular mental technique to help them increase their performance doesn't necessarily mean the same technique will work for you.

The Winner's Bible™ will help you identify your own unique Strengths and Weaknesses. You will see yourself more clearly than you have ever seen yourself before. Armed with this information you will then be shown how to construct your own twenty-page *Personal Winner's Bible*. This will be a small plastic folder which contains pictures and bullet points that are tailored specifically to have maximum mental and emotional impact just for you. It will be quick and easy to construct.

You'll then end up with two books:

The Winner's Bible™
This is the book you are reading now. It is a resource and an instruction book. It will help you construct your own *Personal Winner's Bible*.

Your Own *Personal Winner's Bible*
This is the small folder you will construct yourself. It will have your name and photo on the front cover. You will use your *Personal Winner's Bible* EVERY DAY. Because it has a maximum of twenty pages of pictures and bullet points, you'll

be able to scan through it in a few minutes. But those pages will have more effect on you than any other book because they are tailored specifically for you. The images will connect directly with your emotions in a way words alone never will. Each day you will be charged up and refocused.

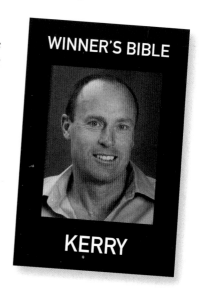

If you use your *Personal Winner's Bible* every day you will find that it actually works. You'll not only know exactly what to do but you'll also gain the emotional strength to do it. You will grow into a better, happier and more powerful person. As this happens, you'll remove pages from your *Personal Winner's Bible* that are no longer needed because you've conquered your old problems. You'll replace those pages with new ones that continue to challenge the 'new and improved' person you've become. That's why you'll use a folder with clear plastic pockets to construct your *Personal Winner's Bible*. It will allow you to quickly slip pages in and out as they are needed. In this way your *Personal Winner's Bible* will become a *living* and *dynamic* manual. It will change and grow as you do. It will help you create and live your own 'designer life'. A life personally tailored to give you power, peace and satisfaction.

Your *Personal Winner's Bible* will be the most powerful book you'll ever hold in your hands!

YOU ARE NOT A COMPUTER

The next problem with traditional self-help books is that they usually treat you as if you are some sort of computer that can be instantly re-programmed. They give you the impression that your life will be wonderful if you'd just run the 'correct thoughts' through your brain. But there are three major reasons why you're not a computer and why this approach is doomed to fail:

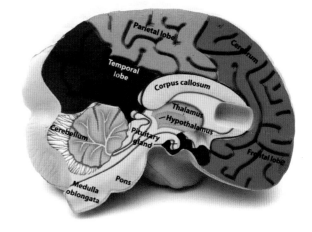

1. Your brain doesn't have one big centralised processor which controls everything like your PC does. Instead your brain is made up of many independent modules – or 'mini brains' – all doing their own independent things.
2. Many of these modules don't even run on logic or words. So trying to reprogram those modules with words or 'clever phrases' is never going to work if they are causing you problems.
3. Some of your modules are hidden deep in your unconscious and so you don't normally have access to them. This means you can't re-program them using normal Tools. You'll need the special Tools I've developed over the years to help my elite athletes.

Let me explain these three crucial points in a little more detail because understanding them is vital if you are going to permanently change your life.

1. Independent Modules

You may know that your brain has a separate self-contained module whose primary function is to decode sound and understand speech. There is another independent module for processing all the information coming from your skin and yet other modules for working out the position of your limbs and others for vision. These modules all operate independently, at their own speed and in their own time. Because these modules are independent, it explains why a person who suffers a stroke may lose the ability to speak while the rest of their life is relatively unchanged. It's why another person can get Parkinson's disease and have trouble co-ordinating their muscles while their logic and intellect is totally unaffected. The individual modules usually aren't too affected by the other modules.

Now here's the key point: there are many independent modules responsible for controlling different aspects of your 'personality'. For example, one structure is responsible for 'executive planning' and working out the consequences of your future actions while an entirely separate region in your brain is responsible for your emotions and what you *feel*. There is *no* one central place which co-ordinates or controls all these modules to produce your 'personality'. They all just chatter back and forward among themselves and usually manage to come to some sort of general agreement as to what is going on in the world and what you ought to do next. They add together to produce your 'behavior' and your 'personality'. How they do this changes from time to time. Sometimes one module is more 'bossy' and gets it 'way' while at other times another module wins out. It's a very messy business and not surprisingly causes many problems – particularly when the modules give conflicting directions as to what *you* should do.

2. Modules Don't Always Run On Logic Or Words

You can tell your brain doesn't run entirely on words or logic because you don't have to *learn* how to be hungry and you don't have to run 'hungry words' through your brain in order to feel starving – particularly if you haven't eaten for a long time. You just naturally 'feel' hungry because you were born with brain circuits for hunger already wired up and ready to go. Just as well, otherwise you'd have starved to death in the first few days of your life. In addition to brain circuits which are concerned with your physical well-being – like the hunger ones we've just talked about – you were also born with millions of emotional circuits which were primed and ready to control your behaviour without you ever being consciously aware of what they were up to. While these pre-wired emotional circuits were ideal for helping primitive man survive in the jungle, they are often poorly suited for making us happy and successful in modern society – as you'll soon see. It's no wonder life is a struggle at times.

3. Hidden Unconscious Modules

But even that's not the end of your problems. Much of what these modules do and why they do it is hidden from you – the owner of your brain! In many cases the secret agendas of these modules explains why you frequently do the wrong things even when you 'know' exactly what you should do. Sometimes even being highly motivated and wanting to do the right thing still isn't enough. Your unconscious modules are somehow still controlling your behavior against your best wishes. Unless you know how to reprogram these hidden modules, you'll be doomed to failure, despite having all the best thoughts and ideas in the world.

THE KAYAK ANALOGY

One way I explain the influence of our hidden modules to my athletes is to tell them about a kayak race I had against Steve Ferguson. Steve is a champion kayaker and so when I challenged him to a race over 100m he was supremely confident he'd beat me by a huge margin. As we lined up in our lanes it looked like a complete mismatch. Steve was all bulging muscles and a big smile while I was having trouble just keeping my racing kayak balanced. But when the gun sounded everything changed and the smile was wiped off his face. You see, unbeknown to Steve, I'd modified the rudder underneath his kayak so it was jammed permanently to the right. As soon as Steve took a couple of powerful strokes his kayak began to swerve violently in the wrong direction. There was much yelling and splashing of his paddles as he struggled vainly to control his kayak and get it pointed in the right direction. Meanwhile, I just glided on smoothly towards the finish line using only modest strokes.

The point of this story is that we can think of our 'paddles' as our 'conscious logical thoughts'. They're above the water, they're visible and we put a huge amount of effort into them. While all this conscious effort is going on, our unconscious emotions are operating *below the surface* like a hidden rudder — exerting a huge influence on our behavior without us even realizing it.

If our mental 'paddles' and our mental 'rudders' aren't aligned in the same direction then no amount of effort and 'splashing' is going to allow us to achieve our Goals. No amount of 'trying harder' and resolving once again to change our direction is going to work.

This book will provide you with specific Tools and instructions which will allow you to go 'below the surface' and align your emotional rudders. When you do this you'll be able to break the cycle of temporary change and suddenly progress towards your Goals far more easily than all the will-power in the world would ever allow.

NATURE ISN'T BEST

I want you to look at the image of the checkerboard and decide how much darker the square with the letter A on it is compared to the square with the letter B. The best way to think about this is to try to guess how much more ink would have been used to shade the A square than was used to shade the B square. If you think twice as much ink was used then you would say the A is twice as dark as the B. If you think it has 30% more ink then you would say it is 30% darker. Have a go.

Well it's hard to believe, but the two squares are exactly the same! If you don't believe me, get a piece of paper and place it on top of the picture to cover it up. Now punch two small holes in the paper so you can only see the A and the B squares and nothing else. You may be surprised at what you see.

This simple demonstration shows that your brain can give you a faulty answer without you even realizing it. Your common sense and intuition aren't always correct. And so what you need is a book like *The Winner's Bible*™ based on sound neuroscience* to help you rise above your normal human state. So you can go from being a normal 'man' to being a 'superman'. From being a 'woman' to being a 'superwoman'. Achieving this requires each module in your brain to be analyzed and tuned with Mental Tools specifically suited to each of your modules. After all, you don't use a screwdriver to tighten a bolt and likewise you don't use a spanner to tighten a screw. In the same way Mental Tools designed to adjust your logical circuits aren't going to be suitable for tuning your emotional circuits and vice versa.

Rising above your normal, natural abilities and becoming super-natural is a recurring theme in this book. One based on sound science that is going to be presented to you in an easily understood form and illustrated with practical examples you can use every day. You see, nature isn't best. It's 'natural' to have tooth decay. But losing all your teeth isn't the best outcome you can have. That's why it's important to rise above your 'nature' and not only brush your teeth but to also tune up your brain.

A COMPREHENSIVE TOOL BOX

Another problem with self-help books is they usually contain only a small number of limited ideas which are padded out and endlessly repeated. This makes good marketing sense because you read the title and think, *Wow, I only need to learn six quick little keys and I'm going to be a happy, smart, wealthy person*. But do you really think life is that simple?

Think for a moment of all those things you need to do to win Wimbledon. First of all there is your fitness and nutrition to be taken care of. Just those two topics alone are going to fill a book. Then there is the issue of working out which strategy you need to use on each player. Which opponents are vulnerable to a serve and volley game? Who has trouble with the drop shot? The more you

*Neuroscience is the scientific study of the how the brain's physiology produces your behavior. It includes neuroanatomy, neurochemistry and neurobiology.

know about tennis the more you realize how complex the game is and why you can't do it all on your own. That's why champions have highly skilled and highly paid coaches.

Now think how much more complex life is than tennis. Is it likely that six simple ideas are going to transform you and prepare you for *everything* life is going to throw at you? If it was that easy those ideas would have been worked out thousands of years ago and we'd probably get them tattooed on us at birth.

Life is an extremely complex process which is why it is so exciting and rich. This richness means you need a comprehensive range of Skills and Tools in your mental 'Tool Box'.

RULES v TOOLS

It's important that I explain early on in this book the difference between 'Rules' and 'Tools'. An example of a rule might be, 'Don't eat chocolate bars for dinner'. That's a good rule if you're trying to lose weight. It's a rule based on logic and you can only obey it by using will-power and self-control. But rules hardly ever work on their own because they're just too much hard work and they go against your nature. After all, that's why you need a rule in the first place. It's telling you to do something you don't *naturally* want to. What you *really* need are Tools that change your natural desires so you don't even want to eat that chocolate bar for dinner in the first place. That's the sort of Tool that's going to produce a permanent change in your life. Because when you've used it you'll no longer fight against yourself. To use our kayak analogy – 'your rudders' will be aligned – and as a result you'll achieve change almost effortlessly. In fact, that's a common theme I hear over and over again from my clients. They can't believe just how easy it was to finally make a permanent change after all those rollercoaster years of struggle and battle.

Let's think a bit more about this idea of Mental Tools by considering what happens when you learn to use a chisel or a scalpel. You don't master those sorts of Tools immediately but rather you become more skillful with them the more you use them. It's the same with Mental Tools. The more you use them the more powerful they will become. This is the opposite of what happens with rules. You can learn a rule like 'Don't eat chocolate bars for dinner' in a heartbeat. But learning a rule like that doesn't actually help you very much does it? After all, how many people are overweight because they didn't *know* that eating burgers and fries every day was going to make them fat?

Because *The Winner's Bible™* contains many ideas and Tools you'll find you come back to it again and again. You'll do this because it often takes time and experiences in life in order for you to fully absorb some of the lessons in its pages. You may think you've mastered a Tool the first time you use it, but more than likely you'll find some of the sentences in this book take on a deeper significance as you become more familiar with the Tools they describe (see Chapter 10, 'Pomegranates'). Just as no one sits down to read each page of the *Koran* or *Holy Bible* from cover to cover, so too you won't read *The Winner's Bible™* that way either. You'll find you revisit various sections as you progress in your development. You'll also find Tools from one section combine and add to Tools from other sections in ways you hadn't expected. Maybe a lesson from sport helps you in your daily life or maybe understanding how your brain works helps you in your sporting life. Gradually the concepts in *The Winner's Bible™* will start to gel so that the book becomes much more valuable than the simple sum of adding all the individual stories or lessons together.

BALANCE AND COUNTER-RULES

Talking of rules, when it comes to life there is almost always a *counter-rule* for every rule. Most books don't tell you about these counter-rules because they want to give you a simple formula which is easy to follow. But life is never that straightforward. For example, you've probably read about the importance of 'never giving up' – that winning is all about perseverance and determination. In many cases that advice *is* correct. Winners *are* much more strong-minded and *do* fight with gritty determination long after other people have given up. But there is also no point in working your butt off making sales calls, running advertisements and investing all your savings to sell gramophone needles if someone else has invented the CD. In this case stopping and changing direction is absolutely the right thing to do. The key with all rules is in knowing when to use them and how to find the right balance between them. When do you dig it in a little deeper and work harder and when do you stop and change direction? *The Winner's Bible™* not only gives you all the different rules but it also helps you choose which ones to use and when to use them.

IMAGES AND ALLEGORIES

The Winner's Bible™ illustrates each concept or idea with stories and vivid images so that they are easily remembered and become burnt on your mind. It's a bit like when you wake up after a dream. If the dream is powerful and real enough it can sometimes influence how you feel for the rest of your day. This feeling can be either positive or negative depending on the type of dream you've had.

The images and stories in this book will be much more powerful than any dream because they will influence you for the rest of your life.

WHAT IS A WINNER?

If we're going to talk about becoming a Winner then we need to briefly explain what a true Winner is. In this book a Winner isn't just someone who has a shelf crammed with trophies. Mike Tyson won $500 million and was the Undisputed Heavyweight Champion of the World, but he wasn't a 'Winner'. His personal life was a total mess and he ended up in jail and finished his boxing days almost penniless. Likewise, many Hollywood movie stars lead exciting public lives but privately they are wracked by emptiness and a lack of purpose. People like this may be successful but they aren't 'Winners'.

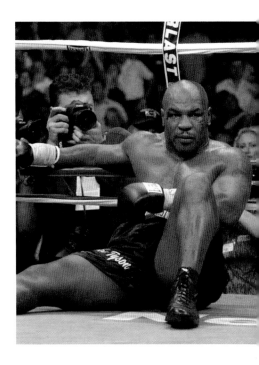

Winners learn how to experience life in Technicolor. Dull, boring shades of grey are replaced by vivid colors. Life is no longer flat and two-dimensional. It suddenly pops out into three or even four dimensions. It becomes more *real* than real. Experiencing life like this is a Skill that has to be learned. It is not acquired by clever phrases or 'being positive' – but by *understanding* and genuinely seeing the world through smarter, wiser eyes.

True Winners are multi-dimensional people who lead full and varied lives both professionally and personally. They not only get the most out of every day but they also enrich everyone who comes into contact with them. They have a genuine inner peace and a satisfaction that provides more happiness and pleasure than any amount of trophies, fame or money.

To truly live is SO startling it leaves little time for anything else.
American poet, Emily Dickinson

So let's get started …

YOU'VE GOT WORK TO DO!

CHAPTER 2
STARTING YOUR OWN *PERSONAL* WINNER'S BIBLE

You don't go into a gym and get the instructor to show you how to do a bench press and then say to yourself, 'Great, now I've learned how to do the bench press I'm instantly going to get a chest like Arnold Schwarzenegger'. You know you've got to put that knowledge into practice and train hard. It's the same with your life. You're not going to revolutionize your life and your brain just by reading a few things with your logical mind and saying to yourself, 'Ah yes, that's right, now I know what to do.' On the contrary, in order to change your life you need to put that knowledge into practice. And the *way* you put that knowledge into practice is just as important as the knowledge itself. That's why this book has step-by-step instructions you need to follow – in the correct order.

Maybe you're already a well developed and successful person and so doing this goes against your pride. Maybe you 'mentally' know many of the components of this book. That's okay. You're in good company. Some of the most successful people in the world – whether athletes or business executives – were surprised to find they were able to take their lives up another gear by following this program. So if it's good enough for people who were already incredibly successful, then maybe it's good enough for you.

This program is progressive with each step building on the previous one. Some of the early steps may seem trivial but they form the crucial foundation for more advanced knowledge later on. So don't skip any steps.

GETTING UNDERWAY

The first thing you are going to do is start making your own *Personal Winner's Bible*. This will be a book that no one else apart from you ever sees. It will probably only have around fifteen to twenty pages in it, but as I mentioned earlier these will be the most powerful pages you'll ever hold in your hands. You'll flick through them each day and it will dramatically change your life. Your *Personal Winner's Bible* is going to contain at least seven different sections and what you put in each of these sections will be completely unique to you. At first you won't really know what to put into your *Personal Winner's Bible,* but as you read through the chapters of this book you'll discover things about yourself you didn't know. It will be an exciting journey of discovery which rapidly gains in pace. Your *Personal Winner's Bible* is only one of the Tools you'll develop – but it is a key part of your foundation.

So let's start by getting your *Personal Winner's Bible* up and going.

You'll make your *Personal Winner's Bible* out of a small presentation folder which is available from most bookstores. It contains twenty transparent pockets which can hold forty pages. That's more than enough for you to be working on at any time.

There are four advantages of using this folder with A5-size transparent pockets. The first is that you can update any page and quickly replace it. This is important because part of being a Winner is constantly improving yourself. As you grow and improve you'll find that what was important for you yesterday is no longer important for you today. Your *Personal Winner's Bible* will be an evolving and organic book that reflects your growth and changes with you.

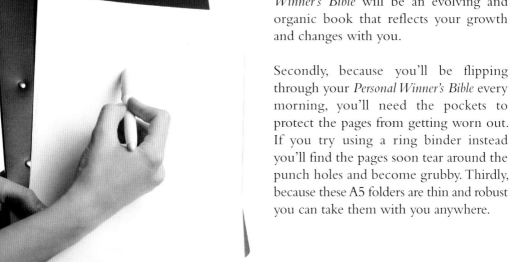

Secondly, because you'll be flipping through your *Personal Winner's Bible* every morning, you'll need the pockets to protect the pages from getting worn out. If you try using a ring binder instead you'll find the pages soon tear around the punch holes and become grubby. Thirdly, because these A5 folders are thin and robust you can take them with you anywhere.

The fourth advantage is the most important of all. Because the presentation folder's pages are small you'll only be able to fit one concept on any page. This is perfect because you aren't supposed to read your entire *Personal Winner's Bible* every day. Instead, what you'll do is flick through the pages until your eyes naturally settle on the most important concept for that particular day.

CREATING YOUR FRONT COVER

Making your *Personal Winner's Bible* begins by creating the front cover. Here's the cover for my own *Winner's Bible*. Obviously my photo and name won't convey any power to you but you'll be surprised how powerful the cover becomes when it has *your* name, *your* own photo and the words *Winner's Bible* on it.

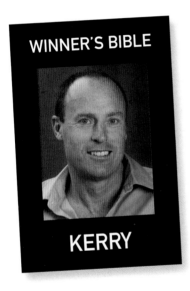

There are two ways to create your *Personal Winner's Bible*:

• Using a computer to create a document
• Manually with pen/paper/scissors

Doing everything on your computer means you can easily update the pages. If you log onto www.winnersbible.com you'll be able to download a blank *Winner's Bible* template with all the sections ready for you to fill in.

Alternatively, you can use a pen or a felt tip to write on a blank sheet of A5 paper and then glue a photo of yourself on the front page.

The photo on the front cover should only have you in it and no one else. Don't use a photo that has your friends in the shot or something else going on in the background. This is *your Personal Winner's Bible* and so the front cover needs to capture the essence of you. There is plenty of space on other pages for your friends and family. Choose your photo carefully. Maybe it's a portrait that shows your best feature. If you're proud of your happy, smiley face, sparkling eyes and brilliant smile, then that's the sort of photo you should use. One that conveys your personality and the things you like about yourself. If you're an athlete then maybe you want a close-up action shot of you at an event you were particularly happy with. Maybe you're on the Winners' podium or perhaps it could be a photo of you at full stretch in the middle of a training event. A photo that shows all your power and speed. It's your choice. But make sure there is no one and nothing else in the photo to distract your thoughts away from the essence of you.

YOUR GOALS AND IMAGES

Your *Personal Winner's Bible* will ultimately contain at least seven major sections which will cover all aspects of your life. The first section will contain your Goals because they are what give you energy and purpose in life. To some extent, your Goals even define who you are. Of course almost everyone has written a list of their personal Goals at some stage in their life. That's a good thing to do but it isn't nearly enough. The problem with lists is they just don't get deep enough inside your soul to arouse your emotions. To change your life you need to *feel* your Goals. You need to *taste* and *smell* them. Words are just too clumsy for that. What you need are powerful images you can immerse yourself in and a very special way of bringing them to life.

VISUALIZATION TECHNIQUES

For example, suppose one of your Goals is to own a boat. Well, you could just write down the sentence, 'Own a boat' as one item in a long list of Goals. Or you could find pictures of the boat you really want to own and put those in your *Personal Winner's Bible*.

But how do you use these images to make your Goals come alive and fire up the circuits in your brain that are going to change your life? One of the many techniques you're going to learn is called *fixated visualization*. With this technique you'll stare *very* intently at the image without taking your eyes off it for about two minutes. As you do, your eyes will naturally move around to take in different aspects of the picture. Of course you can blink as often as you need to.

If you do this, and if sailing is your Passion, you'll find it changes from just being a picture into a genuine experience with emotional power. You might first stare intently at the cockpit and 'see' yourself standing at the helm commanding the yacht. You may even feel the wheel in your hands as you guide the yacht over the waves. Even though you aren't actually in the image you will put yourself there while you fixate. Then a moment later your eyes might move ever so slightly to another part of the cockpit where you imagine a good friend sitting with a cup of coffee. You hear their laughter and smell the coffee over the salty sea air. A few moments later your eyes might take in the sails. You feel the wind gently filling them while the sun shines on your face.

That's the sort of Goal you need to have if you want to get off your butt and achieve something. A Goal that is *alive*, vibrant and tangible. One you can taste, feel and smell. All your senses have become involved with the visualization process. Smells, sounds, touches, sights, feelings, tastes. And the more you practice visualization the more naturally this will happen. You won't have to go looking for the sensations; your subconscious will unleash them all on its own.

So take a few moments and try immersing yourself into the picture of the yacht and see if you can become part of the scene. If boats aren't your thing then go and find an image that will work for you. Maybe it's owning and riding a horse. Maybe it's a fabulous holiday somewhere. Whatever it is, find some pictures of the Goals you'd like to achieve and then see if you can put yourself inside the pictures and make them come alive. Try it now.

CONSTRUCT STORIES

One way you can help your subconscious produce all these sensations is to make up small stories before you start your visualization. This way you don't just see a yacht, you imagine a great day's sailing out with your friends. Even though making up stories like this is a conscious process, you'll find these thoughts naturally slide down into your subconscious where they'll be automatically available during visualization to help you produce vivid scenes.

Another key to getting the most out of your images is that you must really *feel* your Goals on an emotional level. You must totally connect with them so that they aren't just bland mental images. Each image needs to become an emotional experience. There is a sound scientific reason for this which is related to how your brain works. Right now you don't need to understand these brain processes because you are just getting started on your *Winner's Bible*. But we'll come back to this later on because it will help you produce even more powerful and more motivating visualization experiences.

With a bit of luck you're already able to get some sort of energy out of your pictures. When you use images like this each morning it won't cost you any time! Instead, they'll actually add hours of productivity and enjoyment to your day because you'll be more powerful. You'll actually end up with more time because you get things done more quickly rather than fluffing around ineffectively wasting your day.

Hopefully you can now see why your 'lists' from the past didn't really work. Lists are too tame and weak compared to vibrant images.

WHAT MAKES GOOD IMAGES?

Not all pictures work equally well in making your Goals come alive. As you select your images make sure they:

• Tell a story that you can be involved in
• Are of excellent photographic quality

For example, going back to the image of the boat, notice I have chosen one with a man sailing the yacht across the ocean rather than a static image of a boat moored at a dock. This is important because each morning when you use your own *Personal Winner's Bible* you'll actively visualize what it would be like to be part of your dream. So choose images that not only convey the Goal but also how your life will be and what you'll be doing when you have achieved that Goal.

And don't limit yourself to just one image for each Goal. Your yacht is not just an object – it allows you to *do* things like sail to an island and have a BBQ on the beach. So you can add images of people enjoying a BBQ or lying on the sand in the sun. Or maybe your yacht provides you with a quiet place to get away from it all. A place to read a book at the end of a pleasant day's sailing. In that case an image of the cabin is just what you need.

The other point about your images is that they should be of a high quality. Pictures like that have more detail and richness to stimulate your senses. Because they are closer to reality they allow you to immerse yourself more fully in the scene. They become more alive and real.

You can cut images out of magazines or you can use an internet search engine like Google Image Search to help you. The advantage of magazines is that most images are of a high quality and have been taken by professional photographers. The difficulty with using magazines is finding exactly the right images. It's also slightly messier as you'll have to cut the pictures out and glue them onto your A5 pages.

The internet has a huge range of photos which you can quickly sort through by using the right combination of 'search words' but you need to make sure the image quality is good enough. If you print your own photos out make sure you use quality paper and have a good printer.

FINDING YOUR IMAGES

So spend a few moments now and write down a list of Goals. This will be your 'shopping list' for the images you need to find. Like all shopping lists, you'll throw it away when you have all the images you need.

Don't worry at this stage if your list of Goals is incomplete or you're not really sure what they are. Finding your *authentic* Goals and understanding how to achieve them is a key part of this book. As you continue reading you'll learn more about yourself and your Goals will probably change and expand. For the time being, just get your folder started so you can learn how to use it each morning.

One thing you need to be careful of at the start is to choose images that are realistic for where your life is right now. Don't begin by putting an image of a $100 million, 200-foot super-yacht in your folder. A boat like that isn't a Goal – it's a premature and potentially misleading fantasy! You are better off starting with a 55-foot yacht because your images can be updated step-by-step until you finally have the $100 million super-yacht. If you want to, you can put the image of your super-yacht near the end of your *Personal Winner's Bible* so you don't lose sight of your long-term Goal. But on a day-to-day basis the first section of your *Personal Winner's Bible* must contain your immediate Goals. It's important to understand that change is a step-by-step process.

It's also worth bearing in mind that chasing an impossible fantasy is incredibly destructive. So find Goals that are a genuine challenge and deeply satisfying, but at the same time realistically achievable if you perform 200% better than you do now.

IMAGES FOR GOALS THAT AREN'T MATERIAL GOALS

You probably found it reasonably easy to find some excellent images for all the material things you'd like in life. But we all know that material possessions, a successful career, fame or fortune don't necessarily make you happy. Of course, it *is* worthwhile getting all those things and a $3 million house is usually much nicer to live in than a $300,000 house. They are great Goals to have and this book will help you to get them. But real peace, contentment and happiness comes from having genuine 'meaning' in your life, great relationships and realizing the full potential of your natural abilities – what I like to call your 'Optimal Future'. We're reminded of this whenever we see a tabloid or magazine with a report about another celebrity whose life has come unstuck despite all their wealth and fame.

> Many people have Goals that don't actually make their lives any happier. What is tragic is that they spend all their lives chasing them.

Therefore your most important Goals won't be material things like a new house or car. Instead they will be things like:
• Finding and then fulfilling the full potential of your natural abilities
• Overcoming your Weaknesses and the things that hold you back
• Breaking free from your History and creating your own Designer Life
• Increasing your personal power
• Improving your relationships
• Overcoming setbacks

So how do you find vibrant images for these non-material Goals? After all, it's easy to find a picture of a boat but where do you find an image that's going to motivate you to 'never give up and remain positive'? And what sort of image is going to help you 'act with dignity and not get emotional' in a business meeting? These are deep issues and later sections in this book will explain a variety of Tools you can use to solve them. But here's one technique that fits right into your *Personal Bible* that is quite useful.

HEROES AND MENTORS

Find some images of mentors that personify what you are trying to achieve and put those in your *Personal Winner's Bible*. For example, if 'never giving in' and 'acting with dignity' are two of your Goals, then maybe an image of Nelson Mandela would be an excellent place to start.

Here is a man who spent 27 years in jail, most of it in solitary confinement. Think how hard it must have been for him to not have lost faith in his dream, when day after day after day passed and still nothing appeared to have changed outside. Apartheid still carried on, blacks were still being killed. Alone in his empty cell with little outside contact it must have seemed like his life was wasting away – for absolutely nothing. After three years most people would have given up. After ten years, even the strongest person would start to crack when they realized the most powerful years of their life were ebbing away. Yet Mandela held his head high for an astonishing 27 years. And when he was finally released, he didn't seek revenge but instead demonstrated remarkable forgiveness which helped heal an entire nation. You can't help but be inspired by a person like that.

But maybe a sporting hero is better for you. If so, you might want to choose someone like Lance Armstrong. After nearly dying of testicular cancer and following years of chemotherapy, radiotherapy and surgery he went on to win a record seven Tours de France. That's a pretty special result.

Only you know which images will work for you.

YOUR FAMILY AND FRIENDS

While you are in the process of putting in images of your heroes and mentors, don't forget pictures of your family and friends. It is all too easy to be busy on your life's mission and forget to spend enough time and mental energy on the people who really make your life worth living. Seeing pictures of your family and friends as you flick through your *Winner's Bible* may remind you to make that little phone call, or go out of your way to do that little extra thing that makes *their* day better. After all, a true Winner isn't just concerned about themselves. They're genuinely interested in everyone they come into close contact with. Another advantage of having photos of your family and friends in your *Winner's Bible* is that they'll always be with you when you're away traveling.

WHY GOALS ARE IMPORTANT

You may be asking yourself why you should go to all this effort of finding images for your Goals and then using them each morning. To see why this is so important imagine you're woken up at 6 o'clock every morning and dragged out of bed by a really bossy person. He then shouts at you for the next two hours and forces you to lift and move heavy lumps of iron around until you finally collapse from exhaustion. It wouldn't take too many weeks before you'd begin to dread the sound of his footsteps approaching your bedroom door at 6 o'clock each morning. It would be even more soul destroying if, after all his shouting, the heavy objects always ended up back exactly where they started.

Now imagine exactly the same scenario, but instead you are training for the Olympics and that bossy person is your coach. Oh how things have changed. Mornings are no longer dreaded. Instead, each workout is a vital step towards your Goal of standing on the top step of the podium in front of millions of people. Fame, fortune and personal satisfaction await you. The tired muscles at the end of each workout give you a quiet satisfaction.

In both cases you are doing exactly the same work. Both mornings are just as hard and demanding and yet they are completely different, simply because one has a Goal and the other doesn't.

Goals provide you with the motivation you need to complete the tasks that will transform your life. If your Goals are indistinct or faded then your motivation will surely fail because discipline alone can never sustain you over the long haul. Your motivation needs to be constantly topped up with *positive enthusiasm.*

WINNER'S GOALS ARE DIFFERENT

Most people don't have any idea how much effort it takes to be a champion athlete. While we all have this abstract notion that athletes train hard, the reality is vastly more brutal when you're confronted with it on a daily basis. Even though I'd worked with a number of world champions, it was only when I fell in love and lived with one that I experienced the grueling reality of what it takes to be the best in the world. My girlfriend would wake up early each morning and go and swim 100 lengths of the pool before breakfast. But these weren't just gentle laps like you or I would do, cruising up and down in our comfort zone. Every single lap was uncomfortable and every single stroke was spurred on by will-power. That sort of sustained mental effort over that amount of time would drain you or me. But she wasn't finished. After breakfast she'd then go out and ride 80km on her bike. Every turn of the pedal burnt her legs and rasped her lungs. Rain, hail or shine, out she'd go, into a stiff, cold headwind and push herself. And then at the end of the day, when she was already tired, she'd put on her running shoes and blast out a 10km run at speeds you or I couldn't sustain for thirty seconds, let alone thirty minutes. She'd push herself so hard that the next morning she could hardly walk when she first got up out of bed. Every step was painful despite the half hour massage she'd had the night before. For ten minutes she would walk like someone who'd just recovered from a traffic accident. Slow, stiff and with great effort. Gradually her muscles would loosen up and after a black coffee it was once more time to grab her bag and head off back to the pool.

Now while I could maybe force myself to do that for a day or, at the very most a week, she did it for seven days a week, fifty weeks a year – for *fifteen years*! Being able to cope with that level of pain for that length of time is far beyond the average person's tolerance. It's easy to say 'fifteen years' – but stop for a moment and think back over the last fifteen years of your life and all that you've done. Now try to imagine going through her level of pain and effort every day for all those years. Even when she was tired, sore and feeling down, she still somehow managed to get up and keep going and put in that huge effort one more time.

But even that's not the end of the story. Because she was a professional athlete who earned her income from racing she'd have to line up against all the other athletes every fortnight and put her body on the line. It was like a businessman having his annual review – every fortnight! Or like a student having their annual exam every fourteen days. There was no hiding. If she didn't do well she didn't get paid. It was brutal. How on earth can anyone sustain that level of effort for that length of time? No one can tolerate that amount of pain or sustain that level of effort by sheer will-power alone. It's just not possible.

My experience with Winners is they can do this because their Goals are that much more real and vibrant than anyone else's. Winners *believe* in their Goals even when no one else does. Their Goals never fade even when the going gets really, *really* tough. They still have belief and can find one more ounce of energy to keep on going in impossible situations. You might want to take a 'sneaky peek' at Chapter 12, 'An Unshakeable Belief In Yourself' to see what Winner's beliefs are really like. I'm sure you're going to be surprised at how different their beliefs are compared to yours. After reading that chapter, you'll probably realize your existing belief in yourself is probably only 2/10 compared to a champion's 10/10. *You* need Goals and beliefs like theirs. That's why making your Goals come alive is the first part of your own *Personal Winner's Bible*. And as you continue reading this book and doing the exercises in it, you'll find you get that level of belief which will sustain you and make every day enjoyable. You see, your Goals don't just give you the power to carry on – they also give you the ability to genuinely enjoy the journey. And that enjoyment is part of what sustains you. Maybe now you can see more clearly why just having a 'wish list' of goals was never going to work.

> Champion's Goals are durable, vibrant, clear and realistic.

VISUALIZATION INFLUENCES YOUR WHOLE DAY

Let's remind ourselves why we are doing this. It's because five minutes spent using your *Personal Winner's Bible* at the start of every day will dramatically influence all your feelings and thoughts for the next 24 hours! It sounds hard to believe but it's actually true, as you will soon discover for yourself. It simply depends on how *deeply* you connect with your images.

To get an idea of how this can happen, imagine your phone rings at the start of the day and someone tells you you're going to get a visit from the Queen. Even though your mind will be occupied with thousands of other thoughts today, that single thought will over-ride and dominate all other thoughts. On any other day negative thoughts, distractions or worries might bog you down. But today you'll be focused on the big picture: 'The Queen's coming!' This big picture will keep popping up constantly and automatically. It will shape your thoughts. And the same thing will happen to you if you have successfully visualized your Goals at the start of the day. No matter what happens – you'll have the 'big picture' firmly at the front of your mind shaping and influencing you for the best. When this happens you'll subconsciously be more aware of opportunities as you go about your normal day. You may see something or read something or meet someone that normally would have just been inconsequential, but today if it's important, you'll instantly lock on to it with laser focus. As a result you'll find you're 'luckier' and there are more positive 'coincidences' in your life. You'll get twice as much done and more importantly you'll enjoy your day more. And when you finally climb into bed at night you'll find you do so with the quiet peaceful satisfaction of a day well spent.

One of the most common mistakes I come across is that people get a piece of paper and 'do their Goals' or 'visualize them' once a year and think that's going to work. But that's not good enough because this doesn't get these Goals, emotions and images burnt deeply on your subconscious. Doing it yearly or monthly only affects your outer rational, logical layers. In order to profoundly change the way you behave it has to penetrate deep into your emotional, subconscious layers, because these are the layers that control your drives (see Chapter 5, 'Your Limbic System – Emotions'). Getting that deep into your brain takes time and repetition.

VISUALIZATION GIVES YOUR BRAIN AN UPGRADE

Visualizing your Goals provides two other major benefits in addition to sustaining your motivation. Firstly, *your thoughts can actually alter your brain's biochemistry and wiring*. In other words, *you can rewire your brain*. Visualization is different from other thought processes and if it is done correctly will develop new circuits in your brain that will help you perform better. This is equivalent to giving your brain an upgrade. Secondly, your brain will release additional neurotransmitters as you activate your senses and emotions during visualization (neurotransmitters are chemicals within your brain that complete the circuits and therefore allow your brain to function). These neurotransmitters will give you an energy boost that is more powerful and longer lasting than any stimulant. And the more you practice visualizing your Goals the more powerful they'll become and the greater the boost you'll get.

Life is short and you'll want to get the most out of every day (see Chapter 13, 'Carpe Diem').

THIS IS NOT 'THE SECRET'

But let's be very clear. Having vivid Goals is not enough. You then need to *do* something with your Goals and your belief. This is where books like *The Secret* are insufficient. These sort of books tend to make you think that if you *just* believe in something hard enough then this will somehow magically make the Universe provide it for you. That you will attract success and good fortune. But nothing could be further from the truth! There are thousands of people in Ethiopia or Zimbabwe who are starving and it's not because they attracted poverty as a result of their inner beliefs. Rather, it's because of the political and economic plight of their country. Likewise there isn't a single Olympic 100m sprint gold medalist who didn't train their butt off for years as well as having a massive desire and belief.

Having vivid Goals, a positive attitude and a belief in yourself is only the very first step on your way to becoming a Winner. You also need to become more efficient, more powerful and you need to change how you go about life. To do this you need to understand what's going on inside your brain and that means you need to understand your Four Pillars (see Chapter 4). But before we start on that exciting adventure let's recap on your first steps towards becoming a winner.

HOW TO USE YOUR *WINNER'S BIBLE* EVERY DAY

You don't have to go through every single page and visualize every image when you use your *Winner's Bible* each morning. Just flick through and *your mind will automatically select out which pages are important for you.* This will change on a daily basis. So even though your *Winner's Bible* will soon be full with many different things – quite apart from your images – you'll only need to spend five minutes each morning looking through it.

Remember, you must look through your *Winner's Bible* EVERY DAY.

Always find a quiet place where you won't be interrupted. The bathroom (toilet) is a common place for many people.

Keep your *Winner's Bible* confidential to yourself. No one needs to see it. This confidentiality ensures you will have the freedom to write down anything.

ACTION ITEMS
- List your Goals
- Find images for your Goals
- Construct stories for your Goals
- Practice Fixated Visualisation

IMPORTANT POINTS
- Your goals will change and mature as you read this book
- Don't worry if you don't yet know what your authentic Goals are; later chapters in this book will help you find your true purpose and Goals which will enrich all aspects of your life
- This will include goals that aren't just material Goals, such as personal development, friends, increasing your happiness and mental power etc

WHAT YOUR *WINNER'S BIBLE* SHOULD NOW CONTAIN
You've just started making your own *Winner's Bible* but it should already contain:
- Your Material Goals
- Your Career Goals
- Mentors/Heroes
- Your Family
- Your Friends

CHAPTER 3
YOUR STRENGTHS, WEAKNESSES AND REPEATED MISTAKES

ASSESSING YOUR RESOURCES

Now that you've made a start with your *Winner's Bible* and put your Goals in there, it's time to find out a little bit more about yourself – after all, you are the raw material that we are going to reassemble in order to get these Goals.

No good General goes into battle without first assessing his Strengths and Weaknesses and knowing where he is vulnerable. But a General doesn't just quickly glance over his troops and say, 'Yep, that looks about right – let's go to war.' Instead, he goes through each division and each type of weapon and works out how effective they're going to be given the terrain and the state of the enemy. Likewise, you need to do more than just cast a quick eye over yourself. You need to get what I call an Independent Audit of your Strengths and Weaknesses. And once you have that audit you need to see the results clearly in front of you each day in your *Winner's Bible*. That way you'll make the most of your Strengths and avoid tripping up on your Weaknesses.

Being able to accurately assess your Weaknesses and knowing what to do about them is one of the key Skills possessed by all Winners. It is a theme repeated time and again in business, sport and life in general. Many a boxer won a bout simply because they realized they were vulnerable to their opponent's most devastating punch and used that knowledge to position themselves so they were never hit by it. They knew their Weakness and how to work around it.

If your life isn't going exactly as you want it to right now then it's highly likely you're doing something wrong – particularly if there's a recurring pattern to your behavior. Repeated patterns are usually a symptom that you have an underlying Weakness you're not aware of. Finding these Weaknesses and curing them is an incredibly exciting process because life suddenly has a new zing and good things just 'start to happen' to you again. And likewise, if you know your Strengths you'll be more likely to put them to work each day. Once you've fully understood your Strengths and Weaknesses you'll then be in a position to learn some of the special Mental Tools I use with my elite athletes … and to put them to work on yourself. But you need to know the diagnosis before you can choose the right Tool.

THE DISTORTED MIRROR

The reason why you need an Independent Audit is because none of us really see ourselves clearly or objectively. Princess Diana genuinely thought that no one really loved her or cared about her. Her feeling of low self-esteem was so intense that she even became bulimic in an attempt to improve her appearance and be loved more. And yet when she died, millions of flowers were laid all over England in a spontaneous expression of love and affection for her. It was probably the greatest outpouring of love that England has ever witnessed as an entire nation grieved. If only Diana could have seen how people really viewed her while she was alive!

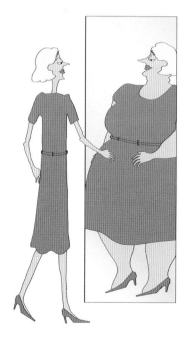

In the same way you may not be fully aware of your own foibles or your own Strengths. It's like looking at yourself through a distorted mirror. So what's the solution? How can you see yourself as you really are?

THE ANONYMOUS ONLINE AUDIT

One answer is to have someone who knows you really well to give you some help. People like your family, best friends and work associates who you respect. But this poses two problems:

1. Your friends would have to be totally honest with you. Unfortunately that level of honesty risks upsetting your friendship. After all, how many friendships would survive if your closest friend says, 'You have a fat bum and need to lose 20 kgs'? Now think how much harder it's going to be for them to talk about the most intimate aspects of your personality.
2. Your friends need to take this exercise very seriously. They need to think this over and not just give you some superficial answer. What you're looking for is genuine insight from them but that's rare to find. And questionnaires and rating scales typically used by psychologists just aren't going to be adequate for this either. After all, if you get a rating of 6/10 on a scale of zero (introvert) to ten (extrovert) this doesn't help you at all. You can be a Winner at either end of the scale. And besides, what do you *do* with a score of six anyway? Feedback is only valuable if you can do something with it and make some sort of change to your life.

Fortunately, I've thought about both problems and have come up with a solution for you.

Anonymous

The first problem is solved if your friends give you feedback in such a way that you never know which of them said any particular comment. In other words, if their feedback was totally anonymous.

Here's how it works. You invite a *minimum* of five people to provide feedback about you – there is no maximum. We'll call these people that you've invited your 'Auditors'. Each Auditor then writes a series of short paragraphs about you on a special confidential part of the *Winner's Bible* website (www.winnersbible.com). The website then automatically combines the feedback from each of your Auditors into a single report about you. Because you only get to see this final report when at *least four* of your Auditors have finished, you won't know who said what about you. The key to making this work is that the comments from the different Auditors are combined in such a way that it doesn't just end up in a big mess.

But rest assured, everything is totally confidential. All e-mail addresses and comments from your friends will be encrypted and protected in the same way that bank details are. No one at *The Winner's Bible Inc* will ever see what has been written about you. None of your Auditors get to see what anyone else has written either. You are the only person to see the final report. Don't worry if you don't understand how this works yet because the process will become a little clearer in a minute.

Free Format Paragraphs
The second problem is solved if your Auditors are given powerful instructions which challenge them to think about you in a deep and detailed way. Then they need to have the option to not only describe your Strengths and Weaknesses, but to also tell you what they think you should do about those Strengths and Weaknesses.

The best way to explain how this works is to give you a real life example.

THE LONELY WOMAN
I was visited by a highly intelligent woman in her mid-forties. She was attractive and outgoing with a wide range of interests. But despite all her obvious charms she had been single for many years and just couldn't seem to find the right guy. As part of my consultation with her, I asked her to undergo an anonymous Independent Audit. One of the responses that came back said she had an annoying habit of 'talking over people'. When people were halfway through their sentence she'd interrupt them and either finish off their sentence for them, or start her own sentence. Her independent auditor said this made her sound aggressive, as if she knew everything. It was as if she was trying to prove her point all the time. Talking with her felt like 'hard work' and people could never just relax and chill out.

This feedback was a complete surprise to my client. She was a nice woman with a genuinely kind and caring soul. She always meant well and had no idea other people thought she came across as 'hard'. But it was true. She was always interrupting. I don't think I finished a single sentence during our first consultation either. After a little probing we discovered this was a symptom of a deeper problem inside her History or Psychology Pillars (see Chapter 4). It transpired that her mother was a highly successful businesswoman who had achieved her success by constantly pushing herself to the limit and never being satisfied with her own performance. She was a solo mother and wanted her daughter to be even more successful. So she reasoned that if self-discipline was successful for her then she would double it for my client. As a result, my client's childhood was based on a never-ending criticism of her errors coupled with harsh penalties for failure. Not surprisingly, she grew up feeling she was 'never good enough'. Now, even though she was a top corporate executive with three first class degrees after her name, she still unconsciously felt the need to 'prove herself' all the time. In conversations she always had to prove she was the smartest, that she knew what the other person was thinking and that she had the perfect answer. Because she was in the top 1% of the population for IQ, she could usually work out what the other person was going to say long before they finished their sentence and she was only too anxious to give the 'clever' reply. This had a devastating impact on her socially. As I said, inside she was a kind, warm and genuinely caring woman but she came across as arrogant and 'hard work' – as her Independent Audit revealed.

Once she realized what was going on, and once we'd dealt with the emotional issues unwittingly left in her History Pillar by her mother, her life was transformed. People suddenly started calling her up. She was invited to more dinner parties and social events. And as fate would have it, she met her soul mate at one of these parties and they've lived happily ever after since. All because she found out something about herself that she hadn't known for forty years – by taking an anonymous Online Audit.

This example also illustrates why standard psychological questionnaires or assessments are never going to work. You're never going to have a questionnaire that is going to cover every possible issue like 'talking over people'. This means you need a system that is incredibly flexible and yet probes deep inside a person with laser focus. That's what your Auditors will get if they use the *Winner's Bible* Online Audit.

They'll be given clear, simple instructions along with two examples like the one I just mentioned which will encourage them to think 'outside the box'. Then they'll have space to write everything down in a series of self-contained paragraphs. Each paragraph has to contain a single Strength or Weakness along with any suggestions corresponding to that self-contained thought. There is no limit to the length of each paragraph. Each Auditor can fill out as many or as few paragraphs as they like. Once all the Auditors have finished, the paragraphs are randomly mixed together to produce a single report. But it still makes sense because each paragraph is self-contained.

All you need to do is go to the *Winner's Bible* website and everything is taken care of for you. You'll get clear, simple instructions on what you need to do and so will your invited Auditors, if they choose to participate. Check out the website now and you'll see what I mean.

CHOOSE CAREFULLY

Before you invite anyone to be one of your Auditors you need to think very carefully about whether they are the right person. Just because someone is a real fun person and a great friend of yours doesn't necessarily qualify them to be a good judge of your character. They might only know you in a light-hearted, superficial way or they may not be people who are themselves developed enough to undertake this analysis correctly. What you're really after is someone who has:

• Enough exposure to you when you are in various situations – particularly when you are under stress or need to make choices
• Enough insight to see deep inside you and understand what drives you and causes you to do what you do. This means they need to be people of a certain level of emotional and intellectual sophistication

As you consider who to put on your list you might even want to think outside the box and ask an ex-girlfriend or ex-boyfriend to participate. After all, they've experienced both the good and the bad times with you. And because they now have some distance from you they might think more objectively about you. Of course, this all depends on whether or not you are both at peace with each other.

You might also want an opinion from a brother or sister, a parent or son/daughter. Another good group of people to consider are your work colleagues – and not just your boss. You want people who know how you react when you're under pressure, when you're ticked off or bored and disinterested. When you say or do things when you're not on show. When you react to people you don't like working with. The point here is that you can get as many different opinions as you like. You don't have to restrict yourself to five people. In fact, that's the *minimum* you can choose. There is no maximum.

The quality of the people you choose will be directly reflected in the quality of the feedback you receive.

SELF-EVALUATION

While you're waiting for your friends to complete your Online Audit it's a good opportunity for you to complete an audit on yourself. You'll find it very interesting to compare your own evaluation with your friends' observations. While you're doing this it's important to think as widely as you possibly can about yourself. The Lonely Woman and her conversational Skills is a good example of how wide you need to cast your net. To help you think laterally, the *Winner's Bible* website contains a list of Strengths and Weaknesses for you to consider.

REPEATED MISTAKES

Another important microscope for looking inside your character is to list your Repeated Mistakes. Even though Repeated Mistakes are related to your Weaknesses they are slightly different. Mistakes are negative things you keep doing over and over again. Maybe you trust people too much or you're a bad judge of character. Maybe you keep falling in love with 'bad guys' who are initially attractive but ultimately hurt you and don't help you grow. Maybe it's the exact opposite – you fall in love with great people but because they are so good to you, perhaps you end up taking them for granted and treating them badly. Maybe you rush off at 200 km/h into a new project without doing your homework properly and then in five months time you've run out of steam and all that work and effort amounts to nothing.

Repeated Mistakes come in many different flavors and cover categories such as relationships, finance, work, recreation and so on. So take an A5 sheet of paper and write on it what you think are your five greatest Strengths, your five greatest Weaknesses and any Repeated Mistakes you make.

YOUR SKILLS

Strengths and Weaknesses typically refer to aspects of your personality. It's just as important for you to assess the strength of your *Skills* and decide whether or not there are any holes in your arsenal. For example, in motor racing I've come across many drivers with exceptional Skill who can balance a car on the absolute knife edge of control, but who lack the technical knowledge to set-up the car's suspension or have the ability to find an optimal solution for a particular corner. Even though they're brilliant drivers, they are missing crucial Skills. At the lower level of motor sport this isn't a problem because they can just rely on their exceptional driving Skill to win. But at the top level of the sport they suddenly find everyone else has a similar level of car control, only now their opponents also have these additional Skills as well.

Maybe you're a businessman doing mergers and acquisitions and can zoom around a spreadsheet with your eyes closed but don't have a grasp of the changing political landscape. In this case, even though you can negotiate brilliant deals buying and selling companies based on their current value, perhaps one day you'll get caught out by a sudden shift in global politics. Maybe a sharp squeeze in global credit affects your consumers' spending patterns or maybe some government's action to reduce oil production suddenly squeezes your business from an unexpected direction. So take a moment to think of all the Skills you need to be successful in your business, your sport and in your everyday life and then write down the ones that you think could be improved and add them to the rest of your self-evaluation. By now you should have a list of Strengths, Weaknesses, Repeated Mistakes and Skills. As always, write them on an A5 page and put them into your *Winner's Bible*. In later sections, we'll show you exactly what to do with these.

My Five Greatest Strengths:
1. ....
2. ....
3. ....
4. ....
5. ....

My Five Greatest Weaknesses:
1. ....
2. ....
3. ....
4. ....
5. ....

Repeated Mistakes:
....

Skills I need to Improve:
....

ALI'S PERFECT MIRROR

Before we look at how you're going to use your list of Strengths, Weaknesses and Repeated Mistakes to improve your life, it's worth pausing for a moment to remind ourselves why this exercise is so valuable. As is usually the case, we can learn a valuable lesson from Muhammad Ali. Prior to his famous fight with George Foreman in Zaire, Ali went into his usual training camp high in the mountains. He was surrounded by coaches, trainers, managers and physiotherapists. As part of his daily training regimen he'd spar with a number of top-ranked heavyweight contenders who were brought into the camp for a week at a time. After each session Ali would ask the guys he'd sparred with how they thought he was doing. The sparring partners always told Ali he was fast, powerful and skillful and for sure he was going to beat big George Foreman.

One day a new sparring partner arrived and after a tough training session Ali asked him the same question, 'How do you think I'm doing compared to George?' The new sparring partner replied, 'He's going to flatten you! He's too big and he's too strong. He'll take your punches no problem and then punish you. You just aren't powerful enough to hurt him.'

There was an immediate outcry from all the coaches and trainers in the room. 'Get that guy out of here! He's ruining our energy. We need to be positive and focused and have belief in ourselves. He's a negative influence.'

Ali held up his hand and told everyone to be quiet. 'Double his salary – he stays until he tells me I'm going to beat George.'

While Ali had the biggest mouth in the business and an Unshakeable Belief in his Optimal Future (see Chapter 12, 'An Unshakeable Belief In Yourself'), this wasn't at the expense of being able to accept his own Weaknesses and see who he really was. He evaluated his Weaknesses and then learned how to overcome them. Unfortunately, too many people live in a fantasy world of hype and self-belief that isn't grounded in reality. We see this at its worst on TV shows like *X Factor*, *Pop Idol* and *American Idol* where people like Robert Unwin come on stage with absolutely no talent whatsoever. They've dreamt without either taking stock of who they are or without having done the hard yards needed for skilled success. Fortunately, Robert was a charming and modest person who readily accepted the harsh but accurate criticism dealt to him by the show's host Simon Cowell.

But the point is, a little genuine reflection from people close to Robert could have prevented him exposing his lack of singing talent in such a public manner and he could have concentrated on other more productive things in his life. That's why the anonymous Online Audit is so incredibly valuable. Too often our closest friends and family can't tell us things to our face because that's such an emotionally personal interaction. The eye contact, the look on your face, your immediate response. It's all just too hard for them. But the anonymous Independent Audit allows them to do this in a loving way without the emotion.

Conversely there are people like Paul Potts, a mobile phone salesman who came on to a show called *Britain's Got Talent*, totally lacking in confidence and self-esteem. He was so unsure of himself that he nearly cancelled his appearance. Yet he went on to display such incredible talent that he won the entire series and ended up signing a $2.4 million record contract. His performance was so moving that it reduced both the judges and the audience to tears. You can watch a replay on the following weblink:
http://www.boreme.com/boreme/funny2007/paul-potts-opera-p1.php

It's an incredibly moving clip and guaranteed to bring tears to your eyes, so it's definitely worth attaching headphones to your computer before you watch it so you get the full impact (this clip is also posted on YouTube).

The point is, sometimes we're held back by not realizing our Weaknesses and sometimes we're held back by not realizing our Strengths. Paul Potts had lived a life of insecurity and low self-esteem until he was given accurate feedback from the judges. Once he had that feedback his life changed immediately and permanently. He became confident in his speech and he exuded a powerful energy in direct contrast to his previously shy demeanor.

THE UNEXAMINED LIFE
Socrates famously said, 'The unexamined life is not worth living.'

The rationale behind his words and the reason why you are going through this exercise of analyzing your Strengths, Weaknesses, Repeated Mistakes and Skills is because this gives you the chance to take control of your life and shape it. Unless you do this you'll just end up living a life that is shaped unwittingly and accidentally by external events. But if you examine your life and understand your actions then you'll have the opportunity to rise above chance and design your own life. Analysis is not the glamorous part of self-improvement, but it is the *foundation* on which you will build change. It is the platform that will allow you to grow and become an advanced soul, rather than an adult with a child's personality.

CHAPTER 4
THE FOUR PILLARS

Author's Note:
The next two chapters are the most demanding sections of this book. In these chapters I'll explain the overarching framework I use when I deal with athletes. I'll also give you some of the science behind the Tools that are waiting for you as soon as you've read these two chapters. You need to get this knowledge because it allows you to work out *exactly* what needs fixing, why it needs fixing and which are the best Tools to make those repairs. Even though you may be itching to get on with trying out some of the upcoming Tools, I'd encourage you to spend a little extra effort now reading about what I call 'The Four Pillars'. If you do, it will prove to be immensely valuable when you start using some of the more advanced Tools.

MY TECHNIQUE WITH ELITE ATHLETES

In my experience I have found there are four crucial things I need to know about every client I help. I call these things 'The Four Pillars' of someone's personality. The diagram overleaf shows these Four Pillars and how they are connected to each other (I'll come back to why I've laid them out in this particular manner in the next section, 'The Interaction Of The Four Pillars').

Because these Four Pillars are so important the first thing I do whenever I sit down with any athlete – regardless of how successful they are – is to get to know what's inside each of their Pillars. If I don't do this I'm only able to make *temporary* changes to their performance rather than the *permanent* and powerful changes they seek. That's why I always spend the entire first session with each athlete making extensive notes and asking them questions. Once I'm sure I know what is inside each of their Pillars, I then spend a few days working out what it all means before I even begin to start developing their program. If you think about it, it's the same sort of approach used by every good surgeon before they operate on a patient. No matter how good the surgeon is with his scalpel and no matter how extensive his toolkit is, the surgeon must also have a thorough understanding of what is going on inside the patient's body. The more clearly the surgeon sees what is right and what is wrong, the more skilfully they can use each tool. It's the same with you. If you understand what is going on inside your head – and why – you'll be in a much better position to use the Tools in the following chapters as you continue building your own *Personal Winner's Bible*. The really interesting thing about this process is that you'll discover things about yourself you never knew – and that will be key to unlocking your potential.

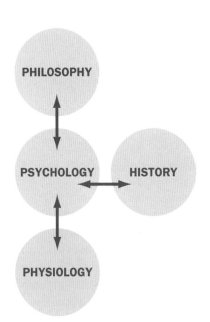

It'll be like having an x-ray of your personality.

So let's start with a very brief introduction to each of *The Four Pillars:*

a) Your Physiology

Your Physiology is your flesh and blood, the 'nuts and bolts' that you're made out of. This not only includes your body but also your brain and the unique concoction of chemicals your brain runs on. Much of your brain's wiring is determined by your genes and the events you experienced as a child while your brain was being wired up for the first time. This wiring has a massive impact on your behavior, your performance and your happiness today. A simple example which illustrates how powerfully your Physiology affects your behavior is what happens when you drink alcohol. Alcohol is an interesting chemical in that it affects different parts of your brain in quite different ways. At moderate doses, alcohol reduces the efficiency of those modules in the front of your brain which are responsible for planning and risk assessment, while at the same time stimulating those modules buried deep inside your brain which are involved in pleasure. The net result of drinking alcohol is that you behave differently because the normal checks and balances in your brain have been altered. The chatter back and forward between the modules that make up your personality has changed, as well as which modules have the greatest influence in how you're going to behave.

A key point of this book is that your brain's wiring isn't permanently fixed like the wiring in your computer. You can use the Tools in this book to rewire your brain to overcome your genes and your History, and in doing so, achieve more happiness and productivity out of your life. So what do I mean by 'History'?

b) Your History

Your History is the sum of all your experiences in life. This History isn't just a calendar list of events that happened to you, but rather what is much more important is how you *interpreted* those events and *how* they now affect you in your daily life. For most of us, events from our past have snuck deep into the unconscious regions of our brains without us ever realizing it and they continue to influence our behaviour today. In this way our History continues to cast a long shadow over our daily lives. Unfortunately this historical influence isn't always to our advantage. We wake up each morning and by default we run the same sorts of thoughts through our heads as we've always run through them – whether or not those are the most appropriate thoughts. And so we repeat our previous patterns of behaviours and we uncritically accept our old view of ourselves - even if this reduces our happiness and effectiveness in life.

It is only by understanding how our History has subtly affected our unconscious brain structures that we can successfully free ourselves to live in the present and build a powerful future.

c) Your Psychology

Your Psychology is essentially the 'thoughts you run through your head' and the unwritten rules that govern your behavior. Some of these thought processes will be logical and have words or sentences attached to them while others will be buried deep inside your unconscious emotional circuits. If you're going to make lasting change you need to have Tools to change both types of psychological processes. More often than not, it's those unwritten rules without words or logic – the ones driven by emotion – that are most likely to cause you trouble. That's why you'll soon learn how to use Tools like Emotional Supercharging (see Chapter 9) which have been specially designed to diagnose and modify those hidden emotional circuits. As you put these Tools to use you'll probably be surprised, just like most of my clients were, at how quickly you can reshape your Psychology and permanently overcome problems that have bothered you for years (see Chapter 7, 'The Dog And Bone').

d) Your Philosophy

Your Philosophy contains your beliefs about how the Universe works and what your role in that Universe is. Your Philosophy is important because if your beliefs don't match reality then you'll be playing life according to the wrong rules. And doing that will guarantee you end up getting second-rate results no matter how hard you try.

Because this subject is so important and concerns the biggest issues such as 'The Meaning of Life', I have written an entirely separate book called *The Winner's Bible Of Philosophy* (see p258).

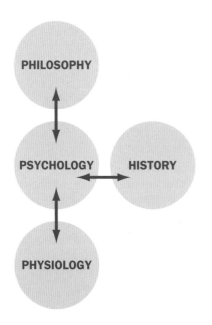

THE INTERACTION OF THE FOUR PILLARS

What's just as important as the contents of The Four Pillars is *how* they are connected to each other. That's why I arranged them in the particular manner shown in the diagram at the start of this chapter.

Let me start by pointing out a few features of that diagram. Firstly, notice your History Pillar is connected to your Psychology Pillar by a double arrow. This double arrow is *vitally* important because each Pillar influences the other Pillar in a way that can cause a powerful ongoing cycle. Having each box connected by arrows pointing in both directions means you can get a feedback loop where small changes can spiral back and forward between the two Pillars to produce enormous changes over time. Sometimes these changes can lead to great improvements in your life but at other times they can cause you great harm and make you become dysfunctional.

Let me give you an illustration of how this spiral can happen and why having an arrow pointing in both directions is so important. Let's consider what happens to a child when a parent criticizes them for doing something they were particularly proud of. Maybe a young girl had practiced playing the trumpet for hours until she thought she'd learnt how to play a piece of music perfectly. The child puffs up her lungs and plays for all she's worth. But at the end of her recital her mother points out a few errors in timing and the notes she'd missed instead of offering praise. The child is inwardly heartbroken. She begins to doubt whether she's got any talent. But things don't end there. Once she starts thinking she doesn't have any talent she then begins to interpret her experiences differently. If she then has trouble with her next piece of new music she'll now interpret this as further confirmation she 'just isn't good enough' – rather than viewing it as a signal she needs to train harder (see Chapter 12, 'Loretta's Story'). And so a spiral has begun. Because she doesn't believe in herself she doesn't train as hard. Because she doesn't train as hard she produces another poor result – once again confirming she's a 'failure'. Before long she doesn't even enjoy playing the trumpet any more. Worse still, this feeling of 'failure' may now spread to other areas of her life.

This example illustrates how your History affects your Psychology and how your Psychology affects your History. What you experience in life (your History) undoubtedly affects the sorts of 'thoughts you run through your head' (your Psychology). But the 'thoughts you run through your head' (your Psychology) also act like a filter and influences how you *interpret* events that happen to you (your History).

This 'double arrow spiral' not only explains how small problems can grow but it also gives us huge hope. It explains why using the Tools in this book to produce even small changes in one Pillar can suddenly produce major changes in your whole life!

PSYCHOLOGY
YOUR THOUGHTS
& EMOTIONS

PHYSIOLOGY
YOUR BRAIN

But this flow doesn't just go back and forward between two Pillars. There is also a flow from a second Pillar to a third or even fourth Pillar and then maybe back to the first Pillar. We've already seen that your History can affect your Psychology, but your Psychology also affects your Physiology. If you think you're a failure and start focusing on what's wrong with your life then this will flow down and cause changes to your Physiology.

• The chemical balance in your brain will be altered
• Your brain will be wired differently

In this way your History not only affects your thoughts (Psychology), but these thoughts in turn affect your Physiology. There is a cascade effect downward. But once you change your brain's wiring and its chemical balance you'll start thinking differently and so the flow goes back up again to your Psychology.

This combination of cascades and feedback loops explains how a person can quickly spiral down into a life-threatening depression which can be frightfully difficult to escape from. A bad experience (History) may produce a negative thought process (Psychology) which then alters their brain's balance (Physiology). The brain's unsettled balance then causes them to think more negative thoughts and so a dangerous cycle has begun.

USING THE FOUR PILLARS

Whenever I work with an athlete, I come back time and again to what's in each of their Four Pillars. I do this because it helps me work out what is the most important issue for them and then – and only then – do I know which Tools are going to help them the most. You'll do the same thing on yourself. So let's dig a little deeper into what The Four Pillars are all about. You'll use this knowledge to continue developing your own *Personal Winner's Bible*.

CHAPTER 5
AN INTRODUCTION TO YOUR PHYSIOLOGY PILLAR

The brain doesn't actually work the way most people think it does, which is one of the reasons why so many people never achieve their full potential or happiness.

The most important thing to realize about your brain is that it isn't like one big powerful supercomputer. Instead, your brain is made up of many different modules and each module has its own function and distinct 'personality'. How these different modules work explains why you sometimes do 'dumb' things or seem to have two (or more) different personalities. These different brain modules also explain why it's *so* hard to break bad habits and improve yourself. Because there isn't a single 'you' inside your brain making all your decisions there isn't just one module or one 'computer program' you need to debug. Therefore, if you're going to upgrade your mind you need to have a reasonable understanding of the different parts of your brain and how they affect your behavior. That is, you need to understand your Physiology.

YOUR LIMBIC SYSTEM – EMOTIONS
Buried deep inside your brain is your Limbic System. This is responsible for your innate emotions and drives. It controls things like your sex drive, hunger, addictions, emotions, anger, happiness, motivation and your fear of dangerous things like snakes or spiders.

A moment's thought shows you don't have to learn any of the things that your Limbic System controls. You don't have to learn to be hungry and you don't have to learn how to find a sexy person attractive or heights scary. If a man sees a sexy woman he doesn't have to stop and think about her for a few minutes before he decides she's good-looking. He just looks at her and he's instantly aroused. There is a reason for this. The Limbic System evolved in prehistoric times to make us automatically do and feel things because historically doing those very things gave us a greater chance of survival.

We can see why the Limbic System does this by considering our innate reaction to hearing a loud unexpected sound behind us – we're naturally scared. That's because thousands of years ago this probably meant we were about to be attacked by something nasty such as a tiger. Being attacked by a tiger is not the sort of experience you can *learn* from by trial and error in the usual way. It's a one-off deal! You either hear the noise and immediately jump out of the way of the tiger – or you're eaten. There are no second or third chances to learn by experience. You don't have time to use complex logic to work out what is going on behind you and what you ought to do. You have to react instinctively and immediately. Therefore any brains that developed automatic systems like these were much more likely to survive and breed. That's how the Limbic System evolved and came to have such a powerful influence over our behavior. Other things like being naturally scared of heights helps prevent us from getting into situations where we are likely to hurt ourselves and so they are also hard-wired into our Limbic System. The same is true of our other 'drives' like sex, hunger, anger and so on. Each helped us survive or reproduce and pass our genes on.

Unfortunately many of these natural drives aren't suited to modern life. We're all born with an innate fear of heights. Even babies who have never fallen or hurt themselves are naturally scared of heights as can be demonstrated by the so-called 'visual cliff'. In this experiment a baby crawls over a clear, bullet-proof Perspex floor which can easily support an adult's weight. Underneath the Perspex floor is a chequered box which abruptly ends to form a 'cliff'. Even though the Perspex

floor is continuous and the baby can feel the floor in front of them with their hands and feet, they stubbornly stop at the edge of the 'cliff', even if their mother is on the other side calling them forward. This inbuilt fear of heights was a tremendous advantage when we were primitive men because it helped prevent us from getting into situations where we fell off cliffs or out of trees. Breaking our bones in primitive times was a major problem because it reduced our ability to hunt and therefore survive. But in modern times this very same fear of heights makes us nervous about flying. The plane accelerates down the runway and suddenly we're looking out the window from a great height. It doesn't feel particularly comfortable and if we encounter bad turbulence our pulse rises and our palms get sweaty, regardless of any outward show of nonchalance we might put on. We're naturally, innately scared of flying because our good old Limbic System hasn't been updated to take account of modern society. But the cold hard facts are that we're 65 times more likely to get killed if we drive between two cities than if we fly between them. We should be much more scared starting our car than taking off from a runway. But our logic and our emotional circuits aren't in tune. For most of us the sheer repetition of flying helps dampen down our Limbic

System when it comes to planes. But we haven't yet learnt how to correctly modulate the Limbic System's other hidden influences on our modern lives.

Our Limbic System isn't just involved in negative or dangerous things. It also controls our happy feelings. It is activated when we are in love or happy because these are important events we want to repeat for the simple reason that they make life worth living. The pleasure centers in your Limbic System are also heavily affected by drugs like cocaine and nicotine which is why taking them is so pleasurable for users and why they are *so* hard to kick. The Limbic System is also heavily involved in helping you learn and remember because it highlights the good things you want to repeat and avoid the bad things that can cause harm.

So you can see that the Limbic System is an incredibly powerful driver of your behavior. You only have to think of how motivated you are to get food when you're starving or how much effort you'll go to when you fall in love. In many cases your Limbic System *makes decisions for you* without you even realizing it. Your conscious, logical circuits do little more than justify afterwards what your unconscious Limbic circuits have already decided you were going to do. Going back to our example of a man seeing a sexy woman – the moment he looks at her his Limbic System fires up making him instantly attracted to her. A fraction of a second later as he starts to walk towards her, his logical circuits fire up and start to justify his actions. They tell him she looks 'interesting' or 'happy' or one of many different logical reasons why he should go and talk to her. He thinks he's made a decision based on the logical thoughts he's aware of, but research shows that the Limbic System made the decision first and his conscious brain just followed obediently along retrospectively justifying everything.

The power of our Limbic System to control our behavior has been revealed in experiments where people had tiny micro-electrodes implanted in parts of their Limbic System. When these electrodes were turned on it was as if the experimenter could control the subject's desires, decisions and even their very personality by remote control. They could be sexually aroused, made angry, hungry or happy – all at the push of a button. We like to think we're rational sophisticated people but if you could look deep inside your brain you'd probably be shocked to find how many of your actions were initiated by this primitive, and to a large extent, hidden module.

The challenge you face then is:
• Your Limbic System is a primitive module compared to other parts of your brain

- It evolved long before 'rational modules' appeared in animals because the Limbic System helped these animals survive in the prehistoric jungle
- You no longer live in the jungle and the challenges you face to be successful or happy today are very different because society is no longer a jungle
- Despite this, your Limbic System still continues to exert a *powerful* influence over your behavior. Most of this influence is still positive. But sometimes it can have a devastating influence on your life and happiness because it makes you do the wrong things

What makes it hard to cure the negative aspects of your Limbic System is the fact that it operates below the radar. You're aware of the words and thoughts that run through your logical rational modules and so you often try to adjust your behavior by talking to your logical modules. Meanwhile your Limbic System stubbornly refuses to change.

This explains why it's so hard to kick a drug habit, lose weight or be positive if you're feeling down. No matter how often you tell yourself to 'get going', 'get motivated', 'be positive' or 'don't worry', you just can't seem to shift your mood. The Limbic System is an emotional system and so it doesn't respond very well to logic or the rational thoughts you run through your head. To rewire your behavior you'll need more than clever phrases and logical arguments, because your Limbic System just doesn't understand normal logic.

Understanding how to take control of your pesky emotional system and change it has been one of the key breakthroughs I've made in my work with elite athletes. It's something I'm going to share with you in the upcoming chapters.

> Rewiring your behavior requires more than clever phrases because your Limbic System doesn't understand normal logic.

YOUR FRONTAL LOBES

While all mammals have a well-developed Limbic System, only apes and humans have powerful 'Frontal Lobes'. The Frontal Lobes are where the more logical and rational parts of your personality reside. They play a crucial role in judgment, long-term planning and all the wisdom you acquire with experience. The Frontal Lobes produce many of the behaviors and attributes we like to think separate us from lesser animals.

Part of the Frontal Lobe's function is to help control and reign in the unconscious, primitive emotions of the Limbic System. For example, when someone upsets us, our Limbic System produces a flash of anger which if left unchecked would rapidly lead to a violent outburst. But our Frontal Lobes quickly bring this under control because we have learned through many social interactions that hitting the other person is ultimately not going to lead to a good outcome. Either they'll hit us back or we'll end up in trouble with the police. My Frontal Lobes also help me consider other people's feelings and so when a pretty woman makes a pass at me, I imagine how my girlfriend would feel if

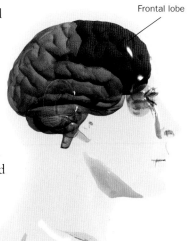

Frontal lobe

I cheated on her. This reflection helps me to over-ride any primitive sexual instinct I might have and the net result is that I don't cheat on my girlfriend. My Frontal Lobes help me to be a less selfish, more sophisticated and higher quality person.

Poor performance of the Frontal Lobes leads to all sorts of behavioral problems. Brain scans of violent criminals often show that key regions of their Frontal Lobes – which are supposed to dampen down and control their tempers – are not working correctly. To some extent, these criminally insane people are acting like primitive men under the control of their unrestrained emotional circuits. Another problem we face is that while the Limbic System develops early all by itself under the control of our genes, our Frontal lobes are largely unprogrammed and take more than 20 years to develop. The Frontal Lobes are like an empty book into which we can write almost whatever we like, whereas the Limbic System has many of the pages fully completed with little room left for us to add much. This has both advantages and disadvantages. It means we are free to learn from experience but it also means that if we don't train our Frontal Lobes correctly we'll act like a primitive, unsophisticated person.

A small part of becoming a Winner is to help our Frontal Lobes develop and interact with our Limbic System in such a way that we rise above normal person and become a 'superman' or 'superwoman'. This is possible because if we go about life in the right way, we can grow powerful circuits that actually connect our Frontal Lobes with our Limbic System. The establishment of these circuits gives rise to what we call wise, kind and intelligent people. People who can still experience their emotions in all their glory, but who are not controlled irrationally by them.

Because the Frontal Lobes are largely unprogrammed, they are by far the last modules to get wired up in humans. This is part of the reason why teenagers can seem so irresponsible. Their Frontal Lobes simply aren't mature enough to control their crazy urges. The trouble is, many adults are only half-wired as well.

At this stage, we should point out that the Limbic System isn't a 'bad' module and the Frontal Lobes aren't 'good' modules. Nothing could be further from the truth. Both have a genuinely positive part to play in your life. The Limbic System is vitally important to us because it gives us emotions and makes us want to do certain things. Without that, life wouldn't have any feeling, value or purpose. Conversely, the wrong thoughts in our Frontal Lobes can cause us all sorts of havoc in our lives. The key, like most things in life, is to have the correct balance between the two systems and for each to exert the correct influence at the appropriate time. This is why there are millions of connections between your Limbic System and your Frontal Lobes. That is one of the reasons why you need to use the visualization techniques outlined in Chapter 2 when you read your own *Personal Winner's Bible* each day. Using those techniques arouses your emotional system at exactly the same time that your logical system is thinking over your Goals. This establishes a powerful link between your Limbic System and your Frontal Lobes which is actually reflected in your brain's wiring. *You are starting to rewire your brain.* Your Goals will gradually acquire more emotional energy, and as we all know, your emotions are incredibly powerful drivers of your behavior.

YOUR SPLIT PERSONALITY

But some of the other things that go on in your brain are even more interesting than this. Your brain has two roughly equivalent hemispheres – left and right. The left hemisphere controls the right side of your body and the right hemisphere controls the left. While the two hemispheres look much the same and have similar functions, there are interesting differences between them. Because you have two hemispheres this means you also have two 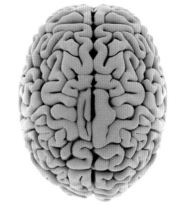 distinct Frontal Lobes. Normally these two Frontal Lobes are connected and 'talk' to each other without you realizing it. But under special laboratory conditions we can anaesthetize one hemisphere while keeping the other one awake. When this happens we get some quite surprising results, as the following example shows.

The right hemisphere of a teenage boy was anaesthetized and the experimenters then asked him, 'What would you like to be when you grow up?' His 'awake' left hemisphere answered, 'An accountant'. Then they reversed the anaesthetic and put his left hemisphere to sleep. Again the boy was asked what he'd like to become when he grew up. This time his right hemisphere answered, 'A racing driver'. It was as if there were two different personalities inside his brain.

An even more striking example of the distinct personalities hiding in the different parts of our brains was revealed when the 'wires' between the two hemispheres of another patient were surgically cut during an operation. After the operation, both hemispheres were fully functional except they couldn't communicate with each other. Now, the left side of the patient's body was controlled entirely by their right hemisphere and their right side by their left hemisphere. One day the patient with this 'split brain' was badly upset by another person. The patient's more excitable right hemisphere instructed their left hand to grab a nearby axe and attack the other person. Fortunately, the left hemisphere saw what was going on and instructed the right hand to grab the left hand and restrain it. For a few seconds the two hands battled it out before the right hemisphere calmed down and the axe was dropped. This sort of dialogue goes on all the time in your own brain except normally you're not aware of it because your two hemispheres 'talk to each other' and come up with an agreed consensus without you realizing it. Your left hemisphere is more logical and rational whereas your right hemisphere is often more adventurous. If the two hemispheres can't agree then the left hemisphere usually has the final say because in most people it is the dominant side. So even though you might *like* to be a racing driver because it sounds exciting and glamorous, you probably realize it's almost impossible to make a living at it unless you are extremely talented and have wealthy parents to get you started. Therefore your dominant left hemisphere tells you it makes more sense to become an accountant after all.

There are many other modules in your brain, each with their own 'agenda' and 'personality'. Because of the unique construction and way each module operates you need to use different techniques to train and improve them. As I mentioned before, it is not a 'one size fits all' process. This helps explain why you can be so developed in some areas of your life but struggle in others. You might have been using techniques that were successful in one area of your life and unsuccessfully tried to apply them to another area. After all, the Tools that help a mathematician successfully solve a formula are quite different from the Tools that help an artist paint a masterpiece.

SPORTS MODULES

Your brain doesn't just control your personality and mental Skills, it also controls your muscles and therefore your sporting Skills. That's why the main difference between Tiger Woods or Roger Federer and other less skilled sportsmen is in their brains. This is where all their exceptional sporting Skills reside – not in their muscles. In the book *The Winner's Bible for Elite Sports*, you'll learn how to get both a Winning mindset for the white heat of competition (mental Skills) and also the most efficient way to rewire those circuits in your brain that are responsible for controlling your muscles, your reactions, your vision and co-ordination (physical Skills).

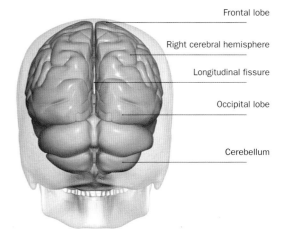

Frontal lobe

Right cerebral hemisphere

Longitudinal fissure

Occipital lobe

Cerebellum

Right now though, I'd like to look at some of the lessons sport can teach us about how our brain affects our behavior. Let's start by considering what happens when tennis champion Roger Federer faces a serve from his rival Nadal. Federer's first task is to calculate the trajectory of the ball – i.e. where is it going? This is primarily done in his 'Occipital Lobe' which is involved in processing visual information. As a result of years of training, Federer's Occipital Lobe is wired differently to yours or mine. Tests show he can identify accurately where the ball is going just *before* Nadal hits the ball. He can do this because he's learnt how to automatically analyse the subtle nuances of Nadal's ball toss and the fine details of how Nadal moves his arms and legs in preparation for the serve. You or I can't do this and so we have to wait until the ball has crossed the net. This makes it look as if Federer has super-human reflexes. But tests show his reflexes are similar to normal people. He only reacts faster because he starts working out where the ball is going much earlier than we do. The additional circuits in Federer's Occipital Lobe give him a head start. But Federer wasn't born with this ability to analyze tennis balls – he had to learn it through practice and experience. In the same way you can learn how to rewire all your brain modules – whether those modules are involved in sport or in behavior – and turn them into Supercharged modules.

Now the point of introducing you to these brain structures wasn't to give you a lesson in neuroscience, but rather it was to show you that elite performance, whether on the sports field, in business or in life – critically depends on the performance of your brain modules and how they interact with each other. It's not just a matter of 'being motivated' or 'training hard' or 'thinking the right thoughts' (although those things are also absolutely vital). Rather, truly elite performance in all aspects of life depends partly on rewiring your brain circuits. Each of us is naturally wired differently because of our genes and each module responds in a different way to different training interventions. We need to be aware of both our natural wiring and also the very best ways to improve it. That is why understanding your Physiology and improving it is one of the foundations on which you will build your success. We'll revisit this module time and again from various angles in this book.

INVERTING GOGGLES AND REWIRING YOUR BRAIN

Before we carry on and discuss the other three Pillars of your personality, I want to show you how much power you have over rewiring your brain and changing your performance.

It is possible to make special goggles with prism lenses that turn the world upside down. When you look through these goggles the ceiling appears below you and the floor appears above. When you first put on goggles like this you can hardly do anything. You can't even reach for a cup on a table and you certainly can't walk. None of this is surprising as this upside down picture of a bedroom illustrates.

You can get a rough idea of how difficult life would be if you wore inverting goggles by trying to trace a picture if you look in a mirror. Initially you'll find it's next to impossible.

Now the really surprising thing is that if you wear these inverting goggles for a few days your brain realizes everything is all wrong. When you reach up with your arm you 'see' your hand move down. So your brain works very hard to find a solution and – incredibly – within a few days, it has developed new circuits which automatically flip everything back up the right way. When these new circuits kick in, you actually see everything the right way up even though all the images are still upside down on your eyeballs.

If you think about this for a moment you'll realize just how remarkable this feat of rewiring is. Vision is an incredibly complex process which involves recognizing objects and working out how they move relative to one another. To be able to re-calculate all this so that an 'upside down image' now appears the right way up, and therefore completely normal, is quite staggering. Particularly when you consider you've seen the world the right way up all your life. Achieving this requires massive changes to how information is processed and how your brain is 'wired'. You have to overcome years of experience and learning and do this in real time with no delays.

If your brain can be trained to automatically invert an upside down world and make it look normal, then it can be trained to do almost anything!

CHAPTER 6
INTRODUCTION TO YOUR HISTORY PILLAR

ACCIDENTAL HYPNOSIS

There is a special type of historical event, which can occur at any stage of your life, where some small and seemingly harmless incident produces a major change in your personality. This can even occur late in your adult life. I call these special events 'Accidental Hypnosis'. In many cases of Accidental Hypnosis you no longer remember the event itself, and yet despite this, it still continues to have a powerful effect on you every day of your life.

It's a bit like what happens when someone hypnotizes you into thinking an onion is actually an apple. If the hypnotist has done their job correctly then you don't know you've been hypnotized and you can't work out why everyone looks at you strangely when you eat an onion. It may be the same with you today. You may do things or feel things without knowing the actual cause.

The reason why this is called 'Accidental' is that no one deliberately meant to change your personality, but that's what ended up happening. It was an accident.

To give you a simple example of how Accidental Hypnosis works, let's suppose a young girl of seven called Patricia is at school and she sees a group of 'cool' girls playing together during lunch-time. Patricia wants to join in with the girls so she walks towards the group. As she gets close Patricia calls out and asks if she can join in. Unfortunately one of the girls in the group called Jill snaps back and says, 'You can't join us because you're too ugly. We don't like you – go away.'

Now Jill's reply was probably just a throwaway line that didn't reflect how pretty Patricia really was. Indeed, Jill may even have said Patricia was 'ugly' because she was envious of Patricia and wanted to remain the centre of attention without any competition. Whatever the reason, this sort of name-calling and criticizing goes on in children's playgrounds on a regular basis – most of it without any real basis in fact. But even though there wasn't any real truth behind the statement that 'Patricia was ugly', it may nevertheless have seared itself deep into her heart. It did this because Patricia was desperate to join the group and she was feeling lonely as she walked over. Her defenses were down and she was emotionally vulnerable and so Jill's words went straight to her heart. From now on, Patricia thinks of herself as ugly or not popular and this may manifest itself in all sorts of unusual and unexpected behaviors. Even if Patricia forgets this episode entirely, she may still continue to be insecure and act as if she is ugly. It's also important to realise that Accidental Hypnosis isn't just the result of what people say. Your mother may have simply 'raised her eyebrows and sighed' when you failed to do something. Non-verbal communication like this can have just as much effect as any amount of words and have just as powerful an impact on you.

A real life example of how Accidental Hypnosis works is illustrated by a successful model from New York who asked for my help. Despite having made it onto the front cover of *Vogue* magazine she acted as if she was unattractive and 'didn't fit in'. Her logical mind would tell her she was good-looking because she was constantly getting modeling contracts and she could even look in the mirror and say, 'Yes, I do look attractive'. But at a deep emotional level she was incredibly insecure and constantly seeking confirmation that she was attractive and acceptable. This insecurity played havoc with her relationships. Lots of men would initially be attracted to her because of her stunning looks, but within a few weeks of dating them her 'needy' behavior would drive them away. She'd constantly talk about herself, seek attention or try to prove she was okay rather than just relaxing and getting on with the relationship. It soon became boring and annoying for any boyfriend. Predictably, the more men she drove away the more insecure she became and so the situation rapidly fed on itself until she was so insecure she gave up dating altogether.

It was clear there was a mismatch between her logical mind and her emotional mind, but no amount of logical reasoning or telling herself she was good-looking or successful seemed to alter the way she truly felt about herself. I began to investigate and discovered that the cause of this mismatch was very simple. When she was 11 she grew incredibly quickly and had long, skinny legs which required her to wear braces for almost a year to help her legs grow straight. Being 5 feet 11 inches tall and wearing braces as an 11-year-old meant she stood out from everyone else. As a result, she received many comments about her appearance, and not surprisingly with young kids involved, much of this was negative. But within a year the braces were removed and she blossomed into a strikingly attractive and athletic girl. However, the emotional damage had already been done. She still felt 'different' and unattractive even though this was clearly no longer the case.

By the time I met this woman she was forty and her modeling career had ended. She was now running her own successful business but was single, lonely and working almost 24-hours a day. She was exhausted and her life seemed empty and hollow. As we talked it became obvious that her excessive working hours and obsession with 'success' was also related to the same inner insecurity and her need to be 'accepted'. That one year of wearing braces and looking 'gawky' while she filled out into her tall frame had cast a shadow which had screwed her life up for the next thirty years! All sorts of therapy, self-improvement courses and counseling hadn't helped fix the underlying problem. And that's the tragedy of Accidental Hypnosis. It is:

• Surprisingly Widespread
Few individuals escape their formative years unscathed. If you're like most people, you'll have had experiences as you grew up that somehow still cast a shadow over you today – even though those experiences are long forgotten and no longer valid.

• Very Powerful In Its Impact
In many cases the consequences of Accidental Hypnosis can be quite debilitating. It is not uncommon for even highly skilled people with great knowledge and wisdom to be leading lives which are only a fraction of their potential and which only produce a small percentage of the happiness they deserve.

• Hidden From You

People are often unaware how their History is affecting them. It's not as if they know what's wrong and can't find the solution. They don't even know what the problem is in the first place. All they know is that life isn't quite working out how it should be.

• Often Quick And Permanent To Cure

The cure is often relatively quick and almost always permanent if the correct Tools are used. This is the real tragedy. People spend decades of their lives backfiring along on three cylinders, squandering their lives away when just a few adjustments could give them the power to lead a life of great satisfaction.

There are two other important points I'd like to make about Accidental Hypnosis. The first is that it doesn't always have to be negative. Sometimes it can have a profound and positive impact (as recounted in Chapter 24, 'Albert's Compass'). The second is that it doesn't just arise from the things people say to you. Remember the raising of a mother's eyebrows?

By now you might be wondering what distinguishes Accidental Hypnosis from all the normal things that happen to you as you grow up. Aren't we just talking about good and bad things having an influence on you? Well the answer is that there are special things about Accidental Hypnosis that make it somewhat different.

Accidental Hypnosis usually:
• Occurs when you are emotionally vulnerable or under emotional stress
• Is caused by someone you look up to or respect or want to impress – a cool person, a parent, a teacher, a coach
• Happens when you are young and impressionable
• Occurs without you knowing it at the time
• Leaves a long-term effect on your personality long after the event has been forgotten

The reason why Accidental Hypnosis is so powerful is because your emotions are aroused *during* the event. When this happens, your good old Limbic System fires up because you've been hurt and it wants you to avoid this bad experience in the future. As far as your primitive Limbic System is concerned, being told you're ugly is no different to having your fingers burnt in a fire. All your Limbic System knows is that you've been exposed to a 'bad thing' and the one thing it wants you to do is immediately and permanently learn to avoid bad things. In the same way the Limbic System helped you to avoid the tiger without you having to go through lots of lessons. And so when your Limbic System fires up it releases special chemicals into parts of your brain involved with long-term memory which make these emotionally charged incidents stick permanently. This is why you can probably remember exactly where you were when you heard about the death of Princess Diana but you probably can't remember a thing about what was going on in your life the day before she died. For most people, her death was an emotional event and so they remember it clearly and easily. In summary, emotionally charged events have this special ability to get stuck inside your soul, and if they are bad events, they can reduce your capacity for satisfaction for the rest of your life.

This also helps explain why events from your childhood often have the most powerful effect on you. When you are young you haven't yet learned how to protect yourself from events or necessarily interpret them correctly because your reason and your Frontal Lobes are still undeveloped. This allows your Limbic System to get carried away and lay down what are often inappropriate concepts about yourself and who you are. For example, if a father runs off with another woman and leaves his family, his actions can accidentally be interpreted by his young daughter as meaning that all men are untrustworthy. At her young age she hasn't yet learned how to judge each person as an individual and she may not be fully aware of all the facts leading to the separation. But because she is emotionally attached to her father her loss is enormous. From then on it may have a powerful effect on how she sees herself and other people. To go back to our analogy with the hypnotist, she may then see the apple as an onion – or in other words, all men as untrustworthy.

KNOTS IN YOUR MIND

So now you know some of the causes of debilitating aspects of your History Pillar. But what is the effect? Well, there's an interesting thing about your History which will make sense to you if you've ever had a massage. Occasionally your masseur will come across a small knot of muscle that feels tighter to his fingers than the rest of your muscles. When he homes in on that little spot you realize it's much more painful than everywhere else he rubs. This sore spot is caused by the muscles in that area being in a permanent state of mini-spasm. For some reason those fibers haven't relaxed and released even though you don't need them to be tense any more. While you might have previously used them for exercise or tensed them when you were concentrating, that was a while ago and they

really should have switched off by now so that they can recover. But they're stuck in this tense state and it's quite counterproductive for recovery. But with sufficient kneading and pressure by the masseur, the tight spot gradually releases and the pain fades away.

There are three interesting points about this:
• Before the masseur found that specific tense spot you didn't realize it was there. All you knew was that your shoulders as a whole felt tense
• There was no need for that tiny group of muscles to remain tight. In fact, their constant contraction and failure to release actually made the spasm worse
• Once the sore spot was fixed your entire shoulder felt better

Now the same thing is true of your brain. We all have localized circuits constantly buzzing away in our brains without us being aware of them – like 'mini-spasms' of thought. Often these unconscious thoughts make the rest of our lives less happy than they should be – just like the small knot of muscle buried deep that makes our entire shoulder feel tense. These brain circuits might have been historically activated by some experience in our past in just the same way our muscles were.

But that was in the past and now we really need them to switch off. The problem is we usually aren't aware what the specific thought is that's causing us this general discomfort or malaise.

The relief when these unhelpful, hidden brain circuits are finally relaxed and switched off is often quite amazing. The sad part is how much energy these knots in the mind consume, and how long we put up with them, because we don't know which parts of our mind to 'massage' and we haven't learned the best techniques to turn them off.

OVERCOMING YOUR HISTORY

Overcoming your History doesn't mean you need to spend years in therapy raking over the coals of your childhood looking for causes and events on which you can blame all your problems. That sort of therapy is rather slow and ineffective from a clinical point of view and there is a risk you end up focusing so much on the past that you don't get on with fixing the present. You become pre-occupied with problems and not with cures.

Overcoming your History, or any experience of Accidental Hypnosis, should be a relatively quick and permanent process if it's done correctly. It requires:
• An understanding of what's in each of your Four Pillars
• Daily Use of your ongoing *Personal Winner's Bible*
• The application of special Mental Tools (such as 'Emotional Transformation' or 'Emotionally Supercharged CDs', see Chapter 7 and 9, respectively)

It's the combination of all three that will be so powerful and effective.

YOUR EARLY HISTORY IS DISPROPORTIONATELY POWERFUL

The reason why your History is so important is because when you were young your brain underwent its greatest changes while it was being wired up. Your brain learned to do literally millions of new things without you even being aware it was doing so. During your early formative years your brain made over two million new wiring connections every single second! All these new connections are required if you're going to learn things like deciphering the mysteries of language or learning how to walk and see. In fact, when you were born your brain didn't know what to do with the signals it received from your eyes. As a result you couldn't see properly as the pictures on the opposite page show. In addition to your images being fuzzy you also couldn't tell the distance between different objects or even where an object started and ended. It was all just one big blurry

| 4 Weeks | 8 Weeks | 16 Weeks |

image without any distinct edges. But over a period of months your brain learned what to do with the signals it received from your eyes and by the time you were seven your vision was as good as an adult's.

But there is something else which is interesting about how you learn to see. If your brain is deprived of signals from your eyes during the first year of your life, then it *never* learns how to see properly no matter how much training you give it in later life. For example, if you wore a patch over one eye for the first year of your life then after that patch was removed, you would be 'blind' in that eye even though there was nothing wrong with the eye itself. You'd be blind because your brain wouldn't have learned how to wire up the vision circuits. Unfortunately this blindness would be permanent because there is only a limited window of opportunity when the brain can do all this vision wiring.

In the same way you learn many other things in your early years without fully comprehending what's going on. You learn what is 'right and wrong' and you learn what 'sort of person' you are. Your brain absorbs millions of messages from your parents, teachers and friends and comes up with an hypothesis of who you are and how you fit into the world based on those messages. Unfortunately, because you are only a child, your brain does this with very limited knowledge and so it often gets these more complex social issues only partly right. And like the other lessons you learn when you are young, most of these social lessons end up hidden deep inside your brain without you really understanding how they came to be there. But once they're in there, they're stubbornly resistant to change.

Conversely what you *don't* learn in your childhood is just as tricky to deal with. If you are deprived of love and affection as a child then key areas of your brain which are responsible for your personality don't get wired up correctly. The effect on these personality circuits is similar to the effect on the vision circuits in the brain if the eye is deprived of light during a child's first year. We know this because brain scans of people who have been emotionally deprived of love and affection show that connections between their rational Frontal Lobes and their emotional circuits don't work correctly. These emotional/logical connections can remain incorrectly wired up throughout your adult life if you've had a very traumatic childhood in the same way that your visual circuits can remain permanently damaged by the wearing of a patch. Fortunately that level of damage is relatively rare in modern society. But the point remains: huge tracts of our personality, our understanding of who we are and how we respond emotionally to situations are laid down early on in our lives and these lessons persist stubbornly for years.

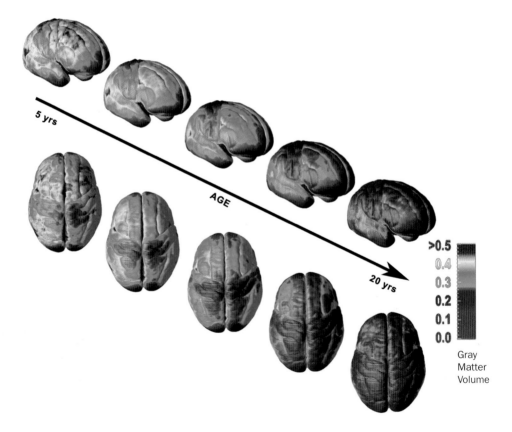

5 yrs

AGE

20 yrs

>0.5
0.4
0.3
0.2
0.1
0.0

Gray
Matter
Volume

While many of our physical, visual and verbal Skills are mastered during the first seven years of our lives, our social Skills continue to undergo rapid changes until we are twenty. This happens because the regions of the brain responsible for our personality and higher reasoning remain highly impressionable and easy to wire right through to our early twenties. This is shown in the figure on the opposite page where the colours illustrate how different regions of our brain mature at different times.

The rate at which these different regions of our brain get wired up is perfectly matched by observations of our behavior. We learn physical Skills most easily when the part of our brain responsible for controlling our muscles – called the motor cortex – is being wired up. That's why it's important for athletes and musicians to learn their Skills early on. Similarly, we can learn a second language while the part of our brain responsible for language – called the temporal lobes – is being wired up. That's why learning a second language after the age of 12 becomes much more difficult.

It's not surprising then that the core foundations of our personality and the strategies we use to shape our adult life are laid down in our childhood and in our teens. But *we needn't be a slave to our History*. One of the aims of this book is to give you Winning Tools so you can break free of your childhood influences and design your own Optimal Future.

KEY POINTS
- Your early years are a very special time for your brain as it effortlessly learns millions of new things
- Much of what you learn during this time is unconscious and hidden deep inside your brain
- As well as developing physical Skills you also develop the core foundation for your personality
- Many of your childhood lessons are resistant to change and continue to exert a disproportionate influence on your adult life – even if what you have learned is not a good foundation for your personality
- A small part of the purpose of this book is to help you break out of your childhood destiny and claim your own Optimal Future

THE OTHER TWO PILLARS

We've now had a brief look at your Physiology Pillar and your History Pillar. There are of course two more Pillars, your Philosophy Pillar and your Psychology Pillar:

Your Philosophy Pillar

Your Philosophy Pillar is probably the most important Pillar of all. Time and again when I've worked with elite champions, or when there was a really difficult issue with a client, I found it was the Philosophy Pillar that held the key. Because this Pillar is so important I had to write an entire book on it which I've called *The Winner's Bible of Philosophy*. We'll need to use some philosophy as we continue on in this book, so what I'll do is occasionally introduce little snippets of philosophy in the form of small self-contained stories or vignettes in various chapters. I know my clients have really enjoyed these little stories and I hope you do.

The reason why philosophy is so important is because a Winner not only needs to understand themself, but they also need to understand the Universe in which they live. Unless you fully understand the rules by which the Universe operates, it will be like playing poker without knowing those rules – and if you do that you're bound to lose, no matter how hard you try. *The Winner's Bible of Philosophy* explains the deep mysteries of the Universe and what it means for you in your everyday life. Is there such a thing as truth? Are we in control of our Optimal Future? How can we ever know? Can we find meaning and value in life? What is man's place in the Universe? I know it may seem strange but having clarity on these larger philosophic issues has time and again exerted a profound influence on the athletes and business people I have worked with. It has allowed them to break through to a higher level of performance.

There is an extract from *The Winner's Bible for Philosophy* at the end of this book so you can see for yourself how I make this topic come alive in a really visual way.

Your Psychology Pillar

The Tools you're going to start learning about in the very next chapter are part and parcel of your Psychology. The rest of this book will be concerned mainly with those Tools because they'll help you overcome your History and maximize your Physiology. They'll ensure you get the very best out of every experience that life throws at you.

Well, congratulations! You've got through all the theory you'll need for the rest of this book and by now you should have built a really solid platform on which you can make some powerful changes to your life. You've got your *Personal Winners' Bible* going and you've completed your Online Independent Audit. It's now time for me to introduce you to some of the Tools and techniques I've used to dramatically change the lives of elite athletes and everyday people. You'll have a chance to sit in with some world famous athletes and watch me in action as I'll illustrate each Tool with real life cases. Then it will be your turn to try these Tools out on yourself.

Ok, let's get on with the fun stuff now.

CHAPTER 7
EMOTIONAL TRANSFORMATION

It's now time for me to introduce you to the first Tool you can use to get a better balance between your emotional Limbic System and your rational systems. I call this tool *Emotional Transformation* (because it reminds me of an ingenious technique called 'Transformation' which is sometimes used by advanced mathematicians to solve really difficult problems). Here's two true stories to illustrate how Emotional Transformation works.

THE DOG AND BONE

A number of years ago I worked on a research project with an exceptionally talented racing driver who had consistently won a number of championships as he progressed up the levels of competition. His form was so impressive that one of the top Formula 1 teams selected him to join their development squad in preparation for becoming their racing driver in two years' time. Unfortunately, in the year immediately before he was due to make his Formula 1 debut he had a shocking season driving in a lower series called GP2. That year was so bad for him the Formula 1 team cancelled his contract and with it his chances of ever becoming an F-1 driver.

Part of the reason he had such a bad year was because of his inability to cope with the increased pressure as he moved up the ranks of competition. He won easily at the lower levels like Formula 3, but as he moved towards the pinnacle of professional motorsport the pressure on him increased exponentially and the consequences of failure became much more serious. A loss at the lower levels went unnoticed or was excused by inexperience, but at the top level each mistake could easily spell the end of his professional career.

If this driver came into the pits for refueling or new tires and one of the mechanics made even the slightest mistake, he'd get very angry and fly into an uncontrollable rage. This anger stayed with him as he left the pits and caused him to over-drive his car and make lots of small mistakes over the next few laps. Wild oversteer and locked brakes would quickly ruin his tires and hence his lap times, ultimately costing him the race. A few tenths of a second lost in the pit lane had quickly snowballed into seconds and then minutes on the track. But that wasn't the end of it. When he'd come back into the pits at the end of the race he'd scream and shout at the mechanic for making a mistake. This only made the mechanics more nervous and more likely to make another error in the next race. By the end of the season the driver's career was in tatters and no one wanted to hire him because of his abrasive nature and unpredictable performance. Despite being blindingly fast and gifted, he was just too difficult to handle.

He'd been to see sports psychologists about his problem but no amount of 'telling himself to relax' when other people made mistakes and to instead 'focus on what he could control' seemed to help. When I questioned him about the underlying cause of his frustration and anger he said it was driven by his intense and overwhelming desire to win. He could see his Goal *so close* – but when a mechanic made a mistake he could see that Goal slipping away while he was powerless to do anything about it. It was the combination of the importance of his Goal, the closeness to it and his inability to get that Goal which drove this particular driver absolutely crazy.

His description immediately generated an image in my mind. This image transformed the driver in just 15 minutes, so that from then on, he *never* had a single issue ever again with anger or frustration while racing. He quickly started winning again and by the end of the following year he'd won the championship. Top teams began knocking on his door and he signed as a factory driver for one of the most prestigious teams in the world. He went on to have a glorious career winning many important championships.

So what was the image and how did it help him?

I told him he reminded me of a dog who could see a bone on the other side of a chain link fence. It's a juicy and tasty bone only inches from the dog's eyes. The dog can smell it and almost taste it as its mouth drools with saliva. The dog desperately wants to get that bone and so it paws and scratches frantically at the fence. But no matter how hard it tries, the dog just can't get through because the fence is made of metal mesh. In desperation the dog digs furiously to get underneath the fence, but again it fails because the fence has deep foundations. It drives the dog crazy because the bone is so close yet remains just out of reach. Yet if the dog would only take its eyes off the bone for a moment and look to its left – six feet away – it would see an open gate. If it walked away from the direct line to the bone and through the gate, it could easily get its objective in just a few seconds.

This image may not mean much to you but it meant a lot to the young racing driver. The dog's furious struggle against the fence and its frustration at seeing the Goal so close but out of reach resonated strongly with him. Another reason this image was so successful for the driver was because it didn't involve him. Because he wasn't personally involved it became a lot easier to see how stupid 'bashing against the fence' was. It was obvious to an outsider how dumb the dog was and how its scratching and fighting against the fence wasn't going to help achieve its Goal. The image was vivid and it perfectly captured the emotions and frustrations the driver was going through. When he thought of the dog, it *automatically conjured up an emotion* of the dog's stupidity.

He was now able to use this natural emotion evoked by 'The Dog And Bone' scene and apply it to his own situation. When he did this it became immediately obvious at an emotional level that he'd achieve nothing except a lot of scratches and bruises if he continued to 'struggle against the fence'. He didn't have to 'convince' himself or 'talk' himself into a better approach. It was just natural and obvious to shift his focus away from a mechanic's error and towards making sure he was in the perfect mental zone so he could drive the car to perfection when he left the pits.

> **KEYS TO EMOTIONAL TRANSFORMATION**
> - Find a Substitute Situation (e.g. 'The Dog And Bone') which vividly captures the essence and emotion of an event that is causing you trouble (frustration at not being able to reach Goal/bad mechanic)
> - It is preferable if you aren't personally involved in the Substitute Situation as this makes it easier to see the situation more clearly (a dog instead of you)
> - Make sure your natural reaction to the Substitute Situation is one which works to your advantage (the dog is stupid and you'd never behave like that)
> - Make sure the Substitute Situation has a positive outcome (dog goes through the gate – driver concentrates on getting in the zone)

THE COCAINE GIRLFRIEND

Let me give you another true example which illustrates this Emotional Transformation procedure. A highly successful businessman came to me after he'd fallen madly in love with an incredibly sexy woman. She was beautiful, sporty, minxy, outgoing, witty, intelligent and had a crazy, spontaneous sense of humor that constantly amused him. There was a huge mutual chemistry between them and so it wasn't long before he was totally besotted with her. But four months into the relationship he began to realize she was 'bad' for him. Despite her perfectly packaged image and despite being Miss Popularity, she was at heart a rather self-centered person. She'd learned the power of her beauty and how to use her mischievous humor to get what she wanted. She loved the businessman, but it was in the way you love an object like a car, a house or a piece of music: that is, for the pleasure they give you. She didn't really care about his intrinsic inner happiness or his human feelings. She gave him love, but in reality this was just a transaction so she would *get* his love, affection, intellectual stimulation and financial security in return. She wasn't a malicious woman and she certainly didn't mean to hurt anyone. She probably wasn't even aware of how superficial her love was. It's simply that she was a 'good time' girl who thought if she could get away with things then no one would be hurt as long as they didn't find out. In short, she didn't have a properly developed moral compass guiding her life.

The businessman realized that if times got tough or some tragedy befell him she'd probably trade him in for another man despite her words of love. When I questioned him about the subtleties of her behavior (see Chapter 22, 'Grandpa's Little Stories' for more on how to spot these subtleties), it became obvious to both of us that she was keeping her options open with other men and, given her long history of unfaithfulness, this was another bad sign.

The businessman *knew* with his mind that a woman like that couldn't possibly be his long-term soul mate and he *knew* she caused him pain and unsettled his life

because her moral compass wasn't aligned with his. Yet whenever he saw her, his Limbic System went into overdrive. He was attracted to her like a moth to a flame. Even though they had genuine times of enormous happiness, they were punctuated with times of great pain when, once again, she did something selfish and let him down. Gradually his own integrity and essence began to waste away. He wasn't the same powerful, decisive businessman he used to be. He even began to excuse or accept her behavior. His 'mind' told him to leave her and find a better woman but his 'emotion' kept holding him back. No amount of rational counseling or support from friends seemed to help. He was addicted to her.

In order to help him, I had to find an image like 'The Dog And Bone' which captured the intense emotions he was feeling. More importantly, it had to reveal the reality of his situation and how damaging his girlfriend was to him. So I painted a picture of a bright young businessman who'd spent years working on a revolutionary new electronics product. To fund this research he'd raised $1 million of venture capital and now, with only a few more months of research and development, his product would be ready. Once it was on the marketplace he'd become an instant millionaire and realize his lifelong ambitions. He'd have his own company, wealth, travel and enjoy the cut and thrust of international business. I painted as vivid a picture of this young entrepreneur sitting in his research lab as I could. Then I had the young man reach into his desk and take out a small packet of cocaine which he snorted. No more work today. Or tomorrow. Each day was squandered with the temporary pleasure of the cocaine high and the low which inevitably followed. Weeks came and went. He spent all his research funds buying cocaine while his Skills, resources and talents wasted away. He lost his career, friends, money and health as all the other exciting activities he'd normally enjoy in life passed him by. He became a pale, gaunt man with hollow, sunken eyes. It was a tragic tale of wasted opportunity and life on a rollercoaster which goes nowhere.

The image was crystal clear for the businessman. Faced with a choice between a life ruled by the highs and lows of cocaine or a rich, full life – it was a no-brainer. If he could genuinely view his dysfunctional girlfriend as a packet of cocaine, if he could view his attraction to her as being an addiction, then there was a chance of him kicking her out of his life.

Fortunately the image resonated for him. He called an end to their relationship and wished her good luck. He even changed her name on his mobile phone to 'Cocaine' so that from now on, whenever she rang or sent him a text, he immediately realized the danger she posed. The spell was broken and he was no longer taken in by her charm. As fate would have it, the businessman soon met a wonderful woman who became his true soul mate. He described his new girlfriend as being like a partner who helped him row their boat to a destination they both wanted whereas his old girlfriend was like a passenger sitting in the back, eating all the goodies out of the picnic hamper while he sweated over the oars.

A QUICK RECAP

Let's recap what I did with both the racing driver (The Dog And Bone) and the businessman (The Cocaine Girlfriend) using the Tool called Emotional Transformation. I related the problem they were having great difficulty with to a problem that was almost identical, but one which they weren't personally involved in. *A problem that had similar dynamics but which naturally evoked the exact opposite emotional response.*

The businessman naturally thought people who became addicted to cocaine were weak and had poor life Skills, yet he was addicted to something equally as dangerous. The racing driver thought the dog was stupid for being so fixated on the bone immediately in front of it and for not seeing the wider picture, yet he was doing the same thing in his racing career.

I want to close this chapter by showing you once again how destructive our natural inclinations are and why we need Tools like Emotional Transformation to conquer them. If you give rats the choice of pressing one lever to get water flavored with aspartame (artificial sugar with no calories or nutrition) and another lever to get wholesome milk, the rats always choose the flavored water. They continue pressing the lever and drinking the sweetened water until they die, even though fresh, nutritious milk is freely available. Their natural instinct is for something sweet rather than something healthy. In the same way, what we naturally like and are strongly attracted to, is not always good for us.

Two key Skills I use when working with athletes is:
1. Firstly, find out what is unbalancing or hindering their performance.
2. Then, most importantly, find an image that is going to arouse a powerful emotion that will overcome their own natural Weaknesses.

CHAPTER 8
THE WHEEL OF LIFE

VIBRATIONS

If you suddenly feel a bad vibration through your steering wheel then you know something has probably gone wrong with your car. If that happens you need to fix the problem otherwise you'll quickly wear out the tires and put more stress on your car's suspension – not to mention making your journeys more tiring as you struggle with the steering wheel. The trouble is it's not always obvious what's causing the problem.

YOUR UNIQUE BALANCE

This situation has a direct parallel for you. Your life is like a wheel with the central axle being your guiding philosophy. Spread around this central axle on the outer rim of the Wheel are all the components of your life: your Passions, hobbies, friends – all the things you think about, worry about, love and do. And because you are a unique person with a unique combination of thoughts, what you have at each position on that Wheel will be unique to you.

Regardless of what is on your Wheel, it is essential that each component is carefully balanced by its complementary component otherwise your life will vibrate out of control. For example, each person needs to balance the amount of 'excitement and stimulation' in their life with the correct amount of 'time out, reflection, recuperation and contemplation'. Different people require vastly

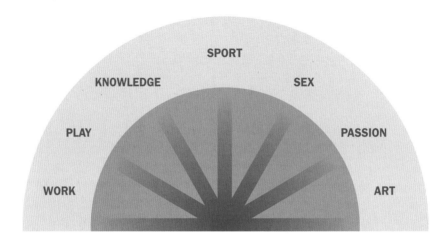

different amounts of each component on their Wheel in order to reach their ideal balance. What is too much stimulation and rushing around for one person is nowhere near enough for another person. Similarly, some people use meditation and contemplation to counterbalance their work while others find exercise is better.

DYNAMIC BALANCE

Although each of us has our own unique balance, this balance isn't static. As we go through life and develop, we should be constantly adjusting the weights of our existing components and removing or adding new ones to our Wheel. What was our focus as a child should not be our focus as an adult. It's a dynamic process — or at least it should be.

When I was a child, I spoke like a child, I thought like a child, I reasoned like a child; when I became a man, I gave up childish ways.
1 Corinthians 13:11

There's nothing sadder than seeing fully grown adults running around on baby training wheels.

YOUR CENTRAL AXLE

The most important part that affects how smoothly a wheel runs is the central axle. The axle not only supports the rim but it also guides and sets the direction for the wheel. In this analogy, your central philosophy is the axle around which your entire life revolves. Your philosophic core supports your activities and

Passions and it also determines the direction of your life and where you will end up. If your philosophic axle bearings are loose then even the smallest bumps in life will cause you to deviate from your true path. Loose bearings cause other problems too. If your bearings are loose then the smallest amount of imbalance on your Wheel will cause you to get the 'speed wobbles'. You'll have no robustness or tolerance. But a solid, well-constructed axle allows you to cope with all the challenges of life and it even allows you to make progress if your Wheel is temporarily out of balance because of some unexpected stress.

THE WISE PERSON

Maintaining your car in peak condition as the mileage increases requires a certain level of expertise. A vibration which was quite normal when the car was new may slowly take on a slightly more sinister quality as the car ages, often without you even being aware there was any change. A small rumble in the background may mean little to you but to a highly skilled mechanic it would be a clear sign there is a very specific problem ahead.

A wise person can listen to the wobbles, vibrations and bumps in their life and know exactly what they need to adjust in order to get the smoothest, most efficient ride possible. The very process of living and moving forward means you will be shaken and jostled. In fact, sometimes feeling no bumps and jerks in your life is a *bad* sign because this means you've become stuck in a rut and are not being challenged or extended anymore. A stalled car or a stalled life is such a waste of all that powerful potential (see Chapter 13, 'Carpe Diem'). A wise person can also tell when they're fruitlessly 'spinning their wheels' without making any progress. For it is often all too easy to confuse action, effort and motion with genuine progress in life.

Knowing how to tell the difference between external bumps on the Highway of Life and internal problems with your own Wheel is the hallmark of a wise person. One sure method is to look for repeated patterns. The bumps on the Highway of Life are usually random in nature and severity while any cycle of repeated ups and downs, stress, sadness, disappointment or failure are probably due to issues with your own Wheel Of Life.

It is essential you learn how to listen to the squeaks, vibrations and ups and downs in your life so you can make the correct adjustments before there is too much wear and tear. A drop of oil or tightening a loose bolt in your life can save substantial remedial work later on. It is therefore very worthwhile to frequently take a moment to see if your life feels balanced. Are you at peace? Are you at the centre of your maximum potential, doing what naturally makes you happy? Are there repeated cycles of stress? Are you moving forward and experiencing the bumps and bangs of life or are you stuck in a rut?

Psychiatry typically involves a process of either tightening or loosening the patient.

OTHER PEOPLE

Some people naturally add a counterbalance to your life and smooth out your ride. With them around everything seems more balanced and natural. Progress is easy and fun. This works because their Strengths are often your Weaknesses and so even though neither of you are individually perfectly balanced, there is an overall harmony when you combine together. Your two Wheels balance each other out, and when combined, allow you to carry far more than you could on your own.

When two Wheels are combined like this it is absolutely critical that the axles are aligned. If they don't have the same direction, the same core values and ultimate Goals, then there will be much chaffing of tires. Misaligned wheels like that will cause your own Wheel to wear out more quickly than if it ran independently on its own and progress will be slow and tiring.

Sometimes another person causes your life to become a rollercoaster of ups and downs. This may not necessarily mean the other person is a bad person – only that their balance does not match your balance. Sometimes this is a permanent state of affairs because both parties are not progressing and learning how to balance their own individual Wheels. If that is the case then the two Wheels should remain separate. But the bumps and jerks caused by another person may also be the result of them challenging you to rotate and move out of your comfort zone when your own central philosophic axle is not yet strong enough for this progress.

The ultimate aim, of course, is for both Wheels to be independently balanced. Neither needing the other to counterbalance their own Weakness. Both Wheels, set apart but pulling in the same direction. People – and their effect on your life – are a good example of life's bumps, both good and bad.

ACTION ITEMS: CHECKING YOUR WHEEL

Take a moment now to look back over last week and think about how balanced your life was. It's necessary to do this from time to time because our Wheels often go out of balance so slowly that we don't even realize it's happening. A relationship that started brilliantly may imperceptibly have now become one that is detracting from your life rather than adding to it. You may now have become used to the rollercoaster ride and accepted that as part of normal life when actually it shouldn't be. Maybe you've become obsessed or overly focused on a certain aspect of your life and this is causing you to wobble along. So take a blank sheet of paper and answer the following questions:

Relationships:
• Are you and your partner balancing each other out or have you somehow got out of synch as time has gone by?
• Are there more repeated ups and downs in your relationship than when you first met?
• Are your axles aligned and are you heading in the same direction?
• Are you becoming less dependent on each other but at the same time more in tune and more in love? (True love shouldn't be based on need or dependence)
• Has your relationship stalled or are you challenging and stimulating each other?

Work/Recreation/People:
• What percent of your week was spent thinking about all the components on your Wheel Of Life?
• Are you overly focused on one or two items?
• Is your work/recreation balance correct?
• Do you have enough components spread around your Wheel or is it rather sparsely populated?

Progress:
• Have you strengthened your central philosophy and are you more secure/content in yourself?
• Are you better able to withstand the challenges of life and people or do you wobble out of control at the slightest provocation?
• Are you heading in the right direction?
• Are you closer to your Optimal Future this week than you were last week?
• What are you doing to make sure you get closer to your Optimal Future?
• What have you done to add further balance to your Wheel this week?
• Has your life stalled and are you in a rut?

- Are you spinning your Wheel with lots of effort – tremendous motion and action – without any actual progress towards your Goals?

The point of thinking about these things is not just to have a list of items you can be dissatisfied about but to:
- First find out *what* needs to be worked on
- Then actually *do* something about it

Write answers to these questions and what you are going to do about them on an A5 page. At the top of the page write the date and then place them in your *Winner's Bible*. It's important you write everything down on paper and keep it safe in your *Winner's Bible* because this will provide you with:
- A snapshot record of where your life was at that point
- A list of things you need to be aware of and watch out for
- A plan of action

The next time you go through the process of balancing your Wheel again, it will be easy to see how effective you've been and how much progress has been made.

CHAPTER 9
EMOTIONALLY SUPERCHARGED CDs

One of the most powerful Tools you can use to overcome problems and generate real 'oomph' in your life is one I call *Emotional Supercharging*. As is usually the case, the best way to explain this technique is to use a real life example.

THE TOUGH OLD COACH

The Head Coach of a European football team came to me because he was under enormous pressure from his country's press and it was starting to get him down. Despite having one of the best international records over the last two years, his team had unexpectedly lost a few key games against countries they were expected to beat. To make matters worse, the Coach was a foreigner and his team was packed full of international star players. Not surprisingly, every newspaper and football fan blamed the team's poor form directly on the Coach. Radio talk shows were filled with comment on what the listeners would do if they were the Coach and there were endless columns of newsprint from journalists giving advice. Whenever the team played badly it was the Coach's fault and whenever the team did well it was the sheer brilliance of the individual players and nothing to do with the Coach. The Coach couldn't win either way and it was really starting to wear him down. Wherever he went people had an opinion about him and, more often than not, they'd find something to criticize.

While criticism is part of any international coach's life, he was now starting to become emotionally drained because the attacks had been ratcheted up to an extreme level and had continued for almost six months without a break. There is only so much anyone can take. When I first met the Coach I actually thought he was doing a remarkable job of coping with the enormous pressure. Other coaches would have cracked and thrown the towel in long ago. But this man was a tough, hardened campaigner with a 'bullet-proof' personality and exceptional mental Skills. Given all this, I wasn't sure whether I could help him or not. However, I was up for the challenge.

My usual procedure is to spend two sessions with someone. The first session usually lasts about one hour and, as you now know, my aim is to find out what is in each of the client's Four Pillars. I don't attempt to help them at all in that session. I then spend a few days thinking about what's in their Four Pillars before coming back for a second session where I try to make a permanent change in their lives. If I've got it right, that second session should be enough to resolve the particular issue my client has come to see me about. It shouldn't need dozens of on-going sessions or months of therapy. If it works, it works! The client then usually goes away and works on any homework I've given them. I only see them again if there is a new issue to deal with or if I wasn't successful the first time around, but so far this hasn't happened yet.

I started my first session with the Coach by exploring what was in each of his Four Pillars and how they were connected. I did this without him actually knowing what I was doing. I never mentioned the Four Pillars and I never explicitly asked him about his Philosophy or his Psychology. I simply asked him a lot of questions and followed the leads provided by his answers – wherever they went. I didn't talk about his immediate problems with the press or the emotional turmoil he was going through. Instead, I wanted to understand how he ticked because if I could do this it would allow me to make a lasting change to the way he dealt with the pressure of his job. I wanted to treat the underlying cause and not the symptoms.

FINDING HIS INTRINSIC SATISFACTION

One of the many questions I asked him was, 'Tell me two things that have given you real pleasure in your life.' His first answer was he felt immensely happy about his daughter's recent wedding. I asked him to explain exactly what made him so happy. He told me he was proud his daughter had married a man who was perfectly suited to her – that she had chosen 'correctly'. He was proud the wedding was not only a celebration but was organized to perfection and progressed flawlessly – like 'clockwork'. Everything was 'correct'.

The second event he mentioned was when his team were up against their arch rival. They were playing away from home in front of a highly charged crowd with the odds heavily stacked against them. The opposition struck early scoring a fine goal. Five minutes later one of the Coach's key midfield players was injured and had to be substituted off. This would normally make winning an impossibility. But the substitute midfielder came on and in his first touch of the ball, broke the opposition defense wide open, allowing his team-mates to score a perfectly executed goal to level the match. Everything clicked together like 'clockwork'. All the Coach's drills and discipline during practice had produced a machine that functioned perfectly when under pressure – even when a key component had to be replaced. His team then went on to an historic win which the Coach described as 'immensely satisfying'.

After listening to these two stories, it was immediately clear to me that one of the key drivers that gave this coach 'Intrinsic Satisfaction' was something described by the words 'perfection', 'correctness', 'precision' and 'order' (see Chapter 14, 'Your Intrinsic Drivers'). I explained my observation to him and said it seemed to me he likes being the 'conductor'. That is, he gets pleasure and meaning out of bringing together a disparate group of highly skilled people and helping them achieve a great result. I could immediately tell from the expression on his face that I'd hit a chord with him. So now the question was, *How can I use this insight to help him survive the media maelstrom that is raging around him and still have genuine peace, despite all the criticism?*

If I was going to be successful I'd have to disconnect the external stimulus of media criticism from the normal, negative emotions these harsh comments produced in his brain. I'd then have to reconnect the 'media criticism' to an entirely different set of emotions because the 'criticism' had to connect to something. It couldn't just be left dangling in a vacuum. To do this I produced a special CD for him. But before I tell you about the CD and what was in it, I need to tell you about one more thing I discovered regarding the Coach's History Pillar.

Against all the odds, the Coach went to the same high school as the guy who was now his harshest critic. This TV sports presenter was the main person co-ordinating and leading the charge against the Coach. He was the one person who was really getting under the Coach's skin. What annoyed the Coach most about the TV commentator was that the presenter simply didn't understand some of the complexities of the modern game, and as a result, his criticisms were not only unfair, they were far too simplistic.

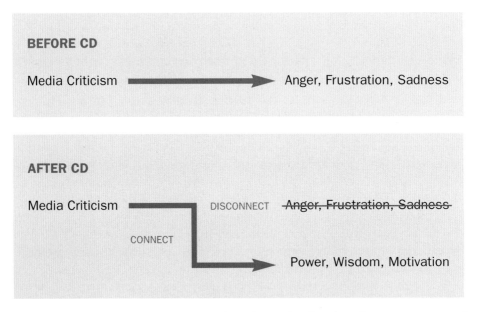

Now they both went to a small, elite boarding school and so they were aware of each other but had never become friends. I asked the Coach if he could remember what the TV presenter looked like when he was at school. Could he conjure up an image of the presenter as a young boy in short pants? He said he could. So now the stage was set.

THE CD RECORDING

I recorded a 16-minute tailor-made CD for the Coach and loaded it on his iPod. I asked him to put on his headphones, lie down on a couch in my living room and get comfortable. I have to admit it was rather strange seeing this gruff, hardened, old Coach lying there. It just didn't seem right. Even though I'd had numerous world famous athletes ranging from heavyweight boxing champions to world swimming champions and professional rugby players lying on my couch, they all seemed so fresh, pliable, open and eager. But here was the old Coach, with a tough, uncompromising exterior who could strike fear into the most powerful athlete with a single word. A man who knew as much about Winning and coaching as anyone in the world. I just wasn't sure my CD would help him.

I started the CD by explaining to the Coach what was on it. I told him I'd take him through three stages:

First, his mind and body would be totally relaxed and switched off.
Second, I'd take him back to a 'happy place and time' in his life.
Finally, I'd help him rewire his emotional connections so he would have a different emotional reaction to any criticism from the media. Instead of being upset, he'd naturally and automatically be motivated and empowered by it.

Throughout the CD, specially composed music played gently in the background while I talked. This music had been carefully designed to help reduce the random words and thoughts that might accidentally pop into the Coach's conscious, logical mind. I wanted him to remain focused entirely on my voice.

During the first stage I used an induction procedure to totally relax the Coach's body. After five minutes he was totally switched off and was breathing slowly but deeply. What was much more important than his body being relaxed was that his 'logical' mind was also gradually being switched off at the same time. While he was listening to my voice and feeling sensations in his body my voice was slowly taking over control of his thoughts without him realizing it. By the time his body was relaxed he was now passively following my voice without consciously analyzing what I was saying. He was comfortable and receptive to the images I was painting and he was enjoying the ride. This may sound a bit like the start of hypnosis, but as I'd explained to the Coach before he listened to the CD, I wasn't going to hypnotize him. I was merely going to help him turn his own logical mind down to such a low level that I could paint vivid images that would arouse his emotions in a new way. It's a bit like dreaming. You can't dream or be in 'artificial reality' if your mind is busy processing sensations from actual physical reality around you.

It was now time for me to move to the second stage and take the Coach back to a really happy place and time in his life. Doing this would allow me to tap into the powerful emotions that were already burnt deeply on his mind and that would further enhance the link between my voice and what he was feeling. Establishing this link between my voice and his emotions was vitally important because making a change in the Coach was all about changing his *emotions* rather than giving him new thoughts. He already had all the logical phrases to deal with criticism and he already possessed incredible mental toughness and logic, but that wasn't enough. In order to help me recreate this happy place and time,

I'd previously asked the Coach during our very first meeting if he would give me a detailed description of two happy events from earlier in his life. As well as his daughter's wedding and the 'clockwork' football match, he also told me of a time when he was on holiday in the Caribbean with some mates and they were lying around a swimming pool while a live band played mellow music in the background. The sun tanned his skin while the warm glow of camaraderie and jokes from his friends combined to make life at that moment seem so peaceful, happy and content. I prompted him for more details so that I could work out exactly which images, sounds, feelings, sensations, smells and emotions would bring that happy event back to life. Maybe it was the feel of the cold beer in his hand and the little beads of condensation that ran down the glass. Maybe it was the song being played in the background. I now used every one of those sensations and images during the second stage of the CD to ensure the Coach was reliving those experiences in full Technicolor virtual reality (the Coach later told me he felt he was 'really there'). Again, this isn't like normal hypnosis where you try to help someone by getting them into a suggestible state and then say something like, 'You will never want to smoke again.' What I was doing was simply using this technique to connect with existing emotional circuits in the Coach's brain. Once I'd achieved that it was time to move to the third stage. I'm going to share with you what I said to him 'word for word'.

As you read these words remember that the images I used for the Coach are only powerful and valid for *him*, because only he's been through his experiences and only he has his unique personality. The image I chose – a conductor – is powerful and moving for him but it may arouse no emotion in you. He got mentally and emotionally fired up by the images of 'perfection' and 'precision' but you may not. This is where the skill of making these CDs comes in. They need to be uniquely tailored for each person. However, even though the images may not work for you, I hope you'll at least get the idea of how I connected with the Coach's unique emotions using the Supercharged CD.

As you read the short transcript below it's crucial that each line is read at just the right speed. You need to allow time for each image to build. Try reading it fairly slowly and pausing at the end of each line as you try to imagine what was going through the Coach's mind. Particularly now you know some of the things that were of special emotional significance to him.

It is your destiny to be the greatest coach that ever lived
You will not achieve that destiny through anxiety or worry

But through impeccable preparation
Like the conductor of a symphony
Who knows the Strengths and Weaknesses of each musician
Who trains and disciplines them
Relentlessly, firmly – but kindly

Like a wise father
Educating and bringing up their children
So that everything is correct and in order

So I want you now to see yourself as a wise conductor
Standing on the stage at school
About to conduct an orchestra of eager, talented but naïve boys
You know how to train them so they can play a wonderful masterpiece
You are older and wiser than them
You've conducted many teams before
You feel at peace when the music starts
For it is what you do best

And as you stand on the stage before you start
I want you to turn around and look at the boys sitting in the rows of seats below the stage
in the big assembly hall
I want you to see the TV Presenter sitting there in his school shorts
Skinny legs and knobbly knees
A noisy boy with lots of opinions, talking when he should be quiet
Beside him are a few of his simple friends
Maybe they're way back in a lower class, Form 3F I think
They don't even have an idea of what they don't know
They're boys compared to you – they really are
So I want you to raise your baton now
Silence the boys
You wouldn't worry what a school boy says to you
So don't worry about them either

For it is time for you to conduct the orchestra
Time to hone your team into the best machine ever
Raise your baton
Play your beautiful music
It is what you do

And as the music plays
A quiet hush falls over the audience
They sit in silence
In awe
And you will have peace and satisfaction
Everything is correct and in order

Assembling a team and getting it to work perfectly is what you DO
You are like a watchmaker
It is painstaking work
At the moment there are cogs and wheels everywhere
You can see them scattered on the bench
You will need to reshape a few
There is much assembly to be done
Tuning, adjusting
You need the very best machinists around you to help with the grinding and cutting
But when all the pieces are together it will be a wonderful sight
Everything ticking perfectly
It takes time and patience
But you will do it

I **strongly** suggest you log onto www.winnersbible.com and download an mp3 copy of the Coach's original CD and listen to it yourself. That way you'll get an idea of how it works. Words simply can't describe these CDs anymore than words can adequately describe what it feels like to listen to Beethoven's 'Moonlight' Sonata.

HAVING 'SENSITIVE RADAR'

One of the reasons why the Coach's CD worked so well for him was that I'd tapped into absolutely vital aspects of his personality and 'key words' that had huge emotional significance for him. When I listened to the Coach during the first session to find out what was in each of his Four Pillars, I realized the words 'clockwork', 'correct' and 'conductor' meant very special things to him. For example, he described his daughter's wedding as going like 'clockwork' and her new husband as being the 'correct' choice. These were just many of the adjectives he chose, but he used them in a rather unusual or unexpected manner which alerted me to them. Most other people would have chosen different words. They might have described their son-in-law by saying things like he was a 'great guy' or they might have said the wedding went 'brilliantly'. But the words 'clockwork' and 'correct' were the words that naturally flowed out of the Coach because they had a special significance for him. Doing the 'right thing' and 'everything working like clockwork' was hugely important for the Coach because he had an impeccable sense of right and wrong and of procedure and order. But it would have been easy to miss those words and therefore not have followed up on them and this would have meant I'd have failed to discover a key aspect of the Coach's personality. We might instead have spent all our time in the first session busily talking about the 'big' issues he was facing – like the media hounding him and how unfair all that was. As you discover what's inside your own Four Pillars, you'll learn how to increase your sensitivity to your own Little Stories, key words and powerful images (see especially Chapter 22, 'Grandpa's Little Stories').

THE COACH'S SECOND CD

The Coach listened to his first CD five or six times over the next week and found it immensely helpful. It gave him energy whereas before his 'batteries had been worn down' and he'd run out of steam. I then made a second CD for him during that week which focused on his future. I wanted to widen his view from the immediate issues he was facing to the bigger picture and his place in history. This second CD was even more important than the first because completely overcoming an issue requires you to move your focus away from the problem once it's been dealt with and to instead focus on a positive event in the future (see Chapter 17, 'Overcoming Disappointment And Disaster').

For his second CD I made use of the Coach's interest in biographies and history. He loved reading about great leaders, studying their personalities and what made them tick (again, I discovered this information during our first session together). Apparently, part of the reason the Coach was going through such a tough time was because his team had recently been depleted due to injuries and his best players had retired or been injured. He was being unfairly judged in isolation from the circumstances around him, as if everything was his fault, when in reality it was probably a much more complex interplay of events. For some reason this reminded me of a period in Winston Churchill's life just before World War II when he fell badly out of favor with the public and other politicians. During that time Churchill spoke passionately about the upcoming threat from Nazi Germany, but no one listened to him. They said he'd lost touch with reality, that he was too old and a product of a previous war-mongering generation. It became fashionable to heckle Churchill during his speeches and the high respect he'd previously commanded began to crumble away. His past days of glory faded and were replaced by what Churchill called his 'dark days'. Of course, that wasn't the end of the story. Churchill would soon come back into his own and save the day for his country.

My aim in the second CD was to establish an emotional link between Churchill and the Coach. Churchill had to weather a storm of criticism because other people didn't see the world as clearly as he did. But Churchill was 'correct' (remember, that was one of the Coach's favorite words) and ultimately history remembers him with great fondness and reverence. I wanted the Coach to see that he was in a similar situation and he had to 'stick to his guns' during this difficult period – in the sure knowledge his time would also come again. In the future when he was an old retired man sitting in his rocking chair, he *would* have a smile on his face. He *would* be remembered as a man who gave his all and got the best out of his players considering the circumstances he was faced with. History would judge him kindly and remember him as a man of tenacity who continued to battle on against all the odds and score great victories.

After listening to both CDs, the Coach bounced back with impressive energy considering the pressure he was under. Instead of his mind wandering during those quiet moments at night and mulling over what he'd read about himself in the newspapers during the day, he found he was instead naturally busy devising

Winning tactics against his competition. He didn't have to force his mind to do this, it just seemed to do it all on its own. In the following year he coached his team to an unbeaten run of international successes in a row thereby silencing his critics once and for all. (You can also listen to the Coach's second CD on www.winnersbible.com)

TRY MAKING YOUR OWN CDS

CDs, like the ones I made for the Coach, are so powerful I strongly suggest you give them a try. If you log onto *The Winner's Bible* website you'll find a section containing the following resources to help you:

• mp3 recordings of background music which you can download
• Written scripts that you can use to relax and get yourself in the zone for Stage 1
• Links to third-party software that will allow you to record your own voice and mix with the background music
• Examples of professionally recorded CDs for you to learn from

Making a personalized CD to Supercharge your emotions is just one of the many Tools you'll use to become a Winner. It's not compulsory and I don't always make CDs for every athlete or business leader I work with. But if they're made correctly, with the right keys and triggers, they usually turn out to be one of the most effective Tools of all. That's why I encourage you to give them a try.

THE THREE STAGES OF A 'SUPERCHARGING CD'

While every CD needs to be custom made for each person, they usually follow a three-stage process:

Stage 1: Relax And Turn Off Physical Reality

Stage 1 puts your mind into a peaceful, relaxed and calm state where you don't have any distracting thoughts of your own. The idea is to turn *physical reality* down so that, in Stage 2, I can begin to construct a *virtual reality*. It's a bit like when you enter virtual reality and dream each night. You can't dream if your eyes are open and your mind is consciously active. You need to let all the outside world fade away so you have the peace and space necessary for your virtual world to unfold.

As your mind becomes relaxed and quiet, it should increasingly become absorbed with the words being spoken on the CD. Having your body 'switched off' helps you achieve this state because your mind and body are intimately connected via a series of special circuits in your brain. Normally your brain needs to be active when you body is active, and vice versa. Therefore, turning your body off quickly allows me to turn your mind off. Once your mind is quiet and focused entirely on following the words on the CD, you're ready for Stage 2.

If you log onto www.winnersbible.com/CDScripts you'll find a choice of 'scripts' you can use to turn your mind off when you make your own CD.

Stage 2: Construct Virtual Reality

The aim of Stage 2 is to gradually increase your immersion in virtual reality. It's the sort of state you get into when you're watching a great movie. You're not aware of anything else around you in the cinema and it's almost as if you're immersed in the action. Another aim of this second stage is to strengthen the connection between the words you hear on the CD and your emotions.

The best way to do this is by tapping into vivid images that are already burnt on your mind. Images from especially 'happy places and times' in your life work particularly well for this because they are laced with emotion and always very vivid. And because they are happy emotions they further enhance your relaxed state.

Stage 3: Emotional Supercharging

After the first two stages you're finally ready to have your emotions Supercharged. This requires a lot of careful homework well in advance if it is to work. It requires a deep understanding of your Four Pillars. It must also be logical and something you already agree with in advance of the CD being made. There can be no surprises. This is where the Skill of the person making your CD comes in. Sometimes even the subtlest difference in words or how an image is portrayed can make an enormous difference in the effectiveness of the CD. The timing of the delivery, the tone of the narrator's voice and the background music are all crucial.

SUZIE Q AND WHY THE CDs WORK

There is something incredibly powerful about these CDs. It would even be fair to say I'm constantly amazed at the profound and lasting effect they have on people when they're made properly. Let me tell you about my all-time favorite example and then I'll explain in a little more detail *why* these CDs work.

A few years ago I met, quite by chance, this wonderful woman called Suzie. Over the years I've grown to like Suzie a lot and, like all my friends, I've given her a nickname. I call her Suzie Q. You can see a short video of Suzie Q on the *Winner's Bible* website.

Many years before I met Suzie she was married to a very successful and wealthy businessman in Auckland and she had a lovely son whom she doted on. Unfortunately, after a very painful divorce Suzie decided to experiment with recreational drugs. The one she tried was a particularly addictive drug called 'P' (which stands for Pure Methamphetamine). 'P' directly targets the dopamine pathways in your brain and as a result goes straight to your pleasure/reward module, which makes it an incredibly hard drug to break free from. It's almost as if this specific drug has been designed with one purpose in mind – to get you hooked.

By the time I met Suzie she had reached rock bottom. Her closest relationships had broken apart under the strain of her drug addiction and the police had taken her son away from her. She was only allowed to see him once each fortnight under strict supervision. Suzie was an intelligent, articulate woman and she really wanted to kick the habit and get her son back. But knowing *what* to do and being *able* to do it were two entirely different propositions. Suzie had tried life-coaching and also been an avid student of the Tony Robbins courses. But somehow they only gave her a temporary burst of resolve. Before long she was back on the drugs.

I did two sessions with Suzie Q. The first was spent getting to know everything I could about her and what was in each of her Four Pillars. Clearly, her Physiological Pillar had one incredibly important aspect to it – namely her physical addiction to 'P' which had hotwired her brain. But there were many other very important things going on in Suzie's History, Philosophy and Psychology Pillars too. With those things in mind, I spent a week making up two things:

• Her *Personal Winner's Bible*
• A CD to Supercharge her emotions

Clearly Suzie loved her son and desperately missed him. Not surprisingly she also wanted to get her life back on track. But her logic and natural desire for these two things wasn't strong enough to match the unnatural pull of the drugs. So what I had to do was make her love for her son become more 'real than real'. I had to *Supercharge* her natural emotions for her son. To make those feelings become so powerful they swamped her desire for 'P'. Just like the Coach, I found the key emotional buttons to push and then I turned the volume of those emotions right up. That's why the CDs work. You align the emotions with the logic – both in terms of direction and also in terms of strength. To use our analogy of the kayak, you need to align the 'paddles' with the 'rudders' (see Chapter 1, 'The Kayak Analogy').

The CD planted a really powerful emotional driver in Suzie's mind which was then backed up by her daily use of her *Personal Winner's Bible*. It was a winning combination. After two sessions, Suzie's life turned around 180 degrees. She never touched drugs again. Twelve months later her hair was tested by the police to prove she'd been clean for over a year; she's since regained total access to her lovely son once more. Suzie is one heck of a woman. She's rebuilding her life, a step at a time. That sort of result where someone gets their life and their family back again is worth far more to me than any world championship. After all, if Athlete A didn't win a gold medal, then by definition some other athlete would have. The world would hardly be any different. But Suzie and her son getting their lives back is not a zero sum game. The world *is* a different place.

BRINGING THE FOUR PILLARS TOGETHER – THE FIJIAN CHIEF

Let's close this chapter with one more illustration which brings together in a single example how to:

• Use your Four Pillars to find out exactly what's going on inside your brain
• Use this knowledge to develop a CD
• Link that CD with your *Winner's Bible*

I was asked by the coach of the All Blacks rugby team to see if I could help one of their players. The coach told me Steve was one of the most naturally talented players he'd ever seen. Yet some days he'd turn up on the field for an international match and he'd have as much energy and enthusiasm as if he was there to just enjoy the sunshine and lay down on the grass. Other days he'd be in sparkling form and tear the opposition to pieces. Various psychologists and mental Skills people had tried to motivate this player but all to no avail. Clearly no coach could afford to have such an inconsistent player on their team in the white heat of an international match and yet the All Blacks didn't want to lose him either because of his natural Skills. But Steve's form had recently become so lackluster that they were facing the inevitable choice. Unless something drastic happened, he'd have to go.

Steve was a wonderfully likeable guy. In fact he was also the most laid-back guy I've ever met. He'd been born in Fiji where he lived a simple life in a dirt-floored hut with his parents on one of the remote islands. He looked back fondly on his childhood and it was clear to me that 'family values' were critically important to him. He'd come a very long way from that grass hut to being an All Black living in New Zealand and being paid a $1 million annual salary.

When I asked Steve what motivated him in life he told me 'nothing really', and I suppose given the riches he now had, and where he'd come from, this didn't surprise me. I asked him how he spent his time away from the All Blacks training camp. He told me he just spent his time 'chilling' at home with his wife and his son. I then asked him what he'd wish for if I gave him a magic wand and he could have five wishes. He sat for about three minutes in total silence and then said, 'I can't think of anything I'd like to wish for. I'm happy as I am.' Even though he was only 26-years-old he could afford to retire, and given his moderate requirements, live till old age without ever having to work again. It was little wonder no one could motivate him. People were trying to motivate him and treat his 'symptoms' without fully appreciating what was inside his History, Psychology and Philosophy Pillars. External motivation like that was bound to provide only temporary change.

In that same first session, I found out three crucial things about Steve:
1. He had a very strong Christian faith.
2. He absolutely adored his son and wife.
3. He had great respect for his father who lived back in Fiji.

I used those three things to totally and *permanently* change Steve's life.

The first thing I did was draw on Steve's Christianity – his Philosophy Pillar. I placed the story from Matthew Chapter 25 into Steve's *Personal Winner's Bible*. This story tells how God gave each person certain talents in life and the responsibility we have to make the most of those talents. It's an interesting story because in ancient Rome a 'talent' was a measure of weight (about 32kg) and so a 'talent of silver' was equivalent to nine years wages for the average Roman. A 'talent' is also the skills we might have. So you can read the following passage from *The Bible* and think of the word 'talent' using both those meanings at the same time. I also found a picture that summed up that story from *The Bible* for Steve so he didn't have to read the whole chapter whenever he looked at that page. Here is what I put into that page of his *Winner's Bible*.

Matthew 25 vs 14 – 30

'For it will be as when a man going on a journey called his servants and entrusted to them his property; to one he gave five talents, to another two, to another one, to each according to

his ability. Then he went away. He who had received the five talents went at once and traded with them; and he made five talents more. So also, he who had the two talents made two talents more. But he who had received the one talent went and dug in the ground and hid his master's money.

Now, after a long time, the master of those servants came and settled accounts with them. And he who had received the five talents came forward, bringing five talents more, saying, "Master, you delivered to me five talents; here I have made five talents more." His master said to him, "Well done, good and faithful servant; you have been faithful over a little, I will set you over much; enter into the joy of your master."

And he also who had the two talents came forward, saying, "Master, you delivered to me two talents; here I have made two talents more." His master said to him, "Well done, good and faithful servant; you have been faithful over a little, I will set you over much; enter into the joy of your master."

He also who had received the one talent came forward, saying, "Master, I knew you to be a hard man, reaping where you did not sow, and gathering where you did not winnow; so I was afraid, and I went and hid your talent in the ground. Here you have what is yours." But his master answered him, "You wicked and slothful servant! You knew that I reap where I have not sowed, and gather where I have not winnowed? Then you ought to have invested my money with the bankers, and at my coming I should have received what was my own with interest. So take the talent from him, and give it to him who has the ten talents. For to every one who has will more be given, and he will have abundance; but from him who has not, even what he has will be taken away. And cast the worthless servant into the outer darkness; there men will weep and gnash their teeth."'

I explained this story to Steve in our second session when I gave him his *Personal Winner's Bible*. It got his attention as if I'd slapped him in the face. Here he was, an incredibly talented person wasting his talents away. And yet in this passage God tells him – not me, not a coach, but the creator of the Universe – that he should not only use his talents to the full, but that he has to increase them! And because this message was based on beliefs rooted firmly in his Philosophy Pillar, it provided a powerful anchor for *permanent behavior change*.

The second thing I put into his *Winner's Bible* was a picture of a Fijian chief along with a few key bullet points.

I really liked this image, because for me, the Chief had a real presence about him.

THE SKILLFUL CHIEF

- Is respected
- Is admired
- Makes use of all his talents
- Leads by example, not words

There was something both dignified and vibrant in his appearance. He really looked like he was in control and was the sort of man you ought to trust. I talked to Steve about the example he was setting for his wife and son. What sort of message was he giving them when he sat on his couch each day watching TV rather than going out training? What sort of example was he setting for the other young players in his Super 14 team when he wasn't with the All Blacks? He not only needed to use his talents, he also needed to become a chief of great dignity. A chief of his family and a chief of his team. Instead of just muddling by each day, Steve actually had a purpose in life. If he truly loved his son, then there was much more he had to do than just lavish affection on him. A chief doesn't just tell his tribe how much he likes them. He also leads them by example. He does things and achieves things.

Steve then toured with the All Blacks throughout Europe for five weeks and played brilliantly in every game, scoring one particularly spectacular try which cut the opposition team to shreds. On his return to New Zealand after this brutal tour he knuckled down and became an inspiration for his Super 14 team and a role model for the younger players. Instead of sitting on his couch in front of the TV he was out inspiring other players.

I hope you can see how rather than treating his symptoms and trying to 'motivate' him to become successful like coaches usually do, I tapped into the contents of his Four Pillars and used those contents to Supercharge his emotions. I used his History, his Psychology and his Philosophy Pillars to make *permanent* changes in his behavior.

Given the sorts of images I've already painted for Steve in the sentences above, I hope you can imagine for yourself how I could use these vivid pictures to record an incredibly powerful CD for Steve which Supercharged his emotions and brought them to life. Emotions that were intimately linked with the images we'd selected for his *Winner's Bible*.

Steve later told me he not only found a new source of inspiration and energy from those two sessions, but he now enjoyed life, his wife and his son even more than before. Rather than just affecting his game on the field I'd managed to affect his entire life.

CHAPTER 10
POMEGRANATES

Author's Note:
From time to time I'll interrupt the natural flow of the book and introduce little self-contained stories or vignettes. The idea of these vignettes is to make you stop and *think*. They also contain great truths. Initially you might not understand why these vignettes are there but as time goes by they will assume greater importance. You'll find you come back to these stories when you least expect it. For example, the following little vignette called 'Pomegranates' is important because one of the characteristics of Winners is that they lead balanced lives. We all know we need to have balance but how do you know if your life really is balanced? What does 'balance' actually mean?

Many years ago there was a young man apprenticed to a wise, old doctor. After watching his master heal many people he became restless to begin seeing his own patients. So one day he said to his master, 'Master, I have watched you for many years and now I am ready to heal my own patients.'

The Master replied, 'My son, you have learned much but still you are not yet ready to treat your own patients.' But the young doctor persisted and badgered his master. Finally the Master relented, 'Very well my son. Standing outside the tent is a patient who has a liver problem. The cure for this man is pomegranates. You may see him.'

The young doctor was very excited and ushered his first patient in. He quickly looked the patient over and proudly proclaimed, 'You have a liver disease. What you need is pomegranates.' On hearing this, the patient threw up his arms and stormed out of the tent shouting, 'Pomegranates my arse! You're a useless doctor.' Understandably the young doctor was shaken and upset. He turned to his companion, 'Master, Master, you told me he had a liver disease and he needed pomegranates. What went wrong?'

The Master replied, 'As fate would have it, there is another patient outside the tent and he too has a liver problem. Please show him in and learn.'

The second patient came in and the old Master examined him thoroughly before sitting down quietly in deep thought. Two or three minutes passed and still the Master had said nothing. Finally he looked up and said, 'I have examined you and it is clear you have a liver disease.' He paused for some time in deep thought. 'What you need is something fleshy … not too sweet …' He looked into the patient's eyes and said, 'Ah … what you need is pomegranates.'

The patient stood up, hugged the Master and thanked him profusely before leaving with a happy smile on his face.

The young doctor was now even more perplexed than ever.

'Master, I don't understand. Both patients had a liver disease and I too prescribed pomegranates.'

The master replied, 'My son, that is where you are mistaken. What they needed was pomegranates … and *time*.'

And so it is, that even though many things are 'correct' they may also need time to be absorbed. Time needs to pass before they can be of value or can work. Sometimes the *timing* also has to be right. Remember this as you work through the exercises in this book and in your interaction with people. Be patient.

> It is a strange truth: you may one day find a particular thought you reacted against and ridiculed is now the very thought that is most precious and helpful.

CHAPTER 11
GONZALES' HAPPY DAY

HOW *THE WINNER'S BIBLE*™ GOT STARTED

For the first ten years of my career in Formula 1 I was primarily involved in analyzing the mathematical and technical aspects of driving. I'd look over the telemetry data and calculate how the drivers could make subtle changes to their style to get that extra millisecond out of the car's performance. The following true story is about the first athlete I helped on a purely *mental* level. It marked the start of my own personal journey into this arena and led to the creation of this book and all the techniques you are reading about. Let me tell you the story of the very first *Winner's Bible* ever made.

In order to protect the name of the F-1 driver in this story, I've decided to call him Gonzales after the Warner Brother's cartoon character Speedy Gonzales – 'the fastest mouse in all of Mexico'.

WINNING AND HAPPINESS

Being a Winner isn't just about solving your problems, setting Goals and achieving things. You also need to be genuinely happy in life. Unfortunately, not being able to enjoy life and being caught up with negative issues is one of the most common problems faced by elite athletes and businessmen. It's a risk factor for successful people because part of their success is due to their ability to work relentlessly on their Weaknesses and solve them. But like everything in life, this requires a balance (see Chapter 8, 'The Wheel Of Life'). Being happy not only makes your life worth living, it also provides you with the energy to achieve more and ultimately become more successful. When you're happy your brain releases different chemicals and the modules in your brain work together more efficiently. Almost without exception, being genuinely happy will provide you with a significant performance improvement over the long haul compared to someone who isn't happy. Whether we measure your academic ability, the speed of your reflexes, your ability to recover from hard training sessions or your ability to learn new Skills – being 'happy' has been clinically shown to change your brain and give you a competitive advantage.

Before we go any further, we need to make an important distinction. The type of 'happiness' we are talking about here is a 'genuine deep-seated happiness' and contentment rather than a superficial laugh-a-minute type of humor. Many a 'clown' appears to be laughing on the outside and be the life of the party, but is actually hollow and crying on the inside. With this in mind it's time to add another section into your *Personal Winner's Bible* which will help you start the process of having a 'Happy Contented Balance'. Let's use the true story of the very first *Winner's Bible* to help set the scene.

THE BLANK SHEET OF PAPER

A number of years ago I was working with a Formula 1 driver who was having a really tough season. No matter how his engineers set up his car it was aerodynamically unstable and seemed to behave differently every time he entered a corner compared to the last time. Because F-1 cars are so incredibly fast this meant he was constantly on the edge, not knowing whether he was going to crash or not. It also meant he couldn't drive the car right on the limit and as a result he was struggling in the championship. As the races ticked by without any improvement to the car it seemed as if his career was draining away. Slowly but surely he became more frustrated and angry, often taking his frustrations out on the engineers and mechanics when things weren't going right.

MISS UNIVERSE

As I talked to Gonzales it became clear this state of affairs was really getting him down. Life seemed to have lost its sparkle and had become a long hard grind of training and practice and disappointing races. After talking at length about the problems with the car, I decided to change direction and asked him to tell me about some of the things he still got pleasure out of. Initially he told me he just wasn't enjoying anything any more – but I persisted and asked him to think of the things that at least gave him some sort of temporary pleasure so I could write them down in a list and we could work on them.

He told me he loved driving fast cars. As I wrote this down I said, 'Loves driving fast cars – is paid a fortune to drive the fastest and most expensive car in the world.'

I then asked him to tell me something else apart from cars that he enjoyed. He said he loved women. I asked him if he was seeing anyone at the moment. He told me he was currently dating a Miss Universe finalist.

K.S: 'What else do you enjoy?'
F-1 Driver: *'I love boats.'*
K.S: 'And do you have a boat?'
F-1 Driver: *'Yes, I've got a beautiful 80-foot Sunseeker yacht.*
                      She's a real beauty.'

With a joking voice I replied, 'Crikey, I'm looking through this list and it seems to me you're having an absolutely miserable life!'

We both laughed.

What was happening with Gonzales was that a major part of his success was due to the fact that he'd constantly look at how he could improve himself and his performance. He did this by focusing on the slightest imperfections in his performance, himself or his car and then he'd work his butt off to improve each of those small details. In essence, he was concentrating on any small negative things and exaggerating them with a microscope. That *was* a good strategy and it had helped him to become a successful person in both his racing career and in his life. But as so often happens with elite athletes after a number of years at the top, this 'focusing on the negative' starts to become an occupational risk. They start to only see •he negative things they need to improve and life begins to lose its enjoyment. They've become used to the fame, fortune and success they so desperately wanted when they were teenagers and now take it for granted. Instead, they're worn out by the constant travel, hotels, endless press conferences, the intrusions into their private life and the relentless training. I explained this was a normal process for elite athletes and told him he needed to spend a moment each morning to get the 'feeling' of being happy back again.

DAILY DEVOTIONS

Of course, he *knew* with his logical mind he was privileged and fortunate, but he'd forgotten to *feel* it each day. So I decided to make up a little folder for him and put his photo on the front cover and call it, *Gonzales' Winner's Bible*. I told him he had to fill the first few pages with 'All The Things I Am Happy About.' Each morning I wanted him to briefly spend a moment and look over those pages to remind himself how lucky he was and how happy he should *feel*. To help him get the *feeling*, we put photos and images inside the plastic pockets of the folder. I told him he wouldn't feel happy immediately, and of course, he'd still have to work with his race engineers to solve his badly handling car. But he had to trust me on this and:

• Do it religiously *every* morning and *before* he did anything else
• Not put his *Winner's Bible* down until he had at least established a flicker of a connection with one of his 'happy things'
• To continue for at least two weeks – regardless of how well it was going

And that was the start of the very first *Winner's Bible*. Gonzales loved the idea.

BEING THE CAPTAIN

While I was at it, I told him he needed to take responsibility for the mood of the mechanics and engineers around him. He wasn't just the driver who turned up, drove the car and then got out and complained about everything that went wrong. He needed to change his attitude that fixing the car was everyone else's job. Even though he wasn't the team owner, he *was* the 'team captain' of his car. He needed to turn up each day with an air of positive energy and dignity. He had to be part of the solution even if he didn't design the car. I wanted him to think about the engineers and mechanics and see them as individuals who had emotions, dreams, disappointments, Goals and girlfriends just like he did. I wanted him to take a personal interest in each mechanic as another human being rather than thinking of them as someone who just bolted the wheels on the car. If they felt 'loved and important', I was sure they'd do a better job for him and ultimately that meant he'd do better.

So the next section of Gonzales' *Winner's Bible* contained a piece on 'Being the Captain'. I put a photo of a distinguished captain in his folder along with a list of attributes a captain has. Gonzales had to *feel* he was a captain and that required him to get inside the picture of the captain.

Within a matter of weeks, the entire team had improved out of sight. Because the mechanics felt 'loved and important', they went about their job with just that little extra bit of energy, and interestingly enough, the car started to become more stable. No one could say why – it just started to perform better. If you walked into the race bay you noticed a positive energy in the garage rather than the previous tension. But what was much more dramatic was the change in the racing driver. Over the next three months his whole demeanor changed. While he was still at heart the same guy, little things no longer drove him crazy anymore. He seemed to have more fun with his friends and they in turn found him more charming and amusing. At home he could relax and enjoy a DVD or just chill out without feeling anxious that he ought to be doing something. He kept using his *Winner's Bible* each day throughout the following year and good things just started to happen to him out of the blue. Because he was famous he'd dated hundreds of women, but he'd been rather unlucky in love. His relationships always seemed to be tempestuous affairs which ended rather unsatisfactorily. Now he fell in love with a woman he'd actually known for some time and before long he started a family with her. To this day they are blissfully married.

THE HAPPY SECTION IN YOUR *WINNER'S BIBLE*

The point of this story is that we all tend to take the good things in our lives for granted and instead focus on the things we don't have and that aren't right. That's just human nature. After all, fixing things which aren't right is what helps us get ahead in life. But it comes at a cost. We risk never being satisfied with our progress or what we've got. Of course we *know* all the good things in our lives, but unless we remind ourselves and experience them each day, our cup seems to be half-empty rather than half-full. This is the motivation for the next section in your *Personal Winner's Bible*. It's going to contain all the things that you are *happy* about. The most important things in this section won't just be your material possessions – they'll also include things like your health, your sports, hobbies and pastimes. They'll also include your friends, your family and the people who are important to you. You should also include things you've done in your life that you are proud of. Events that made you really happy. Be creative and think outside the box. You might suddenly realize that even though you're 40, you still look better than most 35-year-olds. That's worth reminding yourself of each day.

Don't worry if you have difficulty starting your 'Happy Pages'. Most people begin by telling me how miserable their lives are and that nothing is going well for them. That they've got nothing to put into their 'Happy Pages'. But with a bit of prompting they soon begin to realize just how many things they've taken for granted and not appreciated properly.

KERRY'S HAPPY SECTION

Let me give you one of my own personal examples which shows how creative you can be. I like to remind myself I live a better, fuller and richer life than Napoleon Bonaparte. While I might not rule France, I do eat better food every day than he did. I have access to the most amazing selection of culinary delights in my supermarket with fresh foods from around the world. A bewildering variety of fresh seafood (lobster, scallops, salmon, hapuka, caviar etc), fine wines (buttery New Zealand Chardonnays, spicy Australian or South African Shiraz), and desserts he would have died for. I can travel the world in the luxury of a 747 and I've already experienced more cultures and more amazing things than he did in his entire life. I can race my motorbikes at the weekend or go sailing or waterskiing with friends. I have access to the best medical care. My teeth are in perfect order and I live in a wonderful house with all the conveniences of modern life. I've loved and been loved by some of the most amazing women who have ever walked on this planet. I don't have to fight in any wars and I can read great literature and study the latest scientific discoveries. I'm incredibly fortunate I can spend a large portion of my day studying and having my mind challenged and stimulated by new ideas. I wouldn't even want to swap my life for that of Tiger Woods or Roger Federer because I'm able to spend *my* life doing the things *I* enjoy the most. A few hours of tennis a week is brilliant. But I couldn't spend my whole life hitting a tennis ball every day or going round and round a race track for 100,000 laps. Instead, I love having my brain challenged by a variety of new ideas. Maybe I'm slightly 'geeky' and that's why Federer probably wouldn't want to swap lives with me either. The point is, on average I am doing what makes *me* happy even if there are still things I'd like to change or which get me down from time to time.

With this in mind it's time to be creative and prepare a section in your *Winner's Bible* which contains all the things you can be happy about. While you're compiling your 'Happy Pages', don't forget to include things from your past such as achievements you were proud of or magical times you've had. Life isn't just lived in the present or in the future. It is my experience that people who consistently lead the happiest lives are those who can *savor* the past and still get genuine pleasure from it, even if they are going through tough times in the present. Surely a holiday was no less fun just because it came to its inevitable end. It added to your life at the time and you should still be able to roll it around in your mind like a fine wine on your tongue. You should be glad you were lucky enough to have had that experience.

Likewise, if you were fortunate enough to have had a great relationship in the past then *learn* how to be thankful for that experience regardless of the reason it ended. Even if you are lonely now and can't find anyone who can match your previous partner, ask yourself if you'd really have preferred to have not had that good relationship and all those experiences in the first place? The more you go through life, the more you'll realize it's all about your *attitude*. The more you practice finding the good side of life, the more life will be predisposed to deliver you future happiness.

SAVORING HAPPINESS

The really cool thing about your brain is that the more you tap into your happy emotions, the more powerful they become. Your happy circuits respond to being exercised in the same way your muscles respond to weight-training. That's why it's important to learn to savor happiness like you would learn to savor a fine wine. There is far more pleasure to be had from a wine when you roll it over your tongue and give the various flavors and bouquets a chance to develop on your palate, than when you gulp it all down in a single mouthful. Life is very much like that as well.

Learn how to savor happiness rather than just consume it.

Learn how to savor the past, as well as the present and the anticipation of the future.

Whatever is true, whatever is honorable, whatever is just, whatever is pure, whatever is lovely, if there is any excellence, if there is anything worthy of praise, think about these things.
Philippians 4 verse 8

CUSTOM-MADE 'HAPPY CDs'

Just as you can make special CDs to Supercharge your emotions or to overcome historical issues like Accidental Hypnosis, you can also make special CDs that can tap into your 'happy' emotions and give you a real burst for the day. These aren't motivating CDs or the usual 'rah, rah, rah' type of 'Let's get going!' CD. They're not humorous or funny. Rather, they are custom-made to tap into your pre-existing 'happy emotions' – whatever those unique happy emotions may be for you.

YOUR *WINNER'S BIBLE* SHOULD NOW CONTAIN
- Your material Goals
- Your personal development Goals
- Important people in your life – Family and Friends
- Heroes and Mentors
- Your Strengths
- Your Weaknesses
- Your Repeated Mistakes and Skills
- Things you can be happy about – Gonzales' Happy Day

CHAPTER 12
AN UNSHAKEABLE BELIEF IN YOURSELF

So far we've concentrated on getting your *Personal Winner's Bible* up and running. We've also introduced you to numerous core concepts that will provide you with the foundation to achieve your Optimal Future. It's now time to move on to the next level and see what separates out the truly elite from everyone else so you can start thinking and acting like a Winner.

Because I've worked with a lot of champions in both sport and business, I'm frequently asked what makes a particular Winner or champion so special. People expect me to reply by saying something like, 'Michael Schumacher's reaction times were faster than anyone else', or that a particular athlete has some God-given natural talent which stood out when I measured it in the lab. This hunger to know why certain people are Winners is nothing new. When Einstein died surgeons even chopped up his brain to see if they could find anything unusual which accounted for his undoubted genius.

After studying Winners for twenty years I *can* tell you that there *are* differences between them and everyone else. This chapter explains the first of these differences by telling you little known but completely true stories about three famous people.

ARNOLD SCHWARZENEGGER

John Gourgott was probably one of the most interesting and unusual men I've ever met. To everyone who knew him, he was simply 'Dr John'. Although Dr John was an eye surgeon, his Passion was bodybuilding. He was good enough to come second in the Mr America competition and he totaled over 1,000lbs for the three Olympic lifts during the 1960s, which for his bodyweight was an impressive feat at the time. Dr John was a fiercely intelligent man who studied widely, including such disciplines as Sufism along with the more traditional Western philosophies and science. He was also a law unto himself. Many evenings when Dr John and I were having dinner he would suddenly go off on a tangent and tell some interesting or mystical story that instantly stuck with me. Without fail, these stories would provide me with sound guidance over the following years. Even though Dr John has passed away, his stories and spirit live on. One such tale concerns a very young Arnold Schwarzenegger.

When Arnold first came to America he spent some time living and training with Dr John. After Arnold won his first big money tournament, Dr John sat Arnold down to give him some good, fatherly advice. He told Arnold he should invest his money in a gymnasium in California so that he didn't fritter it all away and end up poor like so many other athletes do after their short careers end. Dr John correctly predicted that California would soon see an explosion in the health and fitness industry and thought that with Arnold's Passion for bodybuilding, his good looks, his bodybuilding fame and the fortuitous timing, he couldn't fail to secure his financial future.

Arnold listened patiently to John's well-intentioned advice and then replied in a deep, slow voice, like only Arnold can. His speech was even more accentuated and slower than his most menacing Terminator voice because he had only recently arrived in America and his English was still quite poor. Arnold looked at John and said (try to read this to yourself in your deepest and slowest Arnold voice):

'YOU DON'T KNOW THE MEANING OF AMBITION.
I'M NOT GOING TO RUN A GYM.
I'M GOING TO BE A MOVIE STAR …
AND I'M GOING TO BE THE PRESIDENT OF AMERICA!'

Dr John was incredulous. Here was this young, relatively uneducated man who barely spoke a word of English. He'd never been to acting lessons, and in Dr John's opinion, would be lucky to hold down a job pumping gas if he wasn't a bodybuilder. Dr John tried to get him to see reason but he wouldn't.

As the years went by Dr John marveled at Arnold's progress. He had this utter conviction, an Unshakeable Belief that he *would* be a movie star. *Nothing* ever got in the way. No setback was a problem. If something didn't work he'd just try harder or find another way. He was like an unstoppable tank. Of course, Arnold had good luck along the way and he obviously used his bodybuilding fame to great effect, but Dr John is convinced that no one other than Arnold could have succeeded in the way he did with the limited Skills he possessed. After all, many a bodybuilder has come and gone and not made it onto the silver screen.

As Arnold's career progressed Dr John noticed a real transformation in his social and intellectual Skills. By moving forward and being constantly driven, Arnold became more intelligent and savvy about the world. He mixed with Winners in other fields of endeavor and picked up their knowledge. He hung around scriptwriters and economists. As you know, he did indeed become a movie star, and not just an extra but one of the biggest box office stars of all-time. And with time he even became the Governor of California. A job that takes real Skill and acumen, no matter what anyone says.

I know this story is true because Dr John told it to me long before Arnold publicly announced he had any political ambitions. At the time I said to Dr John, 'Well, he did become a movie star but sheer ambition has its limits. He won't ever become a politician'. But of course I was wrong. What this story graphically illustrates is the power of having an Unshakeable Belief in yourself. A Belief that defies other people's opinions and even common sense. As the greatest boxer and probably greatest sportsman in history, Muhammad Ali once said:

'To be a champion you must *believe* you are the best.'

What we are talking about here is not just the desire or a dream to achieve some Goal, but a deep inner conviction that this is your absolute Optimal Future. That no matter what happens you *will* somehow achieve your Goal. This inner conviction allows you to get up off the canvas when someone has knocked you down because you *will* be heavyweight champion of the world. The punches, the knocks and the setbacks aren't fatal – they are just part of your learning process and your education along the way to achieving your Optimal Future.

ADOLF HITLER

Let's take a further look at the power of having an Unshakeable Belief. How it can even transform a weak man into one of the most powerful men the world has ever known. To do this we need to go back to World War I.

'The Great War' was a truly terrible ordeal for the soldiers unfortunate enough to be on the front line. They had to live in muddy, waterlogged trenches while under constant bombardment. At any minute their lives could be snuffed out. Each explosion they heard could be the last one before they too joined the long list of soldiers that were mutilated and killed. Each day dawned with only more death, disease, pain and explosions. Slowly but surely, this relentless stress and the futility of war drove many of the soldiers to a nervous breakdown. In those days this nervous breakdown was called 'Shell Shock' because the soldiers associated their symptoms with the constant sound of the explosions. This affliction produces many different symptoms in different patients. One of the most severe symptoms was something called 'Hysterical Blindness'.

Hysterical Blindness is a purely psychological problem where the patient is completely unable to see even though there is absolutely nothing wrong with their eyes or the visual parts of their brain. This psychological blindness is so

complete that patients suffering from it don't give a flicker of response even if you pretend to attack them with a knife. If you think about it, this shows the extraordinary power of a psychological illness. Even though it appears you are about to kill them, they still genuinely don't see what you are doing. To all intents and purposes they *are* completely blind.

One person who suffered from Hysterical Blindness in World War I was a young, lowly-ranked Lance Corporal called Adolf Hitler. Hitler thought he'd been blinded by mustard gas in an attack but a clinical examination by surgeons revealed nothing wrong with his eyes. He was therefore classified as suffering from a psychological illness and sent to a military reserve hospital to receive treatment by a psychiatrist called Dr Edmund Forster. After weeks of treatment Hitler was still unresponsive to the standard medical approach to Hysterical Blindness and so Forster decided to try a different angle. Forster said he believed Hitler had been born with a special destiny in life which was to save the German race. He said that if Hitler really focused his mind on this amazing destiny he would gradually see a chair in the corner of the room. Hitler did as he was instructed, and slowly, the fuzzy image of the chair came into view.

From then on, Hitler absolutely believed in his destiny and unfortunately what happened next is history. Before acquiring this Belief in himself Hitler was just a lowly corporal with no distinguishing characteristics or leadership potential. Afterwards he was forever changed and went on to lead a nation and shape the world – in this case for evil. As a footnote, Hitler subsequently had Dr Forster killed in an attempt to cover up this episode of his life. But once again, the point of this story is to show you how having an Unshakeable Belief in yourself can totally transform your life.

THE EMOTIONAL CONNECTION WITH YOUR BELIEF

Before we continue, I need to explain what I *really* mean when I talk about an Unshakeable Belief. A lot of people tell me they 'believe' they are going to do this or that. But when I question them deeply, what they are really saying is that they *want* this or that Goal. Or even that they are *telling* themselves or *convincing* themselves each day with words – over and over again – that they will do a particular thing. But despite all this self-convincing and all their mental words, I can look in their eyes and see there is still a lack of genuine inner conviction. They still don't *feel* their Optimal Future with every fiber of their souls. And so when the going gets tough they lose confidence in themselves. They get dispirited and downhearted if they lose a race or a boardroom battle. Their feelings and emotional happiness depend on their most recent success or failure. As a result their lives are a rollercoaster, dependent on external events and not on themselves. Whereas the true believer always has an air of confidence. A confidence which is quite different to arrogance. In fact, it's often the case that the more confident someone is, the less they need to show off and brag. Think of Roger Federer, Pete Sampras, Michael Schumacher or Tiger Woods. They just get on with their game. If you have that same sort of confidence then you won't need to get upset or angry when you are challenged in a boardroom meeting. You won't need to blame anyone else if you mess up a race. You are big enough to squarely accept your own Weaknesses because you know that sooner or later you *will* prevail.

A Belief like this is more than words or thoughts running through your head. It is a *feeling* or an *emotion* deep inside you which is as powerful as the feelings of hunger or sex. And like the feelings of hunger or sex, it provides you with a powerful drive. This is why you have feelings and aren't just a robot. Deep emotions make you do things. We can think of an Unshakeable Belief as being like the engine of a ship. It is what drives you forward through any storm. If you don't have this engine pushing you forward then you'll wallow motionless at the mercy of every wave or event in your life. And when you are wallowing stationary like this, no amount of twisting and turning of the tiller will be of any use because your rudder only works when you are moving forward.

Another thing to keep in mind is that your Beliefs don't just concern the things you want to achieve in life. They also have a massive impact on other aspects of your personal life such as your relationships and health. For example, suppose your boyfriend leaves you and you think you'll never find anyone as good as him again. Without doubt, this will be a much more traumatic event for you than for someone else who believes with every fiber of their being that one day they *will* find their true soul mate. For them, the loss of their current boyfriend is but a stepping-stone on the way to their true partner.

LORETTA'S STORY

To gain more insight into how an Unshakeable Belief in yourself can be used to achieve remarkable results, let's look inside the mind of one more champion and hear in her own words what was going on in there.

Like many young Australian girls Loretta Harrop enjoyed sports. But unlike most girls, she decided to become a professional athlete (in her case competing in triathlons). To get funding she had to be measured by the Australian Institute of Sports to see if she had genuine potential. They measured Loretta, and after all their tests, they told her that not only was she not championship material – she was actually *below* average. Now the Australian Institute of Sports is widely recognized as one of the best in the world. If they say you have no potential then you *really* should consider doing something else. How did Loretta react to her results?

'I remember being quite annoyed that their tests were an interruption to my training day. However, if I wanted to be funded, then I had to do their tests. But my attitude was completely carefree about it. In fact, I was defiant because I knew my Goals and what I wanted to achieve. I had a *huge* self-belief that I *was* going to make it to the top.

After I did my test they said I was below average. I had to laugh to myself. I *knew* I was going to be great and I would find a way to be great even if I didn't pass their tests. I didn't even know what their tests meant so why would I care what number they gave me? Even if *they* thought I would never be a champion, *I thought I would be.*'

Loretta didn't get her Lottery funding and even though she trained harder than anyone else she still didn't win. Day after day was filled with pain and enormous effort. Imagine how she must have felt a year later – after all that intense training, after all that hard work and all those sacrifices – when she *still* lost. Surely the words of the Institute of Sports would ring in her ears? '*You'll never be a champion. Go and do something else.*'

She had every excuse in the world to give up. Valid excuses measured at the Institute of Sport. Now think for a moment how would you have felt in the same situation? Would you have kept going? What would you have thought when you were alone at night in your bed after a bad race and the words of the Institute came back to haunt you? But Loretta never gave in. Her response to failure was to realize she had to train even harder. That huge work ethic gave Loretta another added bonus. While most athletes suffered from pre-race nerves, Loretta never did.

'I was different to most of my competitors because the closer I got to the race the more confident I was. I knew I had done more work than my competitors because that was the key to my training. My huge work ethic meant I never left it to race day to find out if I had self-doubt. This gave me confidence on the start line. My mantra before a race was … "Bring it on!" I wanted to see what I could do next.'

What a fantastic attitude. A race was an opportunity to measure herself and see how much progress she'd made. Her hard work in training was the solid platform for her race confidence. A platform she would use to demoralize her competition: 'I am very focused in a race. For me it is like going into battle. I would talk myself through the physical pain as it happened and I'd enjoy that pain because I imagined how much the other girls were hurting. I believed I was the fittest out there and if I was hurting then they must be hurting even more. Then I would pick a moment in the race where I would say to myself, "Right, now stick the knife in and twist it." I am aggressive inside, even if no one knew it on the outside.'

Loretta faced another major obstacle. Bike racing is a dangerous business. Even in dry weather, a bike's narrow tires provide only the slightest of traction. In wet conditions a racing bike at top speed can be lethal. Loretta's one fear was her ability to ride fast in the rain. Fortunately she frequently trained with her brother because he was also a top triathlete and had great bike control Skills. But tragedy struck only months before the World Cup when her brother was killed while he was out training on his bike. After something like that, she could easily have packed up her bike and gone home without any medals. She had the perfect excuse. But how did Loretta respond?

'I did lose confidence on the bike a couple of times. I remember just before the World Cup in Geelong – not long after my brother had been killed – it was teeming with rain and the course was hairy even in the dry. I was clear favorite and I thought my Weakness and fear was about to be exposed because I just could not ride in the rain.

After an initial 'flip out', I got alone in my room and looked in the mirror and said, "I have to face this fear head on." I soon realized I was more afraid of having to live with this stupid fear beating me than I was of crashing. I didn't want to be a loser. So I tackled it head on, because I had no choice. That is the best way for me. I work great under that 'no choice' banner. When things go terribly wrong in my life, I have to face them. There was no hiding and I treated fear of any sort in that way.'

With a mental attitude like that it is no surprise that Loretta went on to win the gold medal at the World Triathlon Championships and a silver medal at the Athens Olympics.

So if you ever think you aren't good enough or have an excuse for giving up or losing confidence in yourself, stop for a moment and think of Loretta. Most likely she had more disadvantages and hurdles to overcome than you ever will. Think of her incredible work ethic and how this provided the platform for her confidence. Her relentless attention to detail in her training preparation. Her ability to face her worst fears head on and conquer them. Her battle hardened attitude during a race. Her Unshakeable Belief in herself despite what anyone said. Now imagine how proud she feels looking at those medals sitting on her mantelpiece. The quiet satisfaction of a job well done, against all the odds.

YOUR *WINNER'S BIBLE* AND YOUR UNSHAKEABLE BELIEF

An Unshakeable Belief in yourself is the engine that drives you forward and powers you over any obstacle. Some people are lucky and appear to be born with this inner conviction already buried deep in their souls. Other people have it instilled in them by their parents, teachers or coaches while they are still young. Yet another group get it from a religion or a philosophy because they believe God, or some other 'higher force', has a special destiny for them. If you're going to be a Winner then you absolutely need to get an Unshakeable Belief in your Optimal Future. But how do you get an Unshakeable Belief if none of the situations listed above applies to you?

The answer is, you can *train* your brain to have an Unshakeable Belief in exactly the same way you improve your tennis backhand or teach your brain to automatically invert an upside down image – by constant practice.

If you don't have a good backhand, what you do is practice it over and over again. Before long it starts to improve and your new action becomes automatically ingrained in your brain. In the same way, if you constantly practice having an Unshakeable Belief in your Optimal Future you'll actually start to get one. It's almost as if you can pull yourself up by your own bootlaces. As the great Muhammad Ali said, 'To be a champion you must believe you are the best. If you're not, *pretend* you are.' What's important here is that this process of 'pretending' isn't about fooling your opponents, but rather it's about how you *get* your own Belief in yourself.

For truly, I say to you, if you have faith as a grain of mustard seed, you will say to this mountain, "Move from here to there," and it will move; and nothing will be impossible to you. **Matthew 17:20**

With all this in mind, it's clear you need to have a section in your *Personal Winner's Bible* which helps you practice your 'Unshakeable Belief In Yourself' every single day. Part of the answer is already supplied by the section you've previously completed in your *Winner's Bible* which contains your Goals. Having vibrant Goals which come alive for you each day does help provide some of the energy and Belief you need – but unfortunately it still takes much more than this. You not only need to *taste* and *feel* your Goals, you have to be *totally convinced* you can achieve them.

Step 1: Believing In Belief

Before I consider my own personal Unshakeable Belief, I remind myself of the power of Unshakeable Beliefs in general by having pictures of Arnold and Loretta in my *Winner's Bible*. I have pictures of them both not because they are my Heroes or Mentors, but because their stories demonstrate the power of an Unshakeable Belief. Arnold had far less going for him than most teenagers who turn up in Hollywood hoping to be stars. But he had two things other wannabe stars didn't have – an Unshakeable Belief in his Optimal Future and a willingness to dig in and do *whatever* hard work was required to get there. Any failure Arnold experienced was just another lesson in what he was doing wrong and what he should now do to get it right. Loretta is exactly the same.

Therefore my *Winner's Bible* contains images of Arnold and Loretta because they remind me of the *general power* of having a truly Unshakeable Belief. It's nice to know that if I have an Unshakeable Belief in my Mental Arsenal then I've got a Mental Weapon more powerful than 99% of the people I'll meet today. It's a nice feeling walking around town or going into meetings with this knowledge!

Step 2: Write Down Your Own Optimal Future

Now that you've seen the power of an Unshakeable Belief, it's time to be bold and start believing in yourself. Right now! So, write in your *Winner's Bible* what you believe is your own unique Optimal Future. This will have many components and will include all the aspects of your life that will make you a happy and well-rounded individual. This is quite different to your material Goals. It's about you becoming the person you ought to be and doing the things that make you intrinsically happy.

Unfortunately this is where many people stumble. They simply don't know what their true Optimal Future is. And, of course, if you don't know what your true Optimal Future is then it's not surprising if you're not living it. For the time being, don't worry if you don't know what your Optimal Future is at this stage. Just do your best for now and write down your considered guess (in Chapter 14, 'Your Intrinsic Drivers', I'll show you how to discover your Optimal Future).

Step 3: The Clear Plan

The next method I use to strengthen my Unshakeable Belief is to write down in bullet points the precise steps or stages I am going to go through in order to obtain my Optimal Future. Having a clear, well-constructed plan with each small step carefully laid out helps make the process more believable. I know that if I can just do Stage 1, then it should be quite possible to do Stage 2. And once I've completed Stage 2, I know I should be able to get to Stage 3. By laying out all the stages toward my Optimal Future in bullet point format, I get more peace because I no longer feel like I'm going to climb the whole mountain in one go.

I never ran a thousand miles. I could never have done that.
I ran one mile a thousand times.
Stu Mittleman, Ultra Marathon World Record holder

Let me give you a worked example from real life. A friend of mine, Sam, is a professional photographer. Celebrities come to him when they want a stylish photo shoot. Now Sam's problem is he's overloaded with work because he's so good. He's always got a backlog of three or more famous people who are waiting to work with him. The reason why Sam has so many clients on the go is because he's a very modest person who doesn't like to 'blow his own trumpet'. Unconsciously, this gives out the message to prospective clients that they can get Sam 'on the cheap'. As a result, he needs to work huge hours and take on far too many shoots at once in order to make a decent living. And yet, the quality of his photography is always absolutely first-class and acclaimed. His clients are among the most famous in the world. So there is a clear mismatch between Sam's perception of himself and reality (see Chapter 3, 'The Distorted Mirror').

When I spoke to Sam it was clear he needed to become more selective in his clients. He needed to book fewer shoots and charge more. That way he'd earn more and yet have the time to do an even better job with each of his clients. So Sam's Optimal Future was to become internationally recognised, and more importantly, to live the life of the 'World's Premium Photographer'. This meant he'd need to make a few changes.

First, he'd need to set up a proper website that reflected this status. So far his only online presence was a web page tucked inside someone else's site. If you were a celebrity and your agent told you Sam was going to be your photographer you wouldn't be that excited when you Googled him. Sam needed his own website which proudly displayed pictures and magazine covers from the 100+ celebrities he'd photographed and all the glowing reviews he'd received. He needed to position himself as 'The Best'. Next, he'd have to start turning down 'lesser' stars who approached him and become more selective. This was going to be a bit scary but it was the only way he could legitimately ratchet up his fees. He needed to send a message to various magazines that 'Sam has earnt his wings and is now at the top of his game'. After all, if some up-and-coming football (soccer) player is still charging only £100 to play a game for the local team then he's not going to be in a very strong position to negotiate a £1 million fee to play for Manchester United.

So we now have a clear Optimal Future for Sam and are already starting to populate a list of things he needs to do. Without going into all the details, Sam's Optimal Future and his plan for how he is going to achieve it would start to look something like:

Optimal Future:
• Be and live the life of the 'World's Premium Photographer'

Clear Plan:
• Set up website befitting the best photographer in the world – don't hold back!
• Be more selective in my clients – turn some down
• Believe in myself at a deeply emotional level

• Learn how to be comfortable promoting myself and claiming my quality
• Increase my fees

Making all the stages explicit and laying them out like this will help you to be patient and realistic and consider correctly the effort, Skills and time required to achieve your Goals. This is important because nothing kills an Unshakeable Belief quicker than unrealistic expectations that are then dashed by realistic (but slower than expected) progress. So add a page with your Optimal Future as a heading, then list using bullet points the various stages you need to complete. Laying out the stages like this also reinforces the need for you to enjoy each stage as you go through them.

OPTIMISM v UNSHAKEABLE BELIEF

At this point, it is vital we distinguish between 'Optimism' and an 'Unshakeable Belief'. Optimism is about looking on the bright side of the situation and this has little to do with an Unshakeable Belief. To be truly successful, you need to be realistic and understand the size of the task ahead, what your Weaknesses are and what you need to do to improve. Loretta wasn't optimistic in a wishful thinking sort of way. She knew how hard she had to work and she knew her Weaknesses. That's being *realistic* as opposed to optimistic. Despite this realism, despite the size of the task ahead, she still believed somehow, even in the tough times when everything was going wrong, that she'd find a way through.

> An Optimist says the stone in her running shoe isn't going to bother her and she'll still climb the mountain. Optimists often fail.
>
> A Realist says the stone is hurting her feet and she needs to get it out. The mountain is long and high and she is hurting badly.
> But she WILL get to the top and she WILL enjoy the view when she gets there.

POEMS

Poems are a good way to reinforce the importance of having an Unshakeable Belief. Here's one I have in my *Winner's Bible*. I find it works for me. See if you can find other poems or quotes that work for you and add them into your *Winner's Bible*.

IT'S ALL IN THE STATE OF MIND

If you think you are beaten, you are,
If you think you dare not, you don't,
If you'd like to win, but you think you can't,
It's almost a 'cinch' you won't.

If you think you'll lose, you've lost,
For out in the world you'll find
Success begins with a fellow's will —
It's all in the state of mind.

Full many a race is lost
E'er even a race is run,
And many a coward fails
E'er even his work's begun.

Think big and your deeds will grow,
Think small and you'll fall behind,
Think that you can, and you will;
It's all in the state of mind.

If you think you're outclassed, you are,
You've got to think high to rise,
You've got to be sure of yourself before
You ever can win the prize.

Life's battle doesn't always go
To the stronger or faster man;
But sooner or later, the man who wins …
Is the fellow who thinks he can.
Walter D. Wintle

CHAPTER 13
'CARPE DIEM'

There is a wonderful scene at the beginning of the movie *Dead Poets Society* where the teacher – played by Robin Williams – walks into class for the first lesson of the New Year. Without saying a single word, the teacher walks up and down the rows of desks and looks into the eager eyes of each boy. It's one of America's most prestigious high schools and this is the top class for new entrants. The boys have arrived from all over America and they're filled with excitement and anticipation at their first lesson. When the teacher gets to the last boy he turns on his heel and walks back out the door. The boys are stunned. They don't know what to do. For a few moments the boys look at each other in total confusion.

Twenty seconds later Robin Williams pokes his head back in the door and tells the boys to follow him. He leads them silently through the hallowed halls of the great school until at last they come to a large, glass cabinet. Inside are many old black and white photos of previous school members. Williams draws his students' attention to a particularly old class photo.

'They're not that different from you, are they?
Same haircuts.
Full of hormones – just like you.
Invincible – just like you feel.
The world is their oyster.
They believe they're destined for great things – just like many of you.
Their eyes are full of hope – just like you ...'

Robin Williams then urges the boys to lean in very close to the glass cabinet and look directly into the eyes of each boy in the picture. There is a hushed silence while they stare for a full 40 seconds, imagining what each boy's life must have been like. What were their dreams and fears? What did they spend their time doing and thinking about? Williams is in effect asking each of the boys to engage in the same fixated visualisation you learnt about at the beginning of this book. He gets them to not only imagine the lives of the boys but to put themselves right inside the picture and become part of their story. And then – just when they are right there in this virtual world he brings them up short and tells them;

*'... But there is one thing different about all these boys compared to you.
You see gentlemen ... these boys are all now dead! Fertilizing daffodils.'*

It is an old technique that originates in the mists of time. It can be traced back in literature to Ancient Rome and Greece when young soldiers were encouraged to study the busts of famous generals who were now long since dead. To weigh their own lives against those famous generals and calculate what legacy they will leave behind when they too die. Will anyone look on their statues and remember them? Will there even be a statue of them at all?

Shakespeare used a similar technique with his audience in the play, *As You Like It*, when he had Jacques say;

*"All the world's a stage,
And all the men and women merely players;
They have their exits and their entrances.'*

The purpose of these reflections was to help each person realise the brevity of life and to then make their lives count. And the way to do that was make each *day* in turn count. The Romans had a saying which encapsulated how this was to be achieved: **'Carpe Diem'** – 'Seize the day'.

Notice the power of the word 'seize' in that phrase. You don't just 'complete' a day – you 'seize' it. Seizing implies urgency and purpose. And you need to do this every *day* which is why you use your Personal Winner's Bible first thing every morning.

Carpe Diem is a very compact instruction. It only contains two words but those two words summarise so many things. **Seize** the **Day**.

And so, Robin Williams begins his quest to instil in each boy a passion and a hunger to get the most out of their short lives. As a teacher of literature he then reminds them that life isn't just about building bridges and making money. It is about the richer things in life – poetry, art, love and beauty.

YOUR OWN CARPE DIEM PAGE

In the same way it is now time for you to consider your own day and how much richness and texture you can extract from it. For you to ensure you don't just 'consume daylight' but for you to make your day meaningful. So pause for a moment and answer the following two questions;

• Are you living your life to its fullest, moving toward your Optimal Future and doing what gives you the greatest satisfaction?
• Are you living in such a way as to add value to the world and people you come in contact with?

To help you achieve your Optimal Future I want you to add a page to your *Personal Winner's Bible* that reminds you of:

• The brevity of life
• The importance of quality
• The value of savoring all the richness of life

This page may simply contain the words *Carpe Diem* in large letters. It may contain the photos of Robin Williams or the Dead Boys from the beginning of this section. It may contain poetry or some image of beauty. It may contain pictures of people close to you that you have lost, for there is nothing more powerful in making this abstract concept of the brevity of life become real and meaningful than a vibrant personality you knew well, who is sadly silent and existing no more. You'll know what works for you.

There is a tide in the affairs of men, which if taken at the flood, leads onto great fortune Omitted, and all life's journeys will be trapped in the shallows of misery.
Julius Caesar

You only truly begin to live when you have fully understood and mastered death.

IF

If you can keep your head when all about you
Are losing theirs and blaming it on you,
If you can trust yourself when all men doubt you,
But make allowance for their doubting too,
If you can wait and not be tired by waiting,
Or being lied about, don't deal in lies,
Or being hated, don't give way to hating,
And yet don't look too good, nor talk too wise.

If you can dream – and not make dreams your master,
If you can think – and not make thoughts your aim;
If you can meet with Triumph and Disaster
And treat those two impostors just the same;
If you can bear to hear the truth you've spoken
Twisted by knaves to make a trap for fools,
Or watch the things you gave your life to, broken,
And stoop and build 'em up with worn-out tools.

If you can make one heap of all your winnings
And risk it all on one turn of pitch-and-toss,
And lose, and start again at your beginnings
And never breathe a word about your loss;
If you can force your heart and nerve and sinew
To serve your turn long after they are gone,
And so hold on when there is nothing in you
Except the Will which says to them: 'Hold on!'

If you can talk with crowds and keep your virtue,
Or walk with kings – nor lose the common touch,
If neither foes nor loving friends can hurt you,
If all men count with you, but none too much;
If you can fill the unforgiving minute
With sixty seconds' worth of distance run,
Yours is the Earth and everything that's in it,
And – which is more – you'll be a Man, my son.
Rudyard Kipling

CHAPTER 14
YOUR INTRINSIC DRIVERS

Some paths in life will lead you to great happiness, success, power, fulfillment and peace, while other paths lead you on a more difficult journey punctuated with harmful strain instead of healthy effort.

It is not always easy to know which journey is going to lead us to our Optimal Future and we often end up following a particular direction simply because some historical event or accident placed us on that road. We forget to get off that path or we fail to choose wisely when faced with a new fork in the road. The path that suits me is completely different to the path that suits you, because our natural make-ups differ.

This chapter is about helping you discover your Optimal Future by uncovering your hidden Drivers and Passions. Once you complete this exercise it may mean:

• Making subtle adjustments to your existing career because you have developed or changed but you career hasn't kept up with you
• Changing your career entirely
• Doing nothing at all because you're already 100% aligned

DRIVEN BY PASSION

An analysis of highly successful people showed they shared one important experience in common:

At some stage in their lives, the highly successful people chose to follow their Passions rather than pursue a career based on money or prestige.

In retrospect this finding is not that surprising. If you choose a career you are passionate about:

You Never Give Up

Your Passion sustains you when times get tough. You don't have to force yourself to keep on going and you don't have to motivate yourself. You keep on going because you love doing it. This is important because success is so often about overcoming obstacles and perseverance in the face of overwhelming adversity (see Chapter 12, 'Loretta's Story').

You Pay Attention To Detail

If you love something you'll naturally want to get intimately involved in the fine details. No stone will be left unturned, no Weakness left unchecked and every possibility for success will be endlessly investigated. You'll find little details which will lift you above your competition and make your performance, product or service better.

You Have Extra Energy

Nothing saps your energy more than spending time doing things you don't like. But when you're enjoying yourself your brain produces a cocktail of positive chemicals that have a long-term effect on your energy levels. It's like being permanently on Prozac. You'll get out of bed fresher, sleep deeper and attack everything with more vigor. Because of this extra energy you'll get involved in more things and attract more people to your cause.

And so the following pattern unfolds:
a) Because you are passionate about something – you do it well.
b) Because you do it well – it becomes successful.
c) Because it is successful you enjoy doing it even more, you become more passionate.
d) And so a cycle back to a) is strengthened.

Each time you go around the loop your life becomes richer, more successful and enjoyable. And each time you go around that loop your Wheel Of Life moves forward too (see Chapter 8).

There is an old adage which has a lot of truth to it:
Find a job you love – and you'll never have to work again.

This is because doing something you love is never hard work.

ACCIDENTAL CAREERS

So, having established that doing a job you are passionate about is the ideal, how do we apply that to ourselves? The problem most of us face is that we choose our career paths while we are still in our late teens. At that age we're still naïve, easily influenced by our parents or peers and we often don't fully understand what a particular career is actually all about. It might seem a glamorous choice at 18 to become a doctor saving lives but the realities of the General Practitioner's daily grind of prescribing treatments for minor ailments may be entirely different to what we'd imagined. More importantly, we don't really know what makes us tick because we're not yet fully developed. The things we're passionate about at twenty may not even interest us at forty, so it's not surprising that millions of people end up in careers that aren't perfectly suited to them.

Unfortunately, once we've chosen our careers and started training it's frequently difficult to change them without substantial upheaval, considerable risk and possibly great cost. By then, responsibilities such as children, a mortgage, school fees and all manner of factors may make a career change seem at best inadvisable – and at worst impossible. But conversely, it would be a tragedy to waste the majority of your waking life doing a job that doesn't give you deep satisfaction and enjoyment. Life is just too short and too precious for that.

Because our careers have such a huge impact on our lives it is important we constantly analyze them and consider our options very carefully. Despite what many self-help books tell you, there are no easy or simplistic answers. Even though it's common for books to tell you to 'dream the impossible dream', 'cast caution to the wind' and 'throw in your career' to pursue your Passion – it's not as easy or as simple as that. That sort of armchair advice can often lead to disappointment while giving you the false impression it's helping you aim for life on a higher level. Writers of such advice don't have to live with the consequences if it goes wrong – but you do. This chapter is about how you can be a wise person and truly divine the correct path for your life to follow. Finding that path is not a simple process as the following true stories reveal.

THE SURGEON AND THE BANKER

Many years ago at a dinner party, I met a successful orthopedic surgeon in his mid-thirties called Mike. Over drinks Mike told me he was rather unhappy in his job despite holding a prestigious position at his hospital and having his own private practice which earned him lots of money. As our conversation progressed, it became obvious Mike was a happy and well-adjusted guy in general life. It was just his work which was the exception. He had a great wife, excellent health, good friends and diverse interests.

As fate would have it I met Mike again about six years later. This time he excitedly told me how he'd thrown in his career as a well-paid surgeon and had become a builder. Well, more than a builder actually. He now designed houses, drew up the architectural plans all by himself and then actually went on to the building site with his hammer and saw. Mike said changing his career was the best decision he'd ever made in his life.

During those same six years I also met an investment banker called John. It was a remarkably similar story in some ways but completely different in others. John had a huge Passion for sailing and had already proven himself to be highly competitive by winning a number of local races. He was relatively well off financially and had a lovely family but he was becoming bored with the same old routine of going to the bank each day. So he decided to quit his job, put together a professional yacht racing team and enter into one of the big, international 'Round The World' races. He raised millions of dollars in sponsorship and then assembled a team of experts to build an innovative yacht. To cut a long story short, three years later John won the 'Round The World' race.

Unfortunately, as so often happens in professional sport, you always seem to need more money than you've got no matter how much you raise. In order to win John had spent every last sponsorship cent on the campaign and hadn't drawn any earnings for himself. The inevitable result was that his family gradually consumed their life savings in order to pay their weekly bills. At the end of the three-year campaign his own family's finances were in tatters and his wife and family had made huge sacrifices, as he'd been overseas most of that time. Worse was yet to come.

Once the race was over and the champagne had been sprayed all across the podium, John found he was faced with a rather unexpected challenge. He'd had enough of professional yacht racing but unfortunately he couldn't return to his old banking position as it had been filled by a bright, young guy who was doing a fabulous job in his place. While John had experienced a great adventure, it had come at a massive cost to both him and his family. And now it was all over he didn't actually feel he was any further ahead. He still felt like something was missing in his life. His Winner's trophy somehow represented a rather hollow victory.

These two stories raise the following questions:
• What is the correct balance between following our Passion and being practical?
• How can we discover the true Drivers which give us deep, lasting, intrinsic satisfaction?
• When should we be happy with our career and learn how to make the most out of it and when is it time to move on and look for a new opportunity or a complete change of direction?
• How can we leverage off our existing career or modify it so it's more in tune with our current state of development?
• How can we discover what is our *true* Optimal Future?

THE ORACLE OF DELPHI
We can gain an insight into how you can make a wise decision on these issues by travelling back in time to the famous 'Oracle of Delphi'. The Oracle (a person who can prophesy, tell the future or give wise advice) was actually a specially chosen priestess who lived in the great temple of Apollo in Delphi, which is part of Ancient Greece. Each Oracle was chosen to succeed the previous Oracle in much the same way that the Vatican chooses a new Pope to replace the previous one.

The Temple of Apollo had many features, most notably the fact that it was constructed over a geological fault in the earth's crust. Sweet-smelling geothermal vapors wafted out of this crack 24 hours a day. According to Ancient Greek mythology, this fissure was the exact site where the great body of Python fell and entered the earth after Apollo had killed it. The fumes erupting from this vent were supposedly gases from the rotting corpse of Python.

From 800BC to 100AD, people traveled from around the world to seek the Oracle's guidance on all matters of importance. The Oracle was held in such high regard because of the accuracy of her prophecies that even kings and foreign rulers were required to book an audience months in advance.

Before she would prophesy the Oracle first entered into a trance. She achieved this by sitting on a specially constructed seat supported by three legs which spanned the crack in the earth. Breathing the gases which came up out of the ground slowly caused the Oracle to fall into this trance. At that time it was thought the gas allowed the 'spirit' of Apollo to enter into her soul and give her Apollo's great wisdom. Finally, once the Oracle was in a deep trance the eager questioner was ushered in and allowed to ask her for advice. Invariably the Oracle would answer with a highly cryptic or confusing response. It was then up to the recipient to work out the true meaning of her riddle before they finally understood the wisdom of Apollo. Sometimes this process of interpreting the Oracle's words took weeks or even months. To the modern ear this may sound rather unconvincing, but the long succession of priestesses who were selected to become Oracles all commanded absolute reverence for over 900 years.

Modern day analysis of the gases which are still emitted from the vents inside the ruins of Apollo's temple tell us the Oracle was actually high on ethylene gas. This explains her trance-like behavior and her rambling, cryptic answers. This then raises the question of how she could have possibly been so accurate if we no longer accept it was due to the power of the great god Apollo. Part of the answer is to be found in the three mottos carved in large gold letters over the entrance to the Temple of Apollo. Each person entering the Temple to seek the Oracle's wisdom was first instructed to study these mottos because they were the key given by Apollo to unlock each of the Oracle's riddles.

The first and most widely known of these sayings was, 'Gnothi seauton' or 'Know thyself '. This statement is of course ambiguous and has two interpretations which can mean either:
• Know who you are – in other words, what is inside your inner soul
• Know on your own – that is, work it out for yourself

Both of these interpretations are important when you consider crucial decisions in your life. If you are to truly work out which path you should follow then you need to have a deep understanding of who you really are. What makes you tick? What are your Drivers? What gives you intrinsic satisfaction? What are your Strengths and Weaknesses? This explains why the Oracle was so successful. She essentially uttered random or ambiguous statements because her brain was befuddled by the ethylene gas. But your task was to find some meaning in her words and you did this by following the rules inscribed on the temple, including 'Know thyself'. So you delved deep into your soul and worked out who you really were. From out of that knowledge you gained an insight into what you should do. As long as the Oracle's words were lacking in specificity and were random enough you could almost always find a connection between your own deep insight into yourself and her words. It was your knowledge of yourself rather than her words which guaranteed her 'advice' was going to be accurate. In fact, the more obscure her words, the more deeply you needed to delve into 'knowing yourself'.

THE DIFFERENCE BETWEEN MIKE AND JOHN
This tale of the Oracle brings us back full circle and provides us with useful insight that will allow us to work out:
• Why Mike's career change worked but John's didn't
• How you can uncover the Intrinsic Drivers which power your own Passions
• What you can do with this knowledge of your Drivers to guide you in the future

The reason why Mike's career change worked so well was because he understood what made him tick at the deepest level. Mike realized one of his Skills as a surgeon was his ability to visualize objects in 3-D. He could look at a series of two-dimensional x-ray scans and from this build up a complete 3-D image in his mind of exactly how the inside of the patient's leg would look when he opened it up. He could mentally walk around the 'inside' of his patient's leg and view each bone or ligament from a different angle before he started operating. He also realized that what gave him a genuine buzz and made his life worth living was the act of 'creating' something new that no one else had ever created before. This gave him a deep sense of satisfaction which he likened to the feeling a woman gets after she's given birth to a child. Creating something new like this made him feel unique and worthwhile, and in his own mind, it separated him out from everyone else.

Mike also realized what he didn't like about being a surgeon. He hated being stuck inside a hospital surrounded by injured and ill people. Of course, his heart went out to them and he wanted everyone to be cured, but this wasn't his calling in life. Fixing mangled bones and even doing a brilliant job was never going to produce as good a result as perfectly normal healthy bones in the first place. He loved perfection and newness and hated old, broken things. As you can see, his new career (as a builder/house designer) perfectly suited both his Skills and his Passions while avoiding the things he didn't like. It's no wonder the change was a success.

John, on the other hand, didn't quite understand why he liked his yacht racing. He hadn't probed the underlying components that contributed to making his yacht racing so enjoyable. It was only in hindsight that he realized the reasons why he enjoyed his mid-week yacht races were:
• He was highly competitive. He loved the instant buzz as well as the cut and thrust he got from battling man against man
• The adrenalin rush during a race was temporarily all-consuming; this meant that he was able to switch off and escape from his day-to-day grind at the office
• He was the skipper, totally in charge of his yacht, making snap decisions; he wasn't a small cog in a big bank controlled by regulations and head office
• At work he was obsessive about the complex details of any deal. That's why he was a good banker. But all those details and obsessions tired him out. Racing was a simple matter. The wind, the sails the helm and the opposition.

Or so it seemed. However, it doesn't take much thought to see why John didn't enjoy his 'Round The World' campaign. Organizing a three-year challenge necessarily had thousands of details just like all the deals which wore him out at the bank. And a race around the world isn't a burst of adrenalin like a two-hour race around the harbour – it couldn't possibly be. No one could live with that amount of adrenalin for three years and survive. Even though he was the skipper and nominally in charge of his campaign, he was constantly being told what to do by his sponsors because they ultimately controlled the purse strings. And even the cut and thrust of man against man competition was blunted in a race where you and your competitors are often separated by hundreds of miles because you've chosen to follow different wind and ocean currents. The instant cut and thrust is gone.

John's mistake was that he'd confused 'yachting' as a general, all-purpose Passion without understanding all the subcomponents of 'yachting' that made him like it in the first place. He clearly loved a two-hour yacht race but this is an entirely different proposition to spending a year sailing around the world and running a multi-million dollar campaign. You can't just multiply up a two-hour yacht race and do it twelve times in a row everyday. Things don't work like that.

UNCOVERING YOUR INTRINSIC DRIVERS

The root of John's problem was he'd never worked out what truly gave him long-term satisfaction, and more importantly, *why* those things game him the satisfaction they did. In short, he didn't *know himself*. The aim of this section is to help you discover the *underlying subcomponents* that drive your Passions. This is what I call your 'Intrinsic Drivers'. By this I mean those things which naturally excite you. The things which are an intrinsic part of your make-up. The warp and weft out of which your character is woven. In other words, the things that uniquely make you who you are. Most people find this process unexpectedly reveals many things about themselves they weren't consciously aware of before. As a result they're able to make better decisions in their lives, become better aligned with their true Optimal Future and balance their 'Wheels' better (see Chapter 8, 'The Wheel Of Life').

Uncovering your Intrinsic Drivers is a three-stage process:
Stage 1: List all your Passions/pursuits/things you really enjoy.
Stage 2: For each Passion, identify the Intrinsic Drivers of that Passion.
Stage 3: Consolidate all your Drivers into a single list.

These do *not* need to be in any order. Just write them down as you think of them. To help explain how this process works, I'm going to write down a few of the things I enjoy doing. So the list below is 'Kerry's List'.

Stage 1: List Your Enjoyable Passions/Pursuits/Things I Really Enjoy

Racing my motorcycle	Waterskiing
Mathematics/Physics	Dinner Parties
My girlfriend	Tennis
Hanging out with my friends	Writing my book
Philosophy	Weightlifting

Now for each of the Passions I've listed in Stage 1 above, I need to work out all the underlying reasons why I like those Passions. I call these underlying reasons my Intrinsic Drivers. Let's start with the first passion and see how this works.

Stage 2: List My Intrinsic Drivers For Each Passion.

Passion # 1: 'Racing' My Motorcycle

Intrinsic Driver #1: Speed/Dynamic Motion
I get this huge adrenalin pump and exhilaration out of the raw acceleration and speed of a modern 1300cc sports bike. When I accelerate at full throttle it feels like a giant hand is hurtling me through space in a way I can scarcely comprehend. It's almost as if the bike is so powerful it twists the very fabric of space-time.

Intrinsic Driver #2: Perfection/Precision
I get an absolute buzz if I come off the brakes at *exactly* the right place, take *exactly* the right line, and use just the *perfect* amount of throttle to balance the bike on the exit. Even though I'm miles slower than a professional racer, it is the 'precision and perfection' of what I do, given my own limited Skill level, that makes it so exciting. On the odd occasion when I take a corner perfectly, I whoop for joy inside my helmet as I roar down the following straight.

Intrinsic Driver #3: Switches my mind off/In the zone
When I'm racing my bike, my mind is totally focused on the task. I'm not aware of anything else in life. I'm at one with the bike and the track. The rest of my life is totally switched off and, for the time being, ceases to exist. This gives me a total break from life – racing is the equivalent for me of pushing the 'reset button' on

a computer. Once I've finished racing I feel exhausted yet refreshed in a way that simply going to sleep can't provide.

Intrinsic Driver #4: Freedom

When you are riding a motorbike you are vulnerable, you feel the air and nature. There is a raw freedom you don't feel when you're in a car going at the same speed.

Intrinsic Driver #5: Sense of Accomplishment

Mastering a high performance motorcycle will always be well beyond my ability. But I enjoy the learning process and it gives me a sense of achievement when I master each little step.

Intrinsic Driver #6: Mechanical Beauty

I love mechanical things and how all the components work together. The physics and engineering of it all. I enjoy the beauty of a well-made and well-engineered bike.

So now that I've got six Intrinsic Drivers for my first Passion, I can fill out the first column of the diagram below.

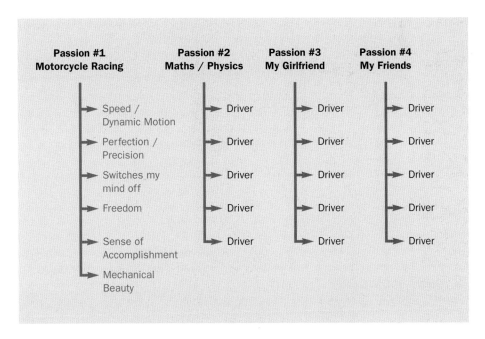

What's interesting about my list is that it's likely to be entirely different to another motorcycle racer's list. Even though two people love racing, the reasons and the order of importance of those reasons are likely to be entirely different for each person. Achieving 'perfection and precision' is the second most important Intrinsic Driver for me, but it may not even figure on someone else's list at all. They may be highly focused on winning, the glory of the fastest lap and proving themselves, but that in turn doesn't figure on my list at all.

You now repeat the process for each of *your* Passions in turn so that each Passion forms a column with a specific list of Drivers underneath it. As you compile your list of Drivers for each Passion it is helpful if:

• You try to put them in rough order of importance
• You try to put a heading or summary title for each
• You write a few sentences explaining what you mean by each title

Like all things, you'll only get out of this exercise what you put into it. The more deeply you think about *why* you like things, the more insight you'll get into your soul. I could have just said 'I like going fast' when it came to my motorbike racing, but it was only after considerable introspection over a number of days that I finally got to the bottom of what made racing so much fun for me. You need to drill down repeatedly and this takes persistence. Let me show you what I mean by giving you another example from real life. When I asked my friend Jill why her ultimate Passion in life was motorcycle racing, she replied, 'Because it's my destiny. It's what I've been born to do.' But I persisted and said that didn't really tell me much. I wanted to know *why* it's her Optimal Future and *what she gets* out of motorcycle racing that she doesn't get out of playing tiddlywinks. She told me she loved 'getting her knee down' on the track and she loved the starts, the huge acceleration. I followed her answer and probed a little deeper by asking her why she loved the starts. For her, it was the moment of truth. The instant where all the preparation is focused into a single event. A vital split second which has an enormous impact on the entire race. I kept digging deeper on each of her answers and when we finally got to the bottom we were both shocked. It turned out that the *most* significant Intrinsic Driver for Jill, underlying everything about her racing, was that she wanted to be a huge success in a male-dominated sport. She wanted to 'show that girls can do anything'.

When we talked about Jill's other Passions in life, she told me she was passionate about the idea of my *Winner's Bible For Society*. And why was she passionate about the *Society* book rather than my *Winner's Bible For Elite Sport*, which would seem to be more directly related to her motorcycle racing? Because the second major Intrinsic Driver for Jill was that she wanted to make the world a better place. All of a sudden we had uncovered a common connection. Jill wanted to be a role model for women. The two are highly related: 'empowering women' is part of helping 'make the world a better place'. Jill wanted to become a national motorcycle champion because, among other things, this would give her a sporting platform from which she could do public speaking and lectures about empowering women to overcome stereotypes and be successful in any career.

This example of finding Jill's Intrinsic Drivers typifies a pattern I've observed hundreds of times. Most people think they understand what drives them. They think they know what is at the very bottom of their personality, but in reality, they've only just scratched the surface. And usually when they do get to the bottom they discover something vitally important about themselves. They have an unexpected revelation. It can also be one of the most powerful experiences in your life. If you visit the *Winner's Bible* website you will see some real life stories of how powerful this process can be in changing your life. I particularly like the two videos recorded by Simon.

CONSOLIDATING YOUR DRIVERS

Once you've identified all your Intrinsic Drivers for each Passion, you need to consolidate them all into a single list. If you're like Jill you'll probably find there is a considerable overlap. Some of the reasons why you like your career might also pop up in why you like a particular sport or pursuit. Let me give you an example from my own life.

I love maths and physics because they are somehow 'pure and true'. With maths I can prove with total certainty that $c^2 = a^2 + b^2$ for a right angle triangle. I love that *perfection* and the absolute truth of the formula. I have no idea why, but absolute truth and clarity just gives me a real buzz. It's also why I like studying philosophy because it aims to discover the very nature of truth and what we can or cannot know. Now here's the interesting connection: if you look back at the list of my Underlying Drivers for motorcycle racing you'll see that my second Driver is about getting a buzz from the 'precision and perfection' of taking a corner perfectly. The perfection and precision of controlling my bike and my love of physics are related. 'Truth' is *absolute perfection* or precision. When something is TRUE there is no error, no slop.

So take all the Intrinsic Drivers from all your different Passions and consolidate them into one big list of Drivers – regardless of where they came from. As you consolidate the list of Drivers try to see if some of them are related or are essentially the same things but only in different forms – just like my 'perfection and precision' from maths and motorcycle racing were. When you've got your final list of Intrinsic Drivers you'll no longer need your original Passion list.

PUTTING YOUR INTRINSIC DRIVERS TO WORK – KNOWING YOURSELF

Once you've finished consolidating all your Intrinsic Drivers it's a good idea to put them into your *Winner's Bible* as a reference because you'll then be able to use them for guidance. They'll act like your 'Golden Compass'. You see, in Ancient Greek mythology, there was a mythical device called an Alethiometer which helped you determine 'truth' or find which 'direction or choice in life' to take (the word Alethiometer comes from the Greek *alethia* which means truth). In modern language, we call this device a Golden Compass. Gold because of its value and also because gold does not respond to magnetic fields as a normal compass does. Your Intrinsic Drivers will act like your Golden Compass to guide you when making decisions and they'll also help you when you're checking how well your life is balanced.

Many people find they end up changing some of the Goals they've already put in their *Personal Winner's Bible* after they consolidate their Intrinsic Drivers because they now have a deeper understanding of who their authentic self is. They discover some of their Goals weren't correctly aligned with their true nature. And if your Drivers and your Goals don't match then your life is bound to be a constant battle of frustration. Sometimes even a subtle re-alignment can change a good life into a brilliant life.

Discovering your Intrinsic Drivers by teasing apart your Passions like we've done is an excellent way of 'Knowing Yourself' (as the motto at the Temple of Apollo suggested). The reason this process works so well is because you sneak up on your soul via your Passions, without all your natural prejudices about who you are constantly getting in the way. You use your Passions as a sort of mirror which allows you to see yourself from a different angle than you normally would.

If you now think back to Mike the Surgeon and John the Banker, you can see why Mike's new career worked so well for him but John's didn't. Mike's new career was naturally aligned with his Intrinsic Drivers while John's wasn't. John had only considered the top level of his Passion for 'Yachting' and thought if he liked afternoon yacht races then he'd love being part of a professional yacht racing team even more. Unfortunately, organizing a major campaign and going for an afternoon sail have little in common except yachts are involved in both. It's the sort of mistake football players can make if they try to become the manager of a football club. Being a manager and being a player are two entirely different propositions. John's other problem was that he was trying to fill a philosophic emptiness and lack of purpose in his life with yachting. This was doomed to failure because he was trying to balance his life by heaping even more yachting on one side of his Wheel, which only made things worse. His Wheel Of Life became even more unbalanced.

UNEXPECTED BENEFITS – SPORTS AND BUSINESS

I've personally helped a number of elite athletes and business people work through this exercise of uncovering their Intrinsic Drivers and the results have always surprised me. It's natural to assume elite athletes wouldn't gain much by doing this because they already have their Optimal Future well mapped out and because sport is such a well-defined and narrow focus. But every single athlete I've worked with has discovered new things about themselves and each time this has led to a dramatic increase in their motivation and on-field performance. Coaches in particular find this really interesting.

But if you think about it a bit more it's probably not that surprising. By the time an athlete reaches the top of their sport they've competed in thousands and thousands of hours of ultra-high intensity events. Each time they compete to absolute exhaustion and each time they face enormous mental and psychological pressure. No wonder they risk becoming mentally fatigued from the constant wear and tear, regardless of how motivated they are or how inspiring their coach is.

Helping each athlete uncover their own Intrinsic Drivers:
• Increases their enjoyment of their sport
• Sustains their deep motivation over the long haul which means they don't have to constantly keep whipping themselves up
• Helps them enhance their Skills and break through a plateau. This last point is of particular note

As a result of observing the impact on athletes when they uncover the deeper layers of their Intrinsic Drivers, I've modified the order of my training programs. When I first began working with elite athletes I started by focusing on the technical aspects of their game and the sorts of things contained in *The Winner's Bible For Elite Sport*. But over time I've realized that getting to the very core of an elite athlete produces such dramatic changes in their performance, their enjoyment of the game and their ability to withstand the constant grind of ultra-high pressure and stress, that the first thing I now start working on is their Intrinsic Drivers.

I've noticed exactly the same results with business people. If you're a manager or business owner then one of the best ways to increase the performance and satisfaction of your employees is to help them:
• Discover their Intrinsic Drivers
• Align their Drivers with your company's Goals

It's a win-win situation. They're happy, more fulfilled in life and moving closer to their intrinsic Optimal Future and you, as the owner or manager, benefit from increased productivity.

TRANSCENDING YOUR NATURE

If you've worked hard on the previous section and spent enough time letting it bubble around in your mind, you'll have discovered new insights into your Intrinsic Drivers. You'll be able to use these insights to guide you in decision-making and to balance your Wheel. For most people that's good enough – to truly discover their natural essence and where that will lead. However, there is one further step you can take if you're an advanced soul. If you wish, you can re-shape the fiber and fabric out of which you are made and thereby modify your Intrinsic Drivers and hence your Optimal Future. You can re-craft your soul and design an entirely new future for yourself. This last step is for very few people and usually comes at a high cost. I won't go into this topic here because it's such a unique journey for each person. But if that interests you then read the book, *The Winner's Bible Of Philosophy* (see p258).

ONGOING REVISION

Identifying your Intrinsic Drivers is not a once in a lifetime exercise because your Drivers should be maturing and developing as you personally develop and mature. This means you should revisit your Drivers at least once a year and formally go through this entire process from scratch – listing your Passions, drilling down to your Drivers and consolidating them. A particularly good time to do this is just after Christmas so you're ready to make top quality resolutions for the New Year and not just the usual list of wishful promises.

KEY POINTS

- Consolidate all your Intrinsic Drivers and put them in your *Winner's Bible*
- These will give you insight into who you are and will act like a compass to guide you when making decisions
- They will not only guide you in your career but will help you in a wide range of decisions, even including things such as choosing your partners and friends
- Review your goals in light of your Underlying Drivers

CHAPTER 15
FINDING AND FEEDING YOUR PASSIONS

Listing your Passions and analyzing your Intrinsic Drivers is often a catalyst for making profound and positive changes to your life. If that's what's happened to you and you're happy with your Passions and Drivers then you can skip this chapter. But if you read the last chapter and found you ended up staring at a blank page and couldn't think of any deep-seated vibrant Passions then this chapter is essential reading for you.

Your Passions should be the most important things to you. They should be at the front of your mind and the easiest things in the world for you to think about. But if they don't come to you automatically then you need to find out what your true Passions are.

The question is, 'How do you find your true Passions?'

CONSTRUCTING PASSIONS OUT OF THIN AIR

The first thing to realize is that finding your Passion isn't like looking in a cupboard or under a cushion to see where it is hidden. Passions aren't just sitting around with a label on them conveniently waiting to be found. And you probably won't discover your Passions by sitting down and thinking really, really hard. In fact, that sort of thinking will more than likely drive you nuts. You'll go round and round in circles and end up where you started. Instead, what you need to do is use a completely different method. The best way to illustrate how to do this is with the following true story about a woman I knew.

She'd woken up one day in Spain after a rather boozy night out. She had a pounding headache and felt rather seedy. At twenty, her life didn't seem to be going anywhere in particular. By day she worked in sales and marketing and at night she went out on the town with her friends and socialized. But this morning was different to other mornings. She looked long and hard in the mirror and realized she couldn't face waking up every day for the rest of her life with nothing more to look forward to than the stale remains of the previous night. As she looked in the mirror, she noticed a small layer of fat covering her stomach. Her eyes were puffy with small dark rings under them. *God, she felt terrible.* She had to do something about this.

That evening she decided to go to the local pool and have a swim to get fit rather than going out on the town. It wasn't that easy or even particularly enjoyable. Her body ached and her lungs felt like they were going to burst. She struggled up and down the pool only managing four lengths at a time before she had to stop for breath. But she was a determined – some would even say stubborn – person. Each week she set herself a slightly higher target. Instead of only coming to the pool twice a week she was going to come in four times next week. Instead of only doing twenty lengths in a session, she'd do thirty.

As the weeks went by her body began to change shape which made her feel good about herself. Instead of just feeling pain and expending effort she was now starting to get something back. She even discovered little pleasures in her training. She got to know the other swimmers and enjoyed the camaraderie.

She also discovered she had a strong competitive streak. Each week she'd try to beat the person who was just that little bit faster than her. Then she'd pick on the next fastest person the following week and try to beat them also. Beating them gave her a real sense of satisfaction. She was having her first small taste of what it was like to compete and win. She liked that taste. In order to increase her chances of beating more swimmers in her pool she began to watch her diet. She stopped smoking and cut down on her drinking. Without consciously setting out to do so, her life and values were slowly changing.

One week, some of the other swimmers in the pool competed in a triathlon. That sounded like fun. Before long, she'd added running and cycling to her training regime and discovered she was a very good runner.

This is where I now reveal something truly remarkable to you.

This is the very same woman that I introduced you to in Chapter 2 when I explained how much harder champions work than the average person thinks. It is none other than my ex-girlfriend Annie, who became World Series Duathlon Champion fifteen years after she first trained in that pool in Spain!

Along the way she'd won hundreds of races and had the most amazing adventures. She'd competed all around the world and met an incredible variety of interesting people. She was on TV and wrote articles for sports magazines. She'd learned about physiology and nutrition. She became a swimwear model. Her life bore no resemblance to that slightly hung-over woman reflected in the mirror all those years ago.

GROWING A PASSION

Now the point of this story is that when Annie first began swimming she never expected it would become a Passion. She never thought it would be something she would derive great pleasure from. In fact, until then she'd merely 'tolerated' exercise. It was okay, but nothing more. But as she persevered she found there *were* things she liked about training after all. Things she could never have imagined if she'd just sat down on her couch at home and tried to analyze them. And the same is undoubtedly true for you. No matter how hard you try to think up a Passion, the chances are if one doesn't exist, it won't come to you by thought alone. You need to try things – even if you can't fully imagine how they could ever become a Passion.

'Growing A Passion' is a bit like learning to play golf. The first time you play, the chances are you'd be lucky to hit the ball cleanly off the tee twice in a row. It's such a frustrating process. You spend all your time hitting balls in the wrong direction. It's not much fun. But if you continue to practice, it won't be too long before you find yourself enjoying an afternoon in the sun playing your friends. And of course, the learning never ends. There are the subtleties of a chip shot, how to get power into your drive, the satisfaction of a perfectly weighted putt that gently curves into the hole and leaves your opponent floundering. The excitement and pleasure of playing a competitive game bears absolutely no resemblance to those faltering first few hits when you were learning.

So, if you can't think of any Passions, then you need to go out and *grow* a few. Put some effort into experiencing different things and give them a chance. You probably won't get much out of your first experience – like golf – so you need to give them time (see Chapter 10, 'Pomegranates') and have a jolly good go.

PASSIONS ARE CONTAGIOUS

Notice also that Annie's Passion for swimming opened up the possibility of other Passions. Her fitness gained in the swimming pool provided a platform that allowed her to get on a bike and enjoy cycling through the countryside. Her competitive success opened up a completely new career in modeling. This illustrates an important rule in life: each additional Passion will provide you with new Skills and abilities that will open up the possibility of yet other Passions. Passions become infectious and contagious. Passions make Passions.

It is a well-known psychological finding that people who are passionate about three things in life are often passionate about twenty things in life. They are more passionate lovers and are able to savor experiences more fully. Their Skills and interests cross–pollinate which makes them more interesting people to be around. Their Passion generates additional energy which gives them increased capacity for yet further Passions. They truly seize the day (see Chapter 13, 'Carpe Diem').

PASSIONS CHANGE

Another important point is that as we grow up our Passions and interests change. Make sure you don't get stuck in your childhood Passions. Just because you've always enjoyed sports doesn't mean you can't learn to enjoy the arts or academic Passions. In Annie's case, her successful sporting career over fifteen years provided her with many hard-learned lessons on how to be a Winner. When she retired from competition she was then able to supplement these practical experiences with learning in other areas. This provided her with a whole new career that added another dimension of richness to her life. Hers became a full and satisfying life which all started that morning in front of the mirror in Spain.

And finally, as you get older, look for Passions which have more complexity in them. Some Passions have limited nuances and details. Other Passions are incredibly rich. Jackie Stewart once said to me that, 'Winning three World Formula 1 titles was enough. To continue driving around in circles and win a fourth or fifth title would have shown a gross lack of imagination on my part. I wanted to experience more in life.' Jackie went on to become a very successful businessman, adding a large fortune from business to the small fortune he'd won in Formula 1.

Make sure your passions grow as you grow mentally and emotionally.

CHAPTER 16
THE HIGHWAY OF LIFE

As Don Juan was walking along a dusty highway he came alongside an old Master with flowing white hair and a weathered face. He adjusted his pace to that of the older man and continued with him in silence. After an hour of agreeable companionship Don Juan turned his head towards the Master and asked what he knew of life.

The Master replied, '*There are four steps on the Highway of Life.*'
'*Pray tell me what these four steps are,*' enquired Don Juan.
'*The first step is **fear**,*' replied the old Master.

Don Juan continued walking in silence for a long time while he pondered these words. The more he thought about it, the more he realized the truth in the old man's answer. His last girlfriend wasn't a good match for him but he dated her anyway. Maybe this was because he was afraid of being alone or maybe he was scared he'd never find the right woman. So he'd settled for her. And why had he recently bought such an expensive house with all those rooms he'd never need? If he was truly honest with himself it was because he was afraid people might not hold him in such high esteem if he lived in a more modest house. He thought of how he behaved in the company of his friends and the strange things they had to do because they were 'cool'. Was this generated by a *fear* of not being accepted or of not wanting to be different? Even the stress he felt at work seemed to be driven by a *fear* of failure. *Fear* seemed to come in many forms.

The old man seemed to be aware of Don Juan's thoughts while he walked effortlessly beside him.

'*Most people never conquer fear*,' added the Master.

The sun was hot and the road dry and dusty, but Don Juan didn't notice. He was thinking of the people he knew and what they did and realized this was true. As time went by these thoughts began to settle in his mind and feel comfortable – like they belonged there. Don Juan was ready to learn about the second step on the Highway of Life and so he enquired of the Master what this might be.

Once more the Master spoke: '*The second step on the Highway of Life is **impetuousness***'

Again Don Juan fell silent while he digested the Master's words. Without *fear* he was of course free to do whatever he wanted and this freedom was intoxicating. But in a flash he became aware of all the projects he'd begun with such enthusiasm that now languished half-finished. The criss-crossing and backtracking of decisions caused by setting off without clearly identifying a destination. Romances begun on a whim. Journeys poorly resourced. *Impetuousness* had wasted much energy and life. As he considered the implications of the Master's words he realized his life was a mixture. Some parts of his life were still on the first step while other aspects had already progressed to the second step. Indeed, some days his whole life was lived as if he had stumbled back to the first step, while on other days he seemed to see the world from the second step. He resolved to progress those parts of his life that lagged behind.

Quite some time passed in quiet contemplation as the two men continued on their journey. Finally Don Juan felt ready to ask the Master for the third step, but just as he was about to open his mouth, the Master turned to Don Juan: '*When you have conquered fear and conquered impetuousness – then you have **power**. You will say to people, "Come" and they will come. You will say to people "Go" and they will go. You will have power not only to do things but also over yourself.*'

Power required even deeper thought for it also brings with it a heavy responsibility. What does one do with genuine *power*?

Many thoughts turned inside Don Juan's mind. He realized each person is unique and so too their powers will be unique. He needed to identify what his special powers were and what they should be used for. He asked himself if had he ever conquered both *fear* and *impetuousness* at the same time so that he had genuine *power*. And if he had *power* in any aspect of his life, was it used or did it just sit there idle, like a magician's wand on a table?

As Don Juan and the old Master continued walking the sun began to set. Don Juan was puzzled. The first three steps seemed to cover so much and explain so much. What on earth could the fourth step on the Highway of Life possibly be? Indeed, what could possibly lie beyond having *power* over oneself and the world?

Don Juan turned to the Master and said, 'You have given me much to think about. I am not sure I can handle the fourth and final step, but as the sun is setting and we will soon part ways, I must ask you.'

The Master looked at Don Juan with a far-away look in his eyes: '*The final step is to know that everything matters and yet nothing matters – that you are but dust on the Highway of Life.*'

And with that Don Juan and the Master parted company.

CHAPTER 17
OVERCOMING DISAPPOINTMENT AND DISASTER

Okay, you're making progress! Your Wheel of Life is more balanced, you've discovered some Passions and you've started using your _Personal Winner's Bible_. However, bad things inevitably will happen to you as you go through life. As a bare minimum, everyone will lose somebody they love. It's therefore essential you know how to react when something tries to knock you back.

THE FUGITIVE

It is incredibly difficult to overcome the death of a soul mate. To lose someone you loved and shared the very best of times with. Now instead of coming home each night to the warm smile of the one person you wanted to spend the rest of your life with, you come back to an empty house. Dinners become quiet, lonely affairs and you miss being able to share those crazy little comments that only your partner would understand while you watched TV together. The future suddenly seems to stretch ahead so empty and sterile.

But even a loss as great as this is not as tragic as that suffered by Sam Sheppard, whose real life was the inspiration for the Harrison Ford film, _The Fugitive_. Sam Sheppard not only lost his wife – he also saw her brutally bludgeoned to death by an intruder _in front of his own eyes_. Despite being unarmed, Sam fought the intruder with all his might and even risked his own life in a valiant attempt to save his wife. It was only when Sam was temporarily paralyzed by a blow to his neck –

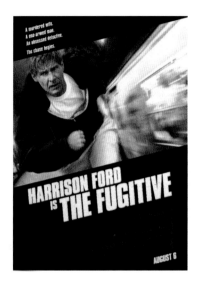

from the same bludgeon that killed his wife – that the murderer escaped from Sam's grip.

Unfortunately, Sam Sheppard's tragedy didn't end there. He was then charged with his wife's murder, despite being totally innocent. Sam was a good man, a successful doctor and genuine guy who was always helping other people. But instead of being respected by society he now found his name plastered all over the newspapers in America's highest profile murder case. As he waited in jail for the court case to begin, he noticed his friends began to visit less frequently. Even they'd started to believe he'd murdered his wife. But at least Sam could hold onto the hope that justice would finally be done in court and he'd be allowed to return home, an innocent man who would slowly reconstruct his life. Imagine then how the immense grief of losing his wife, his friends and his career must have turned to outrage when he was found guilty and sentenced to spend the rest of his life in jail. His whole life destroyed for something he didn't do. Unspeakable loss, immense grief and the denial of his freedom – all compounded by a grave injustice. How could life be so unfair?

Sam spent the best years of his life wasting away in jail before he was eventually cleared of all charges in a retrial. He was released without any compensation and because he was by now an old man, he had no hope of rebuilding his medical career. A man whose life had been stolen from him by a random act of violence by a mentally deranged vagrant. This true story raises two important questions:

1. How could anyone possibly hope to overcome a disaster of that sort of magnitude?
2. What are the best Tools to help you recover from a disaster and carry on to enjoy the rest of your life to its fullest?

VACCINATION AGAINST TRAGEDY

This chapter is about overcoming a disappointment or disaster that was *beyond your control*. A disaster where you weren't at fault or a major contributor to the negative outcome. While there are no 'instant' solutions to overcoming a tragedy and everyone's experiences are unique to them, the thought processes you choose to run through your mind will either help you or hold you back. This chapter contains the Tools and processes you need to make *permanent* progress rather than ones which just 'paper over the cracks' and get you going for the time being. Solutions that allow you to learn from your experience, to understand and appreciate your loss, and yet move on to live the *best* life possible given all the remaining circumstances. This requires far more than just adopting a 'positive attitude' or 'looking on the bright side of life' – as a lot of people will tell you to do when they're trying to be helpful. Overcoming a disaster requires the application of specific Tools in the correct manner.

It is important for you to become familiar with these Tools long before you encounter a tragedy because these Mental Tools act in the same way a vaccination does. Vaccinations require time to slowly build up antibodies in your system before you can become immune to a virus. In the same way, Mental Tools need time to become ingrained deep in your subconscious where they slowly build up your resilience to a disaster. You need to absorb these Mental Tools while you are strong and happy so they have time to reach their full potential.

The power and importance of this inoculation process is revealed by a study of happy and healthy people who were still leading vigorous lives at 100 years of age.

LESSONS FROM HAPPY 100-YEAR-OLDS

A group of researchers wanted to find out what were the key factors that allowed some people to be fit and active at 100 years old while other people ran out of life and died by the time they turned seventy. Was it their genes, their diet, their wealth or the amount of exercise they did that allowed them to still be going strong at 100? Detailed medical examinations were performed and literally hundreds of factors were considered. After all the results were analyzed, the researchers identified three factors which stood out and predicted who was likely to be happy and productive on their hundredth birthday. What surprised the researchers was that the top three factors were *thought processes* and not the biological things they were expecting, such as cholesterol levels or blood pressure. This is good news. Why? Because you can *change* your thought processes while much of your biology is fixed and down to your parents.

The three most important factors they found were:
1. An ability to get over disappointment.
2. An exocentric view of life.
3. A Passion that is actively pursued.

Now why are these three thought processes so important for a long and happy life?

DISAPPOINTMENT IS INEVITABLE
It turns out that there are two parts to the answer:
Firstly, *if you live long enough, you will be disappointed.*
Secondly, it turns out that having an exocentric view of life and having a Passion that is actively pursued are crucial aspects of getting over a disappointment. In other words, (2) and (3) are key parts of the solution to (1).

Disappointment and tragedy are inevitable. Sooner or later, someone who is special to you will pass away. That's just inevitable – everyone dies at some stage. Likewise, the more you do in life and the longer you live, the greater the opportunity for people to double-cross you, do things that hurt you or let you down. If you don't learn to get over disappointment then you'll end up getting stuck in the past, forever going over some fateful event. From then on, your life will limp along in the shadow of a lost love, a financial disappointment, or some other real or imagined catastrophe. This will cause a whole cascade of real physical changes to occur in your brain and your body, which will actually physically age you. It's no wonder that people who don't learn how to get over disappointment never make it to 100 in good shape. They age prematurely, become less fun to be around and go through life with a chip on their shoulder. But if you know how to move on by using the Mental Tools in this chapter, you will become a better, stronger, kinder and wiser person. Even though you may carry a very real scar from the past, that scar will have healed over the wound and will protect you. You'll then have a great chance of making it to 100 with a smile on your face and a spring in your step.

CONSEQUENCES GET MORE SERIOUS AS YOU GET OLDER
Related to the inevitability of disappointment is the fact that as you get older your disappointments will, in general, have more serious consequences. This increasing seriousness of tragedies should not be misconstrued as life

suddenly turning against you. It is just a natural consequence of life's trajectory. When you were a child it was a 'catastrophe' to drop your lollipop in the dirt and ruin it. But hey, somehow tomorrow came and the missing lollipop was soon forgotten. When you were young, your responsibilities and the consequences of your actions were naturally much more limited. What worries children, doesn't – or at least shouldn't – worry adults. Likewise, when you were young your career was just beginning and so any problem at work probably wasn't that final. You'd still have time to learn from your mistakes, re-group and start again. But one day you wake up and find you've got a family, a mortgage and you're forty. Suddenly a setback at work *can* be a real cause for concern. Life *does* get more serious as you get older.

Unfortunately it is all too easy to compare your carefree childhood days with the increasing complexity and gravity of adulthood and think life is now treating you badly. It would be foolish to expect your life to stay in some sort of Peter Pan Neverland world of child-like innocence. Life will send you more disappointments as you develop and they will be more painful. It is for this reason that you need to learn how to overcome disaster so that life can actually become more enjoyable as you grow and master the challenges of life.

God grant me the serenity to accept the things I cannot change,
The courage to change the things I can,
And the wisdom to know the difference.

THE FOUR STAGES OF DISASTER

There are four stages you will go through when you are hit by a major disaster and you need an understanding of them in order to get over them. They are:

Stage 1: Comprehension
Stage 2: Emotion
Stage 3: Reason
Stage 4: Progression

Knowing what each stage is about, which Tools you need to use during each stage and why those stages occur is essential if you are to make progress.

STAGE 1: COMPREHENSION – YOUR BRAIN'S MODEL IN CONFLICT

A key part of your brain's function is to create an accurate model of how the world works and to predict what the future is going to be like. Your brain does this constantly and without you knowing about it. For example, when you turn on a light switch you expect the room to become illuminated – you don't expect to hear trumpets play. If trumpets did suddenly start playing you'd more than likely jump because that's not what you were expecting.

You're not normally aware of all the millions of predictions your brain unconsciously makes every minute of the day because they usually match reality in a nice, seamless fashion. You only become aware of these predictions when your brain makes a mistake. For example, think of what happens when you're walking down a set of stairs in the dark and you think there is one more step to go but you've actually reached the bottom. Your leg unexpectedly hits the flat floor and everything seems so weird and unnatural because your brain had automatically moved your leg in the correct way for the next step – but it wasn't there. Until that unexpected moment, you hadn't realized all the work your brain was doing to build up a model of what to expect next, and thereby ensure your leg was in the right place and moving in the correct fashion.

When your life is suddenly turned upside down by an unexpected and major tragedy, there is the same sort of conflict between what your brain thought was going to happen and what actually happened. The brain's model and reality no longer match. As a result you get the same 'shock' as you would if your foot unexpectedly hits the floor at the bottom of the steps or if trumpets suddenly played when you turned a light on.

Your brain's model, and its interpretation of who you are and how the world works, has been a perfectly successful model for all your life right up until now. This means your brain will be under enormous stress as it tries to overturn such a deeply ingrained viewpoint. Not surprisingly, the brain reacts to this situation with a number of strategies as it struggles to adjust:

Shock

You are in a state of shock because your brain can't reconcile what is happening with what it thought ought to happen. It simply doesn't know what to do and so it temporarily shuts down.

Unreal Dream

Another way of your brain resolving any mismatch is for it to assume this must all be happening to someone else other than you. So things often don't seem 'real'. It's as if you're 'in a dream' or 'someone else is experiencing the tragedy' and you're just a spectator watching helplessly. There is sometimes a sense of numbness.

Go Into A Shell

Another common reaction is for you to 'go into a shell' and cut off as much external input or stimulation as possible. This is a natural consequence of your brain trying to reduce additional stress and processing requirements while it tries to assimilate the situation.

Denial

Another way of resolving the conflict is for your brain to temporarily deny that there is any mismatch between its model and reality. 'This can't be happening to me. I just can't believe it's happened.'

These are all quite natural mechanisms for your brain to adopt as it tries to cope with a situation where its own internal model of reality no longer matches what is actually happening. There is little you can do during this first stage while your brain adjusts. What your brain needs is space, quiet and low stress. Sleep is particularly helpful during Stage 1, as it is during sleep that your brain resolves issues, forms new circuits and makes adjustments. On top of this you will need lots of comfort from other people that 'all is going to be well'. That they are going to protect and take care of you so your brain has less to worry about.

While there is little you can do during the first stage, there are things you can do long before a tragedy strikes that will help you. The most important of these is to prepare your mind to the inevitability of tragedy. To realize that life plays cruel tricks, people double-cross you, friends and lovers die and that you shouldn't have such a strong hold on the material world. You need to construct your life on a foundation of permanent, inner spiritual qualities such as goodness, truth and beauty which survive the 'comings and goings' of the material world. Even though you are positive and plan for a wonderful future – which you believe in with all your heart – you balance this at the same time with a deep inner knowledge that life is temporary and transient.

Stage 1 should be a relatively quick period and should largely be completed within a few days. The key is to accept the reality of the situation as quickly as possible and to give your brain a chance to adapt. You need to have the following sort of approach: 'Okay, I can't undo the situation. I can't turn the clock back. It's happened. I just have to accept it and make the most of it.' The worst things you can do are to continue denying the reality of the situation or to avoid facing up to the consequences. Doing that just gives your brain an excuse to keep the old model of reality going which ultimately just prolongs your pain.

STAGE 2: EMOTION – YOUR INITIAL RESPONSE

We've already seen in earlier chapters that humans aren't machines or computers that can be instantly re-programmed to overcome a disaster. In addition to the systems in our brain involved with logic and reason, we have separate emotional systems – the Limbic System (see Chapter 5) – which is deep-seated, primitive and hardwired. We have this separate emotional system because it is of value to us. It shapes and controls our behavior in ways that ensure our survival without us having to learn what to do. It is activated when you are in love and happy because those are important events you want to repeat in your life. Likewise, when you are faced with a major disaster, your emotional system also fires up because a disaster is something which isn't good for you. Your Limbic System evokes incredibly powerful emotions such as sadness, anger, a sense of loss, grief or pointlessness – depending on the nature of the tragedy – because it wants you to avoid situations like this in the future.

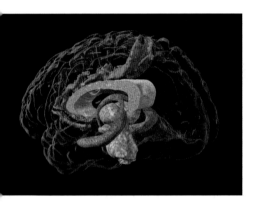

Hugs v Therapy

During this early phase your emotional Limbic System floods your brain with chemicals and to some extent over-rides your logical processes. This flood of chemicals stops you thinking rationally. You're whole focus is on what you've lost and on how your life isn't as good as it used to be before the event. You'll be emotionally hit by the enormity of your disaster. What you need during this initial period is simply comfort, companionship, understanding and reassurance that you are going to be okay.

At this stage, *you are emotional and you need emotional support.*

Detailed therapy, analysis and thoughts are not really going to help you right now because your emotional Limbic System is separate from the logic modules in your brain. Trying to rationalize or counsel somebody at this early stage would be like trying to bandage your arm when your leg is broken. Unfortunately people often don't understand this and so when they see your pain they try their best to help by giving you advice and ideas. What you really need is a big hug and lots of love and affection. Someone who just listens to you pour your heart out and explain what you are feeling. You need to feel loved, secure and a valuable person.

Friends

The most powerful and effective emotional support you can get comes from your family and close friends. From people who genuinely feel your pain as if it was their own. You need quality people who care about your happiness as much as their own. People who feel your pain deep down in their own Limbic System because that is the level where you are being most affected. Very few people even come close to that level of connection. Having friends of this quality is one of life's greatest treasures and is also highly correlated with living a long and happy life. Building relationships like those is also one of the booster shots in your inoculation program for being able to handle the challenges of life.

Let me explain what I mean by this with a real life example. A few years ago, I met up with my closest friend Simon immediately after a tragedy had unexpectedly struck me from a direction I hadn't expected. As I sat in the coffee shop explaining to Simon what had happened to me, his face became ever more sad and drawn. He took a deep breath and sighed. Slowly tears began to form in his eyes and then ran down his face. Here was this big masculine guy – normally bright, bubbly and intelligent – now experiencing my pain as if it was his own. He didn't need to say a single word. In fact he wasn't able to. He was so in tune with my feelings and he was such a genuinely caring guy that he took my pain on as if it was his own. There was no act. There was no 'sympathy' in the third person remote sense where he was just sorry for me. He literally *experienced* my pain with me. Nothing he could have said could possibly have comforted me and helped me as much as his deep experience of my own pain. I'll never forget that moment till the day I die. True friends like that are worth more than any amount of gold.

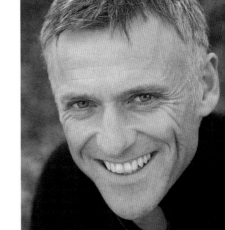

Greater love has no man than this,
That a man lay down his life for his friends.
John 15:13

Duration of Stage 2: The Initial Emotional Phase

Unlike Stage 1 (which can be relatively swift), how long Stage 2 (this initial emotional phase) takes to settle down depends on many things. Because it is a physiologically driven process it will depend on both your genetic make-up and your History. It's a little bit like being hit by a virus. If you're already run down and weakened you'll take much longer to overcome a virus than if you're in peak condition and have a powerful immune system. Likewise, your emotional response will take longer to settle down if you've been weakened by a series of disasters that have come one after another and flattened your 'emotional batteries'. Another factor that affects the duration of this initial emotional response is your genes. Some people have genes which naturally make their Limbic System far more active than other people's. But even taking these extremes into account, the usual rule of thumb is that this initial emotional phase should last days or possibly weeks, but certainly not months.

Let me clarify what I mean when I say this initial emotional period should last days and not months or years. This doesn't mean you won't feel *any* emotional hurt or pain two weeks later. Of course you will. And there will be plenty of times in the distant future when something triggers your emotions and everything comes flooding back to you in full Technicolor. From time to time you can expect to feel sad or disappointed, because after all, you have suffered a genuine tragedy. But these should become increasingly isolated events rather than a continuous state. Your life shouldn't continue to be dominated by raw emotions and you shouldn't be obsessed with the tragedy. Your thought processes should progress and the percentage of your time spent thinking about your tragedy should reduce as you now get on with life. Rather than having the same highly emotional thoughts going around and around in your mind without any apparent resolution, your mind will again become filled with thoughts of how you can achieve a positive future.

Keeping Emotions Going Long After They Should Have Subsided

Where things become dysfunctional and where you end up squandering your life away is if you allow your thought processes to keep your emotional reaction going long after it should have subsided. We can see how this process works if we consider what happens when you nearly crash your car. Imagine you've just had a big skid in your car and you've almost crashed over the side of a mountain. Immediately after the skid your heart will be pounding, you'll have a hollow feeling in your stomach and your hands will be shaking. This is your brain's automatic reaction preparing your blood supply and muscles for what it thought was going to be a serious emergency. Fortunately you didn't crash, and so after a few miles your pounding heart and the hollow feeling in your stomach should settle down. Certainly by tomorrow morning your heart rate should be back to normal when you start your car for the next part of the journey.

But if you get in your car the next morning, and rather than starting your journey as normal, you instead close your eyes and imagine a vivid picture of your car skidding off the mountainside and tumbling down the cliff with your face being smashed against the windscreen – then it is quite likely that your heart will start pounding again. In this case, your thought processes have reawakened your emotional reaction and kept it going. It's as if the near-tragedy is happening all over again.

The same thing can happen when you are faced with a personal tragedy in your life. There will always be an initial emotional reaction. Normally this reaction tapers off and your brain returns to its normal balance. But if your thought processes keep you in this emotional state too long then you risk damaging your mental and physical health. If that happens you can end up in serious trouble because this type of emotional reaction causes a major change in the chemical balance of your brain. That imbalance can in turn produce a physical change in you that can have more impact on your longevity than your genes or diet.

Therefore, once your initial emotional reaction has subsided, it is essential that you stop concentrating on your tragedy and get on with living your life. This is much easier said than done, of course. One of the ways you can do this is by completing Stage 3 in a full and final manner.

STAGE 3: REASON

If you've ever experienced a disaster or an unfair situation, you'll be familiar with the following scenario: your mind goes round and round and round over a series of issues, problems, angers, worries or frustrations. You just can't seem to switch your mind off and yet, despite all these thoughts running around in your head, you don't seem to be making any progress.

If you actually recorded all these thoughts and wrote them down, you'd probably notice they repeated themselves in a random order something like:

My boyfriend's left me
I'll never find another boyfriend like him
What is wrong with me?
I'm so lonely
I'll never find another boyfriend like him
It's not fair
How could he leave me?
What is wrong with me?
It's not fair
I'll never find another boyfriend like him
Etc.
Etc..
Etc…

Now even though you've actually only got maybe seven different thoughts running through your mind, it seems like there are hundreds because they come up in a random order and are usually phrased slightly differently each time. Your mind hasn't kept track of the fact that you've already been over Thought Four perhaps six times already and so you feel like it's yet another 'new' problem. You become overwhelmed by a seemingly endless morass of questions and issues. But make no mistake, there is actually only a very *limited* number of genuinely different thoughts bubbling around in your mind.

A crucial step in surviving a tragedy is to break this endless repetitive cycle of thoughts because repetition only wears you out emotionally and keeps your initial emotional response going long after it should have stopped. The following technique will help you break that cycle.

The first thing you need to do is write all these repeating thoughts down and give each one a number. You may find you had three or four slightly differing versions of the same question just worded in a slightly different manner. Combine those different versions into a single question and write them down with one number beside it. When you do this you'll be surprised at how suddenly 'hundreds' of questions have collapsed down into four or five key unresolved issues. Try it!

Once you've given your problems or thoughts a number you'll find your mind will automatically say, *Oh, that's Thought Four again! I've already been through that thought fifteen times today!* This simple recognition will have a dramatic effect on helping you cut your tragedy down to size and allow you to move on.

The next thing you need to do is try to find an answer or solution to each question that is circling through your mind. For example, suppose you discover your boyfriend has cheated on you then one of the thoughts circling your mind might be:

Thought 1: Why did he do this to me?
There are, of course, many possible answers such as:

• He's a selfish, self-centered person who only cares about his own pleasures
• He's got no moral sense or ethics
• He's a horrible, nasty person
• He made a mistake in an uncharacteristic moment of weakness
• He doesn't love me

The reason why these thoughts keep circling around your mind is because you haven't yet resolved the answer and put that question to bed. Your brain keeps asking the question over and over and can't rest until it has a conclusion. This is where you can help your brain. Suppose in the above list you think it's most likely the reason he cheated on you is any one of the first three answers – but you're not sure. The important point here is that regardless of which of those first three answers is correct, you ought to come to the same conclusion: he's not a suitable partner for you. If he's horrible or he's a selfish brat then you're better off without him. If that's the case, there's no point in continuing to torture yourself with Thought 1 anymore. It's time to draw a line under that relationship and move on. What you then do is put a line through Thought 1, 2 and 3 and write the conclusion:

'Regardless of the reason, he's not a suitable partner and in the long-term I'm better off without him. Even if I have short term pain.'

Now whenever Thought 1 comes up again, in whatever guise, say to yourself: *Ahh, yes, Thought 1 again. No point in thinking anymore about it – whatever the reason, I'm better off without him.* Doing this works wonders and helps chop off repetitive and unproductive thoughts that cycle around in your mind and wear you out emotionally without any benefit.

If, however, you think the answer was Thought 5, 'He didn't love me', then you may need to ask yourself another set of questions such as:

• Did I do anything wrong?
• Could I have improved my behavior?
• What have I learned from this relationship?
• Is there anything I can do to fix the situation?

Again, for each of these questions you need to write down both the questions and the answers. Doing this is enormously beneficial because it helps your brain come to a logical conclusion and that ultimately stops the endless process of questions cycling around and around. It's a bit like when you're trying to solve a complicated maths problem. Mathematicians never try to hold all the equations in their head in one go. If they did that they'd quickly get confused by all the symbols swirling around in their head and make mistakes. Instead, they write down each individual line of the calculation in turn, so they can move methodically towards the conclusion.

KEY POINTS
Preventing Unproductive Repetition Of Thoughts:

• Identify each unique thought
• Write the thoughts down in order and give them a number
• Underneath each thought, write down all possible answers
• Identify the most likely conclusion to each thought
• Whenever a thought pops into your mind, recognize it, say its number and remind yourself of the conclusion – you no longer need worry about that issue because you've already reached a conclusion

---

STAGE 4: PROGRESS
Progress is the automatic outcome of getting through Stages 1–3.

INOCULATION: STARVING YOUR TRAGEDY OF OXYGEN
If you cast your mind back to the Happy 100-year-olds (see page 167), you'll remember they had two other important attributes which distinguished them from normal people:

An Exocentric View Of Life
They genuinely cared about other people and were actively involved in society in a positive, constructive way.

Active Passions
They had genuine Passions that they *actively* pursued.

It is no accident these two attributes are listed alongside the ability to get over a tragedy because they both provide you with balance and direct your attention away from your inner tragedy. They stop you becoming unnaturally obsessed by your tragedy and from keeping the emotions going when they should be fading away. Your tragedy needs constant attention or 'oxygen' to keep it fed. If you give it too much attention then it can grow into a tumor that will slowly devour your soul. Fortunately your brain has a limited amount of attention to go around and so if other things are genuinely important to you, then you won't be able to give your tragedy excessive attention, because other things will be calling out just as loudly. Secondly, when you have an outward-looking perspective and you genuinely care about your friends, your family and society in general, your own tragedy is naturally put into its proper perspective. When you're an active part of the wider community your focus widens like a lens zooming out. Your own ups and downs begin to look more like creases in the fabric of life when they are compared to the wider landscape and mountain ranges of humanity as a whole.

Remember at the start of this chapter we talked about inoculating yourself so that you are already relatively resistant to tragedy before it strikes? Having an exocentric life and having Passions is another part of that inoculation. You can't just switch on an exocentric view of life or 'get' a genuine Passion in an instant. It is even more unlikely you could do that when you are in the middle of a tragedy. Passions and an exocentric view of life need to be carefully nurtured over many years. They take time to grow and root in your soul. In many cases, a Passion will start out small and only grow with time. They are like a line of trees that can only provide protection from the wind after they have reached a certain maturity.

THE PHILOSOPHY OF DISASTER – LIFE IS NOT FAIR
While a detailed discussion of philosophy will occur in *The Winner's Bible Of Philosophy*, I just want to touch on one small aspect here because it's important in helping you overcome your tragedy. This concerns whether you believe life is *fair*.

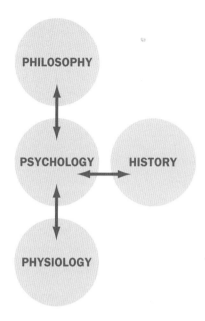

Do things always happen for a purpose? The expectation that life 'ought to be fair' is ingrained in us from birth. We are taught it is okay to become angry if someone cheats us in a game of cards. We are entitled to shout at a referee if he makes a bad decision and we're unfairly sent off the pitch. But unfortunately life isn't a game where everyone follows the rules. It couldn't *possibly* be like that in a world where billions of people are each allowed to selfishly and imperfectly exercise their own free will. If everyone is genuinely allowed to do whatever they want, then there can never be a well-ordered over-arching plan. Free will, which is exercised spontaneously and on a moment-by-moment basis, is incompatible with a tailor-made plan for us. The murderer was free to exercise his own free will on that fateful night when he entered Sam Sheppard's house. It had nothing to do with Sam and it wasn't his fault. A necessary outcome of all this free will is this: *bad things do happen to good people and good things do happen to bad people.* Eleanor Roosevelt summed up the situation very eloquently when she said:

If you think life is fair – then you've been seriously misinformed.
Eleanor Roosevelt

Unless you fully grasp this concept of life's 'unfairness' you'll never be able to completely overcome many of life's inevitable and genuine tragedies. You'll end up constantly going over events in your mind asking yourself questions like, *Why did God or the Universe allow this to happen to me?* And so you're back to the problem of repeated thoughts keeping emotions going (Stage 2 and Stage 3). But no matter how many times you ask yourself that sort of question it still won't make any sense because you'll be trying to find answers, reasons and causes where perhaps there aren't any. All you'll end up doing is going round and round in circles getting yourself angry and frustrated. This is such an important topic we've devoted an entire book, *The Winner's Bible Of Philosophy*, to it.

BECOMING A VICTIM AND TAKING THINGS PERSONALLY

Another consequence of failing to accept that life can be unfair is that we become 'victims' of the circumstances and end up taking things *personally*. If we believe life has unfairly singled us out for bad treatment then it's easy to feel sorry for ourselves and that we've been hard done by. But the Universe didn't personally single out the Fugitive Sam Sheppard for punishment. It wasn't his fault. It was the fault of the murderer who randomly broke into his house. And so it may be that *sometimes* bad things happen to you and it's *not* your fault.

A business partner may rip you off because he's greedy. A boyfriend may be unfaithful to you for no other reason than he's a selfish jerk who doesn't know how to treat you correctly or behave properly in a relationship. In cases such as these you need to see yourself as an innocent person caught in the firing line of another person's mistakes or by the random vagaries of the Universe. Of course, you'll want to learn from events like these and choose your partners more wisely in the future.

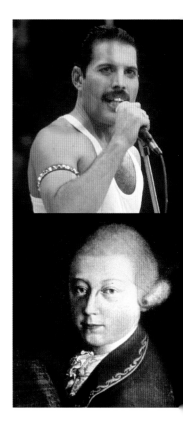

Similarly just because a partner breaks up with you and wants to start a new relationship with someone else doesn't *necessarily* mean there is anything 'wrong' with you (although of course there could be). Maybe you really are a great person but somehow you weren't exactly what they are looking for. That again is just part of the complexity, randomness and variety of life. After all, some people love Mozart while others find his work boring and prefer Freddie Mercury. Neither Mozart nor Freddie would be in the slightest bit upset or offended by this situation if they were alive today. It really is different strokes for different folks. Maybe there is someone else out there who loves you exactly as you are?

Life is a process of becoming,
A combination of states we have to go through.
Where people fail is that they wish to elect a state and remain in it.
This is a kind of death.
Anais Nin

Where things can quickly spiral downhill is if you take this natural variation in tastes and preferences personally and interpret it to mean there is something *wrong* with you. Whenever you do this you undermine your own value and your own meaning in life. This is a guaranteed way to fire your Limbic System into producing a massive emotional feeling of darkness. Whenever you are faced with a tragedy or a disappointment, it is important for you to identify which things were part of the wider Universe and outside your own control and which things were inside your control. Otherwise you'll end up creating a situation that has no resolution. If that happens, your life will effectively grind to a halt with the tragedy. You'll gradually become emotionally drained and worn out because you can never resolve what is essentially an irresolvable issue. No amount of agonizing over why the murderer killed Sam Sheppard's wife was ever going help him. It just happened because that was the murderer's intention. This randomness and unfairness of life is illustrated in the following short parable.

THE PARABLE OF THE SAILOR
We are each sailors on the sea of life. For sure the more skilled we are at sailing and the better prepared our boat is, the more likely it is we will survive each journey. But even the most skilled sailor can get hit by a freak wave and capsize. That's just the nature of the sea. The laws of statistics dictate that the more journeys we go on, the more experiences we have in life, the more likely it is we will encounter rough weather. Equally, the greater the number of journeys we embark on, the more likely it is that we'll discover new islands, learn about ourselves and understand the vessel we sail in. With each experience we'll become better at handling ourselves and knowing how to master each situation. We must concentrate on our sailing Skills and our preparation. We must learn how to ride the waves and run with the wind. There is no point shouting at the wind or the sea when they press against us.

THE HIDDEN BENEFIT OF TRAGEDY
A good friend of mine, Andrew, tragically lost his beautiful, teenage daughter to brain cancer. She died a slow and painful death while in the bloom of her youth. Five years after her death, I was walking through the streets of Eton with Andrew

when he told me her death was more painful and heart-rending than any words could ever tell. No poet or song would ever describe the despair and pain his family went through. Even though he was a Minister and had presided over many funerals before – this was different. This was *personal*. He now experienced in searing reality the jagged edges of nature and they cut him to the core. His good old Limbic System had fired up and made him take note of life.

And yet, out of the black depths of this tragedy, Andrew told me he gained something precious. It was only then that he experienced the emotions of love and despair, hope and anger in their absolute rawest form. Before, these things were more abstract. They happened to other people or he read about them in books. Even though he'd already lived a full life, traveled the world and had many adventures, this one experience changed him fundamentally. He felt he truly came alive for the very first time. As a result, Andrew became a far kinder, better, warmer person. He valued every single day – every single *hour*. Each person he came into contact with was more precious and unique. He no longer took anything for granted. He gained a new vitality and energy. He understood that life, people and events are so fleeting that they need to be savored and enjoyed.

Andrew's experience illustrates a vital point about overcoming a tragedy. It isn't just about *surviving* – it is about taking what life dishes out, sometimes quite unfairly, and turning those experiences to your best possible *advantage*. For a truly moving and personal example of how this can happen, against all the odds, see Chapter 28, 'Grandpa's Cottage'.

THE SEASONS OF LIFE

One of life's certainties is that it will *change*. Just as the seasons come and go, so too will the many phases of your life. One of the keys to being profoundly happy and at peace with yourself is learning to savor all the nuances of each season while you are in them, but then being able to say goodbye with a warm smile when the time comes for the next phase.

The wild-eyed innocence and athleticism of youth must inevitably fade, no matter how hard you train your body. That's just raw physiology. But this should not be a time for regret because if you've lived life correctly, the pleasures of youth will be replaced with even greater treasures such as the wisdom, resources, knowledge and power of middle age.

This concept of the Seasons of Life can also help us cope with tragedies. For example, it is not uncommon for a woman to lose her husband to a heart attack. There is no denying such a death is a truly massive loss to her and that nothing will ever replace him. But in many cases a bereaved wife learns how to rebuild her life and move on to live a different but equally rich life without her husband. The sudden emptiness and loneliness she experiences may spur her on to pursue new Goals or dreams that otherwise would have forever lain dormant. And so she enters into a new phase of independence and accomplishment that is different but equally satisfying. The hard part is learning to let go of one season and welcome in the next.

Ecclesiastes 3:1-10
For everything there is a season,
and a time for every matter under heaven;
a time to be born, and a time to die;
a time to plant, and a time to pluck up what is planted;
a time to kill, and a time to heal; a time to break down, and a time to build up;
a time to weep, and a time to laugh; a time to mourn, and a time to dance;
a time to cast away stones, and a time to gather stones together;
a time to embrace, and a time to refrain from embracing;
a time to seek, and a time to lose; a time to keep, and a time to cast away;
a time to rend, and a time to sew; a time to keep silence, and a time to speak;
a time to love, and a time to hate; a time for war, and a time for peace.

CHAPTER 18
'YOU.INC'

By now your *Personal Winner's Bible* should be getting quite full with plenty of notes, diagrams and images in it. The final instruction I'd like to suggest to you is to give it some structure and organization. Doing this greatly increases your efficiency each morning and ensures you don't accidentally overlook some crucial aspect of your development.

The method I use to help my professional athletes structure their *Personal Winner's Bible* is to get them to think of themselves as a business with a number of divisions or departments. For example, if their name is Ayrton Senna then I'd get them to imagine there is a company called *'Ayrton Senna Inc'*. What I'm asking them to do is think about all the 'divisions' that go into making Ayrton Senna Inc a successful business. In Ayrton Senna's case, his 'business' was to win the Formula 1 World Championship, but simply saying that misses out all the details of what he needs to do to win. It's equivalent to summing up Microsoft by saying it's a company that 'sells software.' While that is Microsoft's mission they need much more just a 'sales department'. They need to have: Programming, R&D, Sales, Marketing, Human Resources, Finance and Legal departments. Each of those departments is just as important for the success of Microsoft as the others. If any one of those departments is weak then Microsoft is vulnerable. This is where many athletes go wrong. They are often so focused on the end Goal of running or jumping or winning a medal that they sometimes don't look after all the other 'departments of their company' that are equally vital for success.

YOUR BUSINESS MIND MAP

So one of the things I do with every athlete is to ask them to tell me what their 'business' is. They usually reply by saying something like, 'To swim faster than anyone else' or 'to drive faster'. And for many of them that's what they really think their job is – nothing more, nothing less. But then I ask them how they are going to ensure they're faster than anyone else. This starts them thinking and they respond by telling me they have to get physically fit and do a lot of practice. But even now they're not thinking deeply enough about their success. So I draw them a diagram that, in the case of a racing driver for example, looks something like this:

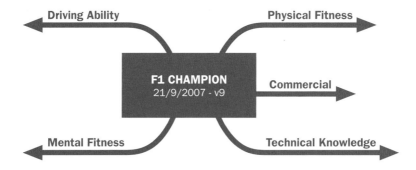

While they do need to have excellent technique and physical fitness, that isn't enough at the elite level.

They also need to have extensive technical knowledge on how to set up the car and provide information back to their race engineers. They need to understand differential settings, suspension geometry and engine mapping. Without this knowledge their engineer won't be able to give them a properly balanced car and that would mean they wouldn't be able to beat other drivers who do have perfectly set–up cars – no matter how 'fast' they can drive. They also need to look after their commercial affairs because race driving is an expensive business. This means they need to look after their sponsors by giving speeches and attending promotions. That in turn means they need Skills in public speaking and presentation. They also need to build a strong relationship with their account manager and their press advisors. You can see already that 'driving faster than anyone else' is not enough.

As I continue exploring with the driver what's in each 'division' of their business, I quickly end up with a more complex and layered diagram that looks something like this:

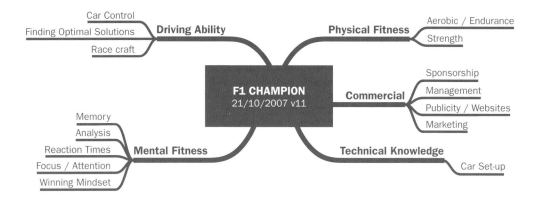

Of course you don't need to understand all the specifics of a race driver's diagram like this one. I've simply sketched this one out because it's a way for me to show you how complex 'You.Inc' can be. But why do you need a diagram like this in the first place?

The purpose of drawing this Mind Map is to ensure that each morning the athlete wakes up and quickly looks over the entire diagram to check that *every* box is being looked after correctly. A single diagram with all the relationships like this allows him to do so in a few seconds and not miss anything. After my athletes have been doing this for a few weeks they often tell me how surprised they were to discover the number of things they weren't taking proper care of. Little things had slipped beneath their radar without them knowing about it or they were incorrectly allocating their limited time to the wrong areas.

LIFE MIND MAP

This concept of constructing your 'Business Mind Map' now needs to be extended to your *entire* life. This is because life is not just about a career or winning on the track. A true Winner's life should be a rich and varied experience where you gain satisfaction from recreation, friends and a variety of pursuits. The trouble is, we sometimes don't spend enough time or energy on the non-career things because they don't 'shout the loudest' at us or because they aren't 'urgent'. Things in business or sport often have deadlines and very tangible consequences if we don't do certain things by a certain time, whereas this isn't usually the case with our private life (at least not in the short term). And so it is all too easy to let career tasks crowd out our private life. But if we remind ourselves for thirty seconds each morning of all the components that go into making our lives truly worth living, then we'll allocate our time more wisely and not just to the things that scream loudest at us. That's where your Life Mind Map comes in.

This has an added benefit because being successful over the long haul in any venture, whether sport or business, requires you to lead a balanced life. Too much emphasis on work at the expense of social and recreational activities will flatten your batteries in the long run or make you so one-dimensional that you become fragile. If a driver's entire life is nothing more than racing then his entire happiness depends on Winning each weekend. If he loses on Sunday then his sense of self – worth and satisfaction is severely dented. Over the long haul this rollercoaster of wins and losses is extremely damaging unless it is balanced with other things that give the racing driver satisfaction. But if he has other interests outside of racing, then these act as a buffer and a steadying influence on his life. You are exactly the same.

CONSTRUCTING YOUR LIFE MIND MAP

So spend some time now and construct a Mind Map which shows all the components in your life. The figure below should give you an idea of the sorts of things you'll include. While it's nothing more than a template, it is a good place to start you thinking. Don't stop at just two levels. You might need to go down three or even four levels in order to make sure you have captured all the details necessary for correctly overseeing your life.

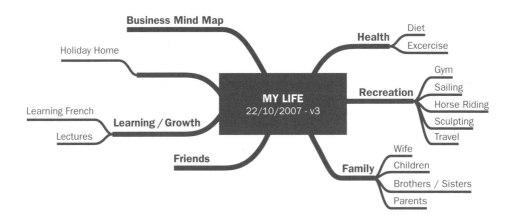

You can sketch your diagram freehand on a piece of paper or you can use PowerPoint or one of the specialist Mind Mapping programs like those available from Mindjet (www.mindjet.com). There are a number of advantages when using programs like Mindjet's Mind Map such as: ease of updating, hiding levels or zooming in on them, attaching notes to each box, adding dates, etc.

Once you've drawn your diagram, *you should put it on the first page* inside your *Personal Winner's Bible*. It goes on there because that's going to be the first thing you look at each morning. It's going to provide you with your checklist to make sure you are properly balanced and allocating your precious emotions, time and energy to the right things. Once you have 'You.Inc' at the front of your *Winner's Bible* you should then re-organize all the pages according to the flow and order of that diagram.

HOW TO USE YOUR MIND MAPS EACH MORNING

Now that you have your Mind Map in your *Personal Winner's Bible* you are going to use it *every day*. Its main purpose is to help you quickly look over your entire life in one quick, fifteen-second scan to:

1. Check you are allocating your time and effort correctly. It is best to do this by looking at both the past and the future. Did you allocate your time correctly yesterday? How much time did you spend in each box yesterday? Last week? Just the simple act of asking yourself this question can often be very revealing. Then think about how you want to spend your time today, tomorrow and the next week? Will this allocation help you get your Goals and be happy? It is important for you to do this regularly because your life will change on a weekly basis – particularly if you are moving forward and growing.
2. Check whether you have neglected any key areas just because some things are screaming more loudly at you than they should. Urgent is not necessarily important!
3. Check whether you need to add or entirely remove some boxes from your life.

As you look at each of the boxes in your Mind Maps, consider the three questions above. You may be surprised at how often they subtly alter your day – for the better!

CHAPTER 19
PUTTING YOUR *WINNER'S BIBLE* INTO ACTION

Author's Note:
I can't overemphasise how important this section is. Indeed, using your *Personal Winner's Bible* correctly is the single most important factor in determining whether or not you'll achieve your Optimal Future.

Time and again I've noticed it's the people who use their *Personal Winner's Bible* in the correct way who are the ones that make the biggest gains in their life. This is not surprising. Even the very best *Personal Winner's Bible* in the whole world is of no use if it's left in your bedside cabinet and only used when you feel like you need a boost. The following unsolicited e-mail from a highly successful businesswoman captures some of the key points in how you should use your *PWB*. Follow this e-mail and see if you can spot the keys to her success – I'll summarise them for you at the end so you can see how well you got on.

AN UNSOLICITED E-MAIL

Hi Kerry,
Excuse the typos, this is a lot of rambling ... you don't have to respond ... just keeping u up to date.

I just wanted to tell you that the more I read your book, *The Winner's Bible*, the more I can say this book is 'THE TRUTH'. I am the living proof you can take the same Tools you use with elite athletes and change someone's life in a few months. Your book is not like other crazy self-help books that promise outrageous change without delivering. I am physically and mentally changing *every day*. Let me give you just a few examples since I returned to work from the holiday break.

1. Work performance is OFF the CHARTS, my President and Vice President have both mentioned this to me (in just 2 wks back at work). I am coming up with fresh and innovative ideas ... one of which has now been implemented company-wide.

2. I was asked by a new acquaintance from the event I had in December to give a lecture tour throughout some of the top universities in the USA. All of my lodging and travel will be paid and in addition I will receive a very healthy stipend.

3. Two of the outside consulting projects I've been working on are starting to breathe life. It looks like one may even get picked up by a TV network in fall 2009.

4. My *Personal Winner's Bible* is something I look at *every day!!!* I use it first thing in the morning and just let my mind find which pages are the most important for me right now. However as the days go on I feel a stronger need to create new things, take out stuff, add new quotes, change photos ... it's been crazy! I have this envelope I am keeping of new stuff I have to add. I am changing my heroes/mentors page, I am rearranging my Goals page. I am adding new photos from Christmas of my boyfriend and myself ... we are back together again. I am crazy about him and he's crazy about me.

5. Photo Shoot: so the picture I had with the gray sweater on in the front of my *Personal Winner's Bible* was a photo from one year ago ... I was 20lbs heavier. I wanted to put a new fresh photo in my *PWB*, to reflect the changing me, so before I finished my holidays, I had a friend who is a professional photographer take photos of me. When she showed me some of the photos, I nearly cried. It's a happier, 20lbs lighter, more confident version of myself.

6. I have been purging old clothes, junk, around the house, a little every other day or so since I returned to work.

7. My creative side, my Limbic brain, my right brain ... I always knew I was creative but I am sure I had buried it. So, working on my *PWB* forced me to return to my childhood a bit. I was cutting things out, pasting, organizing, I felt like I was putting an arts and crafts project together. Then I made my boyfriend this over-the-top card with images of all of his favorite things, phrases from his heroes, etc., and he loved it, then he told his mom about my artsy side (which I didn't know I had) and that's when she gave me the beautiful wooden easel, canvas and paint set for Christmas. Meantime, the art continues. I am looking into taking some painting classes at this place not far from home. Also when I was 'purging' I came across an old shirt my mother wore ... this is the only shirt of hers I have, everything else was given away or sold. It is the shirt she used to paint in. It has paint stains all over it, but it's a cool button-down, light-greenish colored 1970-ish shirt ... my mom was a teacher, but she also made these hand-carved wooden pieces of work and would paint them and give them as gifts to people, her sisters, parents, friends ... she never sold them. However, they are good! Good enough that people ask my aunts where they bought them ... my mother never fully developed her art side ... but I am going to develop mine, and I am going to wear her paint-stained shirt when I paint my first stroke.

8. Every morning, I go thru my *Winner's Bible*, I may read a line or two of scripture or something positive from another book, I journal daily and meditate or pray with music similar to the sounds on the CD you made for me, and then I either do yoga, some other stretching or cardio/weight workouts ... I think the consistency, the daily doing has made the overall difference in my life change. CONSISTENCY – this has made all the difference.

Kerry, I cannot thank u enough, you allowed me to see the God in me, and things that have been buried behind dark clothes, 20lbs, and fake smiles are now being fully authenticated ... surely, I am starting to feel free again ... I am not worried about set-backs, because I know how to get out of it now and not wallow in it forever, and I realize it's only from those experiences, that I learn and grown and share with others ...

Have a great day,
Debbie
xxx

HOW DID YOU SCORE?

Did you notice the key points that made Debbie's *Personal Winner's Bible* successful? Well, here they are:

a) Consistency

The most important point of all was that she used her *Personal Winner's Bible* EVERY DAY! As she says, consistency is the key. And why? Because consistency is what gradually allows your brain to be rewired. It's the same when you practice any sport. For example, if you only go skiing one day a year you'll never make progress. But if you go to the slopes every day for twelve days in a row you'll make massive progress. This happens because your brain needs to know any new process is going to be a permanent and regular feature of your life before it's going to bother changing its wiring. Unless you reinforce your new messages regularly and repeatedly you'll only take one step forward then another step back. You *must* use your *Winner's Bible* every day!

b) Vibrant/Living

Notice how her *Personal Winner's Bible* was changing as she was growing. She had a whole pile of new ideas positively bubbling around in her mind. There were so many she even had to start an envelope to hold all the new ideas as they came to her. She didn't fight these new and sometimes strange ideas, but accepted them as they came along. It was a really interesting journey for her. Entirely new things like 'painting' opened up for her. This is why you won't wear out your *Personal Winner's Bible* or get bored with it. You can use it every day because after a week or a month, it's an entirely different book.

c) Only A Few Pages A Day

She didn't read her entire *Winner's Bible* from start to finish each day. She would flick through a few pages and just let her eyes settle on the ones that were important for her that day. It's a weird thing, but your subconscious seems to know which page to stop at. This is why you only need to spend a few minutes each morning reading it.

d) Used In Conjunction With Her Emotionally Supercharging CDs

You can tell from her e-mail that she'd done her homework correctly and worked out her Strengths and Weaknesses and she'd listed them in her *Personal Winner's Bible*. She used this list *and* her special CD together to help rewire her emotional brain. It's the combination that is so important: the fixated visualisation, reading her lists and consulting her Mind Maps as well as deep surgery with her CDs.

e) Put Things Into Action

While this businesswoman was already successful, she was naturally conservative in her behaviour. You can tell from reading her e-mail that she began to acquire an Unshakeable Belief in herself by the combination of Mental Tools she used; then she took the plunge by *actually putting into practice* the things she had written down. That takes courage – but it's what allowed her to move forward – and then update her *Personal Winner's Bible*.

If you follow these steps as Debbie did, you will experience the same transformation.

It's up to you.

CHAPTER 20
THE END OF
THE BEGINNING

This is not the beginning of the end,
This is only the end of the beginning.
Sir Winston Churchill

So far we've introduced Tools that can improve your performance and help turn you into a Winner. I'd like to take a moment to remind us what a Winner really is. It's therefore time to pause briefly to catch our breath and let the following stories provide some insight into this question.

THE BILLIONAIRE TEAM OWNER

Some time ago, a Formula 1 team flew me over to the Australian Grand Prix for an interview. They were curious about how my peculiar combination of mathematics and neuroscience could be applied to motor racing. When I arrived for the interview there were about twelve executives, engineers and designers sitting rather formally on nice leather chairs. The meeting progressed smoothly as they asked me a number of questions about how I might possibly help with this particular problem or that specific issue. The questions went back and forth for twenty minutes until the team owner suddenly interrupted and said, 'So, how much are you worth?' I was rather taken aback and said I wasn't quite sure what he meant. Did he mean how much value was I going to contribute to the company or did he mean how much was I going to charge for my services?

He said, 'No, how much money do you have in the bank?' I replied by saying I still wasn't quite sure I understood the nature of his question. He replied, 'Well, it's obvious isn't it? A man's success is measured by his wealth. So how much are you worth?'

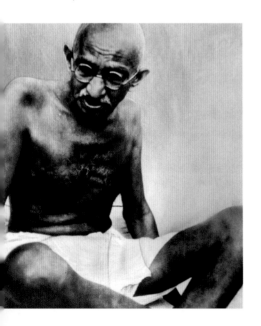

I thought for a moment before replying, 'I don't think Einstein woke up each morning and counted his money. He valued his 'success' in life by the discoveries he made about how the Universe works. Discoveries which changed the lives of everyone in this room. I don't think Leonardo da Vinci counted up his money on his deathbed – I rather think it was all the great works he'd painted which gave him a sense of satisfaction and a life well lived. And I'm absolutely certain Gandhi was far more concerned by the millions of lives he'd improved rather than the few material possessions he'd acquired. If that's how employees in your company are valued then I'm sorry – I'm the wrong man for the job.'

I got up, excused myself from the meeting and returned home to New Zealand.

On the flight back home I thought about that extraordinary exchange. Did the owner really believe a man is measured simply by his wealth, material possessions and the trophies he's won? At first blush it seemed a ridiculous idea but the more I thought about it, the more it seemed this really was the unspoken message behind modern Western society. Maybe it was just that no one else was as brave or as blunt as the team owner to articulate it so starkly.

OUTER SUCCESS

Our Western world is driven by Capitalism which is all about success, winning trophies, being promoted further up the business ladder, making more money and having more possessions. It may even be part of the reason why you bought this book. It's the message hidden behind every advertisement which tempts us with another product or service to buy. It's the dominant message our children hear while growing up because they spend more time in front of advertisements on TV than they do in front of their parents or their teachers. We idolize our sports heroes and TV stars because they're the ones who've reached the pinnacle of capitalist success. They're at the top of the tree; they're famous and have piles of money. Unfortunately, this measure of success is just as much an illusion as the story of the Emperor's New Clothes. We've been brainwashed into thinking these are the 'beautiful' people when, in reality, many of them, like the Emperor, are actually naked, empty souls whose achievements matter little in the long run. We've been tricked by the hype and we haven't realized it.

PORPHYRIUS

Let's think about it for a moment. As I've said, if one famous athlete fails to win a race then, in the grand scheme of things, it really doesn't matter one iota. By definition, another athlete *must* win and they in turn will become famous. It's a cycle of manufactured heroes where the individual hardly matters and the world is barely changed regardless of the Winner's name or face.

One of the most famous athletes the world has ever known was the great chariot racer Porphyrius. At the height of his fame, Porphyrius

used to attract crowds of over 250,000 people to his races in Ancient Rome. In those times, there were no cars, trains, TVs or radios and so his fame was spread by excited word of mouth. People walked or rode horses for days just to catch a glimpse of him. And 250,000 people represents a *huge* percentage of the population of Ancient Rome. It would be something like thirty million people turning up to watch Tiger Woods tee off. But who has heard of Porphyrius today? His name is long forgotten and his exploits are of no lasting significance. I have no doubt he was a tremendous athlete and I have no doubt he thrilled the crowds with his bravery, Skill and panache. But when all is said and done, it has accounted for nothing. But Socrates, who breathed the same air as Porphyrius lives on. Gandhi lives on. We take our actors, celebrities, business moguls and sports heroes far too seriously compared to what they're worth.

Of course, the Billionaire Team Owner at the start of this chapter should take great pride in the team he's made and the facilities he's constructed. He's clearly done a great job, just as Porphyrius did, and for that he needs to be congratulated. But despite all the wind tunnels and autoclaves and trophy cabinets, what has his 'empire' actually contributed to mankind? Is a modern Formula 1 race any more enjoyable than a race from the 1970s? Despite the huge increase in speed of the modern car many spectators argue that events like the Goodwood Revival – with cars from the 1960s and 1970s – are actually a far more enjoyable spectacle than a modern grand prix. All those billions of dollars and millions of man–hours' development since the 1960s have made the cars faster but they haven't improved the actual racing or the fun we derive from the contest. However, on the other hand, Gandhi, Socrates and Martin Luther King have each made a *lasting contribution* to mankind. In the same way, a surgeon or a social worker quietly putting patients' lives back together also leaves a lasting legacy.

INNER BEAUTY

And so this brings us back to the Formula 1 boss. He only saw the outer measure of a man's success and wasn't able to see their deeper inner development. Both aspects are important. Neither should be discarded in favor of the other. Financially successful people and champions ought to be admired because of what they've achieved. Success of any kind is never easy. But there are also other people working just as hard with Skills as finely honed as any F-1 world champion – quietly changing the world without any financial reward or fame. For me, these are the true champions of the world.

Natural man judges primarily according to the superficial view. Our unsophisticated animal nature causes us to judge a woman by her looks and a man by his success – or possibly in more modern liberated times, the other way around. But the advanced person is able to rise above these base instincts and see people in their entirety – both their inner and outer worth. A self-centered catwalk queen who arrogantly assaults cabin crew on planes or throws telephones at people's heads in a petty fit of rage ought to be seen as an unattractive person when you add both her inner and outer beauty together. Such a person should not be admired or even tolerated as a celebrity. The problem is, modern Capitalism trains our eyes so we only see the outer values because that is what consumerism is all about. But like most material things which rust and crumble, the outer view is of little lasting significance. It is the inner beauty of a person – their soul – which is far more important. This conclusion reminds me of the life of my good friend Don Oliver.

A VERY LARGE MAN

Don Oliver was a huge man with hands the size of baseball gloves. For ten consecutive years, Don was the New Zealand Heavyweight Weightlifting Champion and won numerous international championships and gold medals. He was also a successful businessman, owning several swanky gyms. Despite his immense strength and fitness, Don was struck down in his prime by pancreatic cancer. Don's funeral was a massive affair. The large auditorium was packed to overflowing. People lined the car park and the streets outside to listen to the service on loudspeakers. What was particularly interesting about the service was that there was hardly any mention of Don's championship wins. Instead, people spoke with tears and at length of his kindness and generosity. The following story contains a snapshot of Don's personality and a small kernel of the meaning of life.

I remember walking into Don's office one day after he'd just finished having a meeting with one of his staff called Angelique. She'd first joined one of Don's gyms as a receptionist on the front desk. Unfortunately, she kept making terrible mistakes with the memberships despite plenty of instruction and assistance from other staff. So Don transferred her to the gym floor where her tasks were less onerous. Despite her best efforts and much encouragement from management, Angelique failed at that also. She was a simple girl and just wasn't up to the demands of a modern gym. After many months of warnings Don finally called her into his office to fire her. When Don told Angelique of his intention to give her three months notice she burst into tears. To cut a long story short, by the end of the meeting, Don had not only kept her on but he'd given her a raise in salary. While this clearly made bad business sense, Don was thinking of the bigger picture. He felt for Angelique as a fellow human and realized how poor her prospects of finding other employment were. While Don may have lost a little money in business as a result of this decision, I think overall he gained in life. Certainly the world gained, as evidenced by the huge crowd who attended Don's funeral to show their respects to him.

For what does it profit a man, to gain the whole world and lose his life?
Mark 8:36

LESSONS FROM A FUNERAL

And speaking of funerals, two things always strike me when I attend one. First, how short life is. Surely it was only yesterday that my school mates and I were young guys working together on our worn-out old motorcycles, dreaming of our first kiss and maybe one day being able to buy a new bike. Yet here I am, sitting in church with my own teenage son who no doubt has the same dreams. Life is indeed short. Secondly, and even more startling than the brevity of life – its finite quantity – is what it all *means* when it's been finally added up and the last chapter has been closed. What was the *quality* of the life that was lived? When a person dies you bury so much more than their body. You bury their dreams and hopes and all the things that were so dear to them. Their achievements, degrees and bank balance remain – but in the grand scheme of things those items mean very little.

Don Oliver's trophies, all shiny and gleaming, don't remind me of his great athletic prowess. They remind me of his wise, warm and kind personality. That was worth far more to all those people who came into contact with him than any championship he won. His smile, his kindness and wisdom left a lasting impression that has been passed on down through the ages. If Don hadn't won those medals, someone else would have won them and most likely the world would have continued on in much the same way – not tangibly any different. But Don's personality left a mark on many people and so the world was altered slightly. He added value and happiness to those who came into contact with him and they in turn passed that happiness and knowledge on in slightly diluted form. These things are the true measure of a person and what the world loses when someone dies. The rest is mere superficial fluff which quickly blows away and is forgotten.

I have seen everything that is done under the sun; and behold, all is vanity and a striving after wind.
Ecclesiastes 1:14

OZYMANDIAS

The great poet Shelley wrote of a mythical king called Ozymandias, who according to legend, was the most powerful king to ever rule the world (in all probability Ozymandias was based on the Egyptian ruler Rameses the Great). The poem is about the vain and pointless arrogance of mankind. Centuries after Ozymandias ruled, all that remains of his vast empire is the shattered fragment of one of his statues. A broken pedestal on which a statue of the king once stood lies half-buried in the sand. Carved on that pedestal are words which arrogantly proclaim his power and glory. But all around is just a vast empty desert.

I fear to tread in the footsteps of such a great poet but I was so moved by Shelley's words that it sparked in me the desire to write my own version which I hope is somewhat more closely related to this chapter.

Ozymandias – with apologies to Shelley

The vast and empty desert drained the camels dry
And endless sand beneath each step,
Numbed our weary minds
Until one day we stumbled on
Hand-carved stones
Half-buried in the sand.

A fractured leg, a severed face
The statue's crumbling plinth
Proclaimed with arrogance:
'I am Ozymandias, King of all Kings
Weep at my feet ye lesser mortals
My Empire fills your sight.'

Yet only sand now remains
For time weathers all but love and truth
So monarchs come and go
While Socrates survives.

Therefore consider all the works
Your hands have done today
And weigh with balance fair
Which shall last the test of time –
And which shall pass away.

Now take out your *Personal Winner's Bible* and at the end put these points to challenge yourself for the future:

• Consider how your life will appear when viewed from the end looking backwards
• Are you adding to your Inner Beauty?
• Ask yourself whether you are adding value to all those who come in contact with you?
• Are you living your Optimal Future?
• Are you behaving with integrity?

You have just reached the End of the Beginning.

CHAPTER 21
PEOPLE ARE THE MOST IMPORTANT THINGS IN YOUR LIFE

Now that you've started on your journey towards your Optimal Future, it's time to consider the two most important things in your life:

1. The type of person you will become – the quality of your personality.
2. The people you are intimately connected with.

You see, the richest people in the world aren't those with the most assets, the most fame, the most success or even those who are the most popular. The people who possess the greatest treasure in the world are those who:

• are quality people leading their own authentic lives to the fullest
• are intimately connected with other people of equal quality who deeply care for them

The choice of words used here is very important. I didn't just say 'surrounded by people' but 'intimately connected with people'. You can have lots of friends and associates and be very popular, but this popularity is often at a superficial level. While those friends will keep you busy and happy to a certain level, they won't enable you to lead the full richness of life you deserve. Superficial friendship is nothing more than the constant sound of simple advertising jingles or elevator music. It fills your background void but isn't ultimately satisfying. There is no comparison between background music and the rich complexities of a well-crafted song and likewise there is no comparison between superficial friends and quality people who are intimately connected with you. 'Intimately connected' implies there is a bond which penetrates to the heart of your essence or soul. Those friends know your deepest feelings and they desperately care about your well-being. Because of this depth of connection, your mutual laughter and joy is more vibrant. The good times are more relaxed and easy. There is never any 'trying' or 'effort' to get along with each other. You can sit quietly without talking and enjoy life or you can be crazy, whooping it up together. It is never a heavy thing that always requires you to have a deep and meaningful interaction. It can be spontaneous and outrageous and yet, because you are connected, those crazy times will automatically be meaningful without you even trying.

Run those words around your mind again – *connected* – *quality* – *intimately* – *authentic* – *deeply care*. These are the people you need in your life and this is the sort of person you need to be your friend, lover, partner or work colleague.

If you have quality people in your life then it will usually work out for the best. The problem is, the world is not full of quality, enlightened people. Therefore you will need to learn how to recognize those quality people you are going to let into your inner sanctum; you will also need to learn how to deal with those who aren't quality people, but who by force of life will swirl around and intersect with you. This will require tolerance, patience and forgiveness, circumscribed by firm boundaries and love.

CHOOSING PEOPLE

As you go through life you will come into contact with literally millions of people. Most of these people, like your work colleagues or members of your sports club, will interact with you in a fairly superficial manner. You don't choose who they are, and in most cases, you'll bounce easily and happily off them as you go about your daily life. They are just part of life's rich tapestry. But there is a smaller group of people you do personally select – your friends, business partners and lovers. These people need to be chosen *extremely* carefully because they have such a massive impact on your life. Their thoughts will influence and shape your thoughts. What they do, how they think, who they meet and where they go will influence every aspect of your life – what you do, how you think, who you meet, where you go and ultimately who you become. Because you are surrounded and immersed in their environment it is not surprising that you'll gradually absorb their behaviors, ethics, desires and dreams. Slowly but surely you *will* be shaped and influenced by them in a subtle process that relentlessly moulds you, without you even realizing it. This is human nature.

Your close circle of friends, lovers and business associates has another major impact on your life. They are the ones that can hurt you the most (and also conversely the ones that help you get ahead in life). If you think back over all the times when you were seriously upset or let down, you'll probably find it was caused by someone close to you.

So it turns out that the inner character of the people you closely associate with is of prime importance. If their soul is made of quality stuff you'll find your life somehow always turns out for the better. You'll become a happier, more productive and enriched person. But if their inner character is weak or flawed, then sooner or later you'll get hurt.

The trouble is, many people aren't quite what they seem on the outside. A potential business partner may be charming and very smart; they may have the right expertise, fabulous resources and all the right connections. But if they're not a quality person on the inside, you'll almost certainly end up being worse off if you go into business with them. Sooner or later they'll let you down or find a way to make a personal gain at your expense. And the same is true of lovers. How many potential soul mates looked like a million dollars and had all the right lines and a scintillating repartee only to end up being the very person who ultimately hurt you more than anyone else?

Therefore being able to reliably assess a person's inner character is one of the most important Skills you'll ever learn. It is also one of the last Skills most people master. So this raises the question:

How do you really know what a person is like inside?

There are a number of methods that have stood the test of time. Whenever they are ignored, you risk paying a heavy price. The first method was taught to me by my grandfather.

CHAPTER 22
GRANDPA'S LITTLE STORIES

My grandpa, Sir Trevor Henry, was New Zealand's top judge. He lived to 105 and throughout his long and rich life he'd pretty much seen everything there was to see. He'd heard every story and every excuse in his courtroom and he'd met every type of character possible. When he was young there were no cars or electricity in New Zealand. This meant that even something as simple as going to meet his girlfriend required riding a horse for three days and sleeping in the bush each night, living off pigeons and berries. By the time Grandpa was in his seventies he was flying around the world on 747s.

Few can have seen as many changes in their lives as Grandpa and even fewer can have embraced those changes with such fierce intelligence. Grandpa was the only person I ever knew who literally *wore out* an entire set of *Encyclopedia Britannica*. But Grandpa wasn't just an academic genius – he was also a superb athlete in his youth, winning many trophies. Despite all his achievements, Grandpa was a quietly spoken man and when he said something it was always worth listening to.

When Grandpa was in his nineties I'd have him over to my house each Tuesday for lunch and a chat. After our usual 'salmon and scallops', he'd settle back and relax with a cup of tea while I'd carry on and do a few more hours of work. Because I worked from home, I often had friends or business colleagues visit me. As a matter or courtesy I'd always introduce them to Grandpa before moving to the adjacent room to continue my meetings. I liked the idea of Grandpa listening in to my conversations and being part of my life. It gave him an interest and something for us to share.

Occasionally, but not very often, Grandpa would make a small observation about one of these visitors as I drove him home at the end of the day. *Without fail* his assessment would turn out to be absolutely perfect. If he raised a little warning flag about someone, you could be sure that sooner or later they'd do

something which wasn't quite right or which let me down. If he told me he warmed to a certain person you could be certain they'd turn out to be a brilliant business ally or a fabulous friend – sometimes in complete contrast to my own first impression of them.

After a while Grandpa's unerring accuracy began to intrigue me and so I asked him how he was able to do this. Grandpa smiled and said: 'Everyone you meet has a Big Story. They all have an image they want to project about who they are, what they do and why they are so special. Because this Big Story is important to them they put in a lot of effort and care to polish it to perfection. They make this Big Story interesting and so we naturally pay a lot of attention to it. But while they are going about their lives, living and telling their Big Story, they are also leaking out Little Stories. Small subtleties in their behavior that tell you what they are *actually* like inside. Of course, we don't usually notice these Little Stories because they get completely swamped by the Big Story. But if you learn to listen to these Little Stories you'll be able to see inside people's souls. And the more you practice this Skill of listening to the Little Stories, the more you'll see.'

The following true story is an example of how subtle and yet how powerful these Little Stories are.

Simon And Kirsty

A friend of mine called Simon is a professional model with handsome looks complemented by a natural charm and intelligence. Unfortunately, Simon was badly hurt many years ago by a woman he was desperately in love with. The pain from that relationship was so intense he decided to protect his heart and never fall in love again. From then on he only aimed for a series of casual affairs.

However, as time went by, Simon began to tire of superficial relationships and started to long for something more deep and meaningful. After a number of years he finally met a woman called Kirsty who ticked all his boxes in such a big way that he decided to cast caution to the wind and start a serious relationship with her. As you would expect, Kirsty was a vivacious, intelligent and feisty woman. The sort of woman that men are always fawning all over. Slowly but surely Simon began to open his heart to Kirsty and she responded in equal measure by saying she was committed to a journey of love and discovery with him.

Now a key aspect of their blossoming relationship was communication. They'd talk about everything. Two months into their relationship Simon asked Kirsty why she had joined a very expensive and up-market dating agency before he met her. Clearly she was the sort of woman who was never going to be short of a date and so he was curious as to why she joined. Kirsty replied: 'I joined because I need to spread my net wide.'

And there, buried in that sentence, was one tiny detail – a Little Story – that alerted Simon to a problem that would later come back to haunt him and once again break his heart. A problem most of us wouldn't notice at first glance. You see, the problem with Kirsty's answer is that she used the word 'need' which is in the present tense rather than 'needed' which is in the past tense. Without her realizing it, she had told Simon that she *still* felt a continuing need to spread her net wide – even while she was dating him. A little detail had leaked out without her even knowing it. And so it turned out to be. While he was putting all his effort and emotion into her, she was still taking phone calls from guys and flirting with them despite her Big Story of how she was totally devoted to him. Of course, there is nothing wrong with Kirsty having lots of male friends, but she was secretly, or maybe even unconsciously still on the lookout for someone else. It wasn't long before Simon was once again let down and hurt by the very woman he had invested so much love, time and emotion in.

To be fair to Simon, he did actually spot this warning sign when it happened, but being human, he decided to overlook it because he was so captivated by Kirsty. And therein lies another problem. We often choose – unconsciously – to ignore the Little Stories because we don't want to hear what they are saying. We'd rather believe in the Big Story because we want so much for it to happen.

LITTLE STORIES WITHOUT WORDS

Another interesting thing about these Little Stories is that they are often revealed by the words people *don't* say to you, rather than by the words they do. Let me explain.

A friend of mine is a fabulously wealthy billionaire and so he is naturally attractive to women because of the exciting lifestyle he can provide for them. Private jets to any exotic destination as often as they fancy. An opulent super-yacht on which every whim and indulgence is catered for. Unfortunately the billionaire, who we'll just call Martin, faces a tricky problem. He is looking for a long-term soul mate. Someone he can genuinely share his life, his dreams, his thoughts and his Passions with, rather than someone he just has fun with. The problem is, how can he tell if any woman he dates likes him for who he actually is or whether they are just keen on him because of the lifestyle and excitement he can provide? Working this out is a tricky process because people always make a huge effort when they are captivated by something and want it badly enough. Women always tell him they love him and they'll charm him with every trick in the book to keep him interested. But are they fighting for him or the lifestyle he provides? How can he ever tell? Do the women themselves actually know?

As I said above, the answer is often contained in what they *don't* say.

For example, Martin is passionate about exotic birds and has his own aviary at home. If one of his birds becomes sick then he'll obviously be concerned about it. Now if a woman *really* loves Martin then she will also become genuinely concerned about one of his birds if it becomes sick, simply because it is important to Martin. What interests Martin now becomes important to her, because *he* is important to her. Even if birds weren't things she was naturally interested in, she will become interested in this bird. And if she really loves him she won't just talk about the bird as a conversation piece because it makes for easy chats with Martin. She'll spontaneously talk about the bird because she too has somehow started to share his Passion. But if she never talks about the bird except when Martin does, then somehow her lack of words on this matter tells Martin a Little Story about how important he actually is to her.

The point is, everyone can talk about things you are mutually interested in — whether these things are stocks and shares or tropical holidays. But you begin to know if someone is *genuinely* interested in you when they begin to talk passionately and spontaneously about the things that interest you. Particularly when those things don't naturally interest them. The things people don't talk about often tell you more than the things they do talk about.

Inspector Gregory: 'Is there any other point to which you would wish to draw my attention?'
Holmes: 'To the curious incident of the dog in the night-time.'
Inspector Gregory: 'The dog did nothing in the night-time.'
Holmes: 'That was the curious incident.'
From *The Adventures of Silver Blaze,* by Sir Arthur Conan Doyle.

YOUR OWN 'LITTLE STORIES'
How well do you know yourself?

It might seem like a stupid question because if there's anyone who knows your own thoughts, it ought to be you. After all, you're the only person who is aware of everything you've ever thought. But if you've ever been to a really good counselor or therapist you'll know they often see things in your personality which you've completely missed yourself. How do they do this?

The answer is this: skilled therapists do it by listening carefully to the Little Story behind your own Big Story. And here's the surprise. If you start listening to your *own* Little Stories, you might be stunned to find you aren't really the person you thought you were. For example, Kirsty had probably convinced her *conscious self* she was on a genuine voyage of love with Simon. She probably played that message over and over again in her conscious mind and even repeated it to Simon. She didn't realize her use of the word 'need' as opposed to the past tense 'needed' indicated a hidden reservation she had about Simon. And if she was questioned about keeping in touch with other guys she would easily justify it as simply being friendly and having a healthy social balance with other men. However, all the time her internal radar was constantly scanning for someone better than Simon because her subconscious was on a different path to her conscious thoughts. As so often happens, her inner consciousness was the better predictor of what she would ultimately do.

The key point is that your Big Stories are almost always the ones you are most comfortable with. The ones you like to hear about yourself. When you find your Little Stories don't match your Big Stories then this is usually because the Little

Stories are telling you things about yourself you don't want to hear. But they are the very things you need to change in order to grow and develop. So try listening to your own Little Stories and you'll be surprised how much you learn about yourself and how much you grow.

One of the marks of a wise person is that they see themselves as they truly are. If you learn to listen to your own Little Stories you will learn much about yourself and grow into a happier and better person.

DETECTIVE WORK

The second method of assessing people's character was taught to me by three-time Formula 1 World Champion, Sir Jackie Stewart. I met Jackie in the 1980s while I was demonstrating some electronics I'd developed for Ford in America. Jackie liked my product and we decided to go into business together. After the presentation I flew back to New Zealand to continue developing the electronics. A week later I received a phone call from Jackie asking me if I had all my financial affairs in order. Specifically, had I paid all my tax on one of my trust companies? I assured Jackie I had. He said to me rather cryptically, 'Well, you'd better double check.' So I rang my accountant and he assured me that everything was all fully paid up.

A week later I received a surprise call from my accountant: 'You'll never guess what. I've just had a call from the Inland Revenue and they said they have no record of your last tax payment. It took me an hour on the phone to establish they had actually received your payment but somehow it had been accidentally misfiled by them in the wrong department.' My accountant was astonished: 'How on earth could anyone know about that on the other side of the world when I didn't even know about it?'

The answer was, Jackie had done some very thorough checks on my background before deciding whether to go into business with me. He said his reputation was everything and experience had taught him not to take people at face value. He wanted to know as much as possible about anyone he was going to be associated with. Of course I had nothing to hide and so I didn't mind his background checks.

Over the years I've found Jackie's advice has been absolutely invaluable. Time and again it has either saved me from making a big mistake in the first instance or, if I'm already involved with someone and they do one of 'Grandpa's Little Stories' which raises an alarm, it has then prompted me into doing more thorough homework on them. The interesting thing is, in 80% of the instances where my suspicions have been aroused, I've discovered something that would have ultimately caused me trouble. Something that would have remained hidden until it was too late.

Scientia est Potentia – Knowledge is Power

SHOW ME YOUR FRIENDS

Good detectives don't just look at the obvious clues when they are weighing up a case – they also collect indirect and circumstantial evidence. And so when it comes to people the best circumstantial evidence you can obtain about them is from the character of their *friends*. This is summed up in the old saying: 'Show me your friends and I'll show you who you are and who you will become.'

A person's friends tell you a lot about the behaviors they find acceptable, their values in life and the things that interest them or turn them on. Their friends not only inform you of the things you need to be worried about, but also the positive and valuable things about that person's character.

A really interesting exercise for you to do is list the six people you chose to spend the most time with over the last month. Beside each of these six people, now write down four adjectives that best describe each of them. This

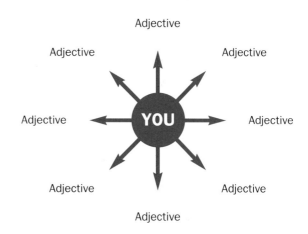

will give you 24 adjectives but you'll probably find quite a few of them are repeated. Now take another piece of paper and put your name at the centre of that page. Then write down all those adjectives in a circle around your own name.

This diagram tells you a *lot* about yourself!

For example, it may be that one trait which three of your friends share is that they're insecure about themselves and are needy or always seeking some form of reassurance. This may mean that you are *needy* yourself because you feel a sense of worth when these needy people want you. Maybe you get a lot of self-esteem out of supplying their wants. Maybe not. But the question you must ask yourself is why do you have that particular list of adjectives surrounding your name? Sometimes the true answer isn't the obvious one!

I've known people who've made a conscious decision to change their friends after they did this exercise because it made them realize their friends weren't people who were adding to their life. A year later every one of them reported their lives were much happier. By removing these 'low value' friends, they made room for higher value, higher quality friends. Unless you actively prune low quality people from your life you won't have the time or effort to attract new people into your life. This doesn't mean you need to be constantly analyzing your friends, but it does mean you occasionally need to do a stock take of who you have accumulated in your life. Sometimes we end up spending time with people simply because they are there. They filled a need or a space at that stage of your life and you forgot to move on or grow. Change requires *effort*. It will be well worth it.

You never know how your actions will affect the world …

THE MANGERE MATAU

I was at Mangere airport about to leave New Zealand for an extended period of work in England. I find airport farewells rather emotional so I had already said goodbye to all my family and friends during the previous week. Now there was just the simple mechanical matter of checking-in and settling back for the long flight and my new adventure.

But before I continue telling you about my check-in, I'd like to take you to a very special beach in New Zealand called Muriwai beach. I'm going to take you there not once, but twice – to taste the strength of the seasons. Muriwai is this vast beach which stretches for almost 100km. It is on the rugged west coast of New Zealand and is covered in shiny, jet-black sand. It is framed by huge sand dunes and the crystal clear waters of the Pacific Ocean stretching all the way to Australia. An unfettered ocean which means the waves are wild, massive mountains. Muriwai is raw nature at her best.

Summer

In summer, you hear kids squealing in and out of the shallow, frothy surf. Thousands and thousands of oiled bodies bronzing in the sun. Games of beach cricket, rugby and volleyball. The jet-black sand is so hot you can't walk on it in bare feet. Everywhere people are happy to be there – for no reason other than the sheer fun of it.

Winter

In winter it's totally different. You see miles and miles of empty beach. The only people there are those that need to be. Pressed into the hard, cold wind, they absorb nature while contemplating life. A few lonely gannets buffet above the dunes. Nature at its wildest and most untamed.

The same place, but the seasons make it oh, so different in every way.

Back To Mangere Airport – October 17

The events of September 11 were still blowing a very cold wind through the departure lounge as I arrived. Gone were the happy holidaymakers. Lovers waiting expectantly or tearfully departing were nowhere to be seen. Duty-free was totally empty and the food hall displayed shelves of food that no one would come to eat. The only people at the terminal were those that *needed* to be there. Business people hurrying to destinations, hassled at every step by heightened security. Purpose not pleasure.

A winter out of season, caused by terrorists.

I'd never seen anything like it before. It reminded me of the empty malls from Nevil Shute's *On The Beach* at the end of the nuclear war. It reminded me of the empty desolation of Muriwai on a cold winter's day.

But as I sat there brooding on this cold, steely feeling, the wind suddenly stopped and the sun shone. For two dear friends strolled through the departure lounge towards me. They had interrupted their business day to come and see me off. An unnecessary but treasured visit. In reality, they had no spare time to come and see me. I knew they started work every morning at 6 o' clock and finished late each night, working hard in a new start-up venture where every single minute counted. We'd already said goodbye but here they were taking time out of a busy day for no reason other than sheer kindness and love.

The exact antithesis of September 11.

Before I left, they placed a Matau around my neck – a small Maori carving which is a symbol of a bond that ties people together – a bond so strong that the recipient must return. The Matau will not leave my neck till I hug them again. It will remind me daily not only of them, but also of all the other wonderful people I leave behind.

The Matau was a lovely gift, symbolic of the power of love.

That little necklace, that little symbolic Matau had the power to change that winter day into summer. I wanted to share it with you so that its power spread. So that maybe we can all be motivated to share a little more love than we would normally do. It certainly motivated me.

Always too busy.

Too many things going on.

Despite what TV and magazines constantly tell us, love is not just Eros, but also Agape. That selfless love which expects no return. A love that extends between the old and the young, the boss and the employee.

It is the same love that made another friend of mine who is a busy CEO take the day off – without me knowing – to come to my father's funeral. She'd never met my father. When I later found out she'd traveled the entire day to sit quietly at the back of the church filled with people she didn't know, before slipping quietly away again, I asked her why she came. She said she wanted to find out more about the man who shaped my life. A spontaneous example of the intimate connection we talked about in the introduction to this section.

People … they are the most important things in your life.

He tangata, he tangata, he tangata

CHAPTER 23
WEATHER FORECASTING

THE IMPORTANCE OF KNOWING THE FUTURE

Being able to predict the future always gives you a major advantage. If you know what's going to happen then you can prepare yourself and always be in the best possible position. Nowhere is this observation more true than in our relationships with other people.

How many times have you invested time and effort into a friend, business colleague or lover only to later find they let you down? This is particularly true in love. So many people who were once madly in love end up scratching each other's eyes out in bitter divorce cases. How can it be that two people who vowed they'd spend the rest of their lives together end up being the very people who cause each other so much pain? While each case is different, a common theme is that as time goes by, the person they married didn't turn out to be the person they *thought* they'd married. With this in mind, wouldn't it be nice if you could tell what someone was going to be like in the future?

One area of 'predicting the future', where people have spent literally billions of dollars and millions of man-hours on research is weather forecasting. Meteorologists employ incredibly sophisticated software, the very latest supercomputers, satellite images and the most advanced sensor technology known to man. The question is: can we learn anything about predicting the future behavior of people from the hi-tech science of modern weather forecasting? The answer turns out to be a surprising yet resounding 'Yes'.

WEATHER FORECAST COMPETITION

A number of years ago a competition was held to see who had developed the most successful computer program for predicting the weather. Dozens of complex computer programs were submitted. Some of these programs ran into hundreds of thousands of lines of code and required supercomputers to execute all the calculations and combine the information from various satellites and ground-based sensors. Each day, the competing models were required to make predictions as to what the weather would be like on the next day in thirty different cities across America. After six months, the scores were tallied to see which program was the most accurate. One program stood out as being the most reliable. It was also by far the smallest and most simple program of all. In fact, it only contained *one* line of code.

The winning computer program simply said: 'Tomorrow's weather will be the same as today's weather.'

If you think about it that's not a bad program. If it's a hot, sunny day today then, in all probability, tomorrow's likely to be another hot and sunny day as well. Of course the weather does change and so the program is going to be wrong on occasion. But on balance it's going to be right more often than it's wrong because the weather usually changes slowly and rather predictably.

So, if you want to know how a person is going to behave tomorrow – then look at how they have behaved in the past. If you want to know how your prospective partner is going to behave towards you in the future, look at how they behaved to *other* people in the past. Let me give you an example of how this works.

ANGELA AND THE PARKING WARDEN

Angela was a stunning, sexy woman. She captured men's hearts wherever she went. Her friends thought she was absolutely charming and would be a wonderful wife for any man lucky enough to put a ring on her finger. Then one day, quite by chance, as I was walking along the streets of London I spotted Angela on the other side of the road. I crossed over and started walking towards her. She had her back to me so she couldn't see me coming. As I got closer to her I realized she was in a furious row with a parking warden. Angela had parked her car illegally and received a ticket. Instead of accepting her fate, Angela had launched into a vicious verbal attack on the poor parking warden. She was calling her every name under the sun. I was totally gobsmacked!

What I had witnessed was the real Angela and how she treated people who weren't important to her. How she reacts when someone causes her some pain – even if that pain was precipitated by her own actions. In that brief, candid moment, I saw how Angela would behave towards people she no longer had any use for. After all, the poor parking warden was only doing her job. She had feelings and emotions like all of us. She went home each night after giving out tickets and looked in the mirror each morning like we all do. If Angela had thought about it for a moment she'd realize we need parking wardens otherwise our streets – her streets – would be total chaos and she'd never find somewhere to park in the first place. And yet she treated this human being – someone with feelings and a soul – as if she was a piece of dirt.

This episode showed me how Angela would act in the future towards her husband if, for some reason, they fell on difficult times. And one thing is for certain, if you live with someone long enough, there will be testing times of some sort or another. It showed me that she treated people according to their 'value' to her and not because of how she viewed people as a whole. This type of observation is closely related to 'Grandpa's Little Stories' (see Chapter 22).

So if your partner was unfaithful in a previous relationship, then the chances are he/she is going to be unfaithful to you as well. If your partner has seriously let you or someone else down in the past, then *expect* the same to happen to you in the future.

Can the Ethiopian change his skin or the leopard change his spots?
Jeremiah 13 v 23

THE WEATHER CAN CHANGE

Part of the reason for telling you these stories is to help you set your expectations at the correct level, so you don't sail blindly into the future expecting things to be different just because someone is full of apologies when they get caught doing something wrong. The problem is, we tend to listen to the words people tell us about how they're going to change because we desperately want the future to be different. They persuade us with great conviction and emotion because, at that moment, they genuinely believe they will change. But the sad truth of the matter is, more often than not history *will* repeat itself.

But as we said in the introductory chapter at the very start of this book – for every rule there is a counter-rule. Some people *do* change. That single line weather forecasting program is clearly wrong on occasion. The weather does change every now and again. It's just that five times out of six it doesn't change, which is why it's such a reliable and compact rule. For this reason, it should be your default position in the absence of any further information.

Now comes the key part of this story. What's really important is to find out how much a person has been growing and changing in their life. Some islands experience very stable weather while other islands frequently get four seasons in a single day. That's the outcome of their geography. Likewise some people are on a real and genuine journey of growth and change, wanting to improve themselves and make the world a better place. For other people, growth and development isn't something that's intrinsically important to them at all. They only change when they're forced to. You can generally spot which camp people fall into by the types of conversations they have (just as you can spot which islands have variable weather by their surrounding geography). If a person doesn't exhibit a general and constant underlying desire to become a better person outside of times of stress, then the chances are history will repeat itself.

CHAPTER 24
ALBERT'S COMPASS

In 1883, a father gave his ill son Albert a compass to play with while he was sick in bed. The father thought nothing more of it as he watched the boy move the compass this way and that. For him it was just another boy playing with a compass – like thousands of boys had done before and countless thousands would do after. The father couldn't have known that this very act would change the world. It has even changed your life as you sit here today.

For as the four-year-old boy moved the compass, he was astonished to discover the needle inside seemed to move all on its own. No matter which way he turned the case, the needle inside was guided by some unseen force so that it always pointed in a certain direction. In young Albert's limited experience, things only moved when something physically touched them. A cup only moves along the surface of a table when a finger makes contact with the cup and pushes it. Even a door that slams only does so because the wind pushes on it. Yet here was a needle – completely sealed in a glass case with nothing touching it – being moved by some unseen force.

Albert was only four and so he could not put into words the fascination and wonder he felt. But if he could have articulated his thoughts, perhaps he would have said he was captivated by how 'forces could act at a distance.' How could something move something else without ever making contact with it? Understanding these hidden forces became his life's Passion. He thought about it day and night.

Albert's compass had no power on its own and it could have been bought for less than a dollar. But it ended World War II, enabled man to walk on the moon and was instrumental in the development of medicines that saved millions of lives, because 22 years later the same Albert Einstein unleashed a blitz of scientific papers that completely revolutionized the world. Three papers in a single year – each worthy of a Nobel Prize. Both the Atomic and the Quantum ages were born because of Albert's Passion for understanding how forces act at a distance. Truly the world was never the same again.

Your life today is different because of that little four-year-old boy wonder. Computers, DVDs, electronics, atomic bombs, Hiroshima and GPS are among thousands of other things which all owe their legacy to that fateful day. Things which may never have occurred no matter how many other scientists had considered the same questions.

There are a number of important lessons in this story.

The obvious one, of course, is how a burning Passion can drive our lives to great success. But the greater lesson here is how our smallest actions can have an influence without us ever knowing. Albert's father could never have imagined the impact his act of giving a compass to his son was going to have on the world. He never lived to see computers or the atomic bomb. Even on his deathbed, the influence of that day was still hidden from him. And so it is, a single word or a single deed may ripple out from you across the pond of life and make a change which is far greater than the ripple itself. It may have consequences you never dreamed or intended. Consequences you may never understand yourself.

What ripples will your actions unleash today?
How far will they spread and who will they touch without you ever knowing about it?
Choose wisely how you interact with people.

CHAPTER 25
THE WORLD'S HAPPIEST PERSON

THE GUINNESS BOOK OF WORLD RECORDS

As a kid, I used to enjoy reading *The Guinness Book of World Records*. It contained all sorts of mind-boggling statistics such as the heaviest man (1200 lbs), the tallest man (8 feet 11 inches), the wealthiest man ($62,000,000,000.00) and the world's fastest runner (faster than 50 km/h!).

But I often wondered who was the 'World's Happiest Person'. While I can't actually give you a 100% guarantee that I've met the World's Happiest Person … I'm pretty sure I have. But before I tell you about Happy Harry, I'd first like to talk about happiness itself.

WHAT IS HAPPINESS?

The first problem with finding the happiest person in the world is that you can't just go out and measure 'happiness' with a set of scales or a tape measure. There is no such thing as a 'happiness meter', nor can you simply measure it by the number of laughs and smiles a person has. I've met many a laughing joker who was the 'life and soul of the party' only to find out later over a quiet cappuccino that their life was privately wracked with pain and sadness. The jokes and the bluster was just their way of papering over the cracks and getting by.

It seems happiness comes in many flavors and so an exact definition of what constitutes 'happiness' is rather hard to come by. But if we're going to talk about the 'World's Happiest Person', we need at least to have a general idea of what we are talking about. True happiness can't just be a life of absolute perfection and the absence of challenges or pain. Imagine for a moment a person who had absolutely every whim and fancy instantly met and whom had everything handed to them on a platter. They probably wouldn't be happy. After all, if you always shot a hole-in-one on every single tee, golf would quickly lose its appeal. The same is true in life. Challenges and difficulties *do* seem to add to the spice and satisfaction of life – as long as they are handled correctly. So I guess the sort of happiness we're trying to measure is that 'deep-seated contentment' where you wake up fresh and bubbly each morning just itching to savor the excitement of the new day; where you go to bed at night bathed in a warm sense of completeness and fulfillment; where you can look back over the previous year, or even ten years, and can honestly say, 'I wouldn't have changed a thing'. And even out of bad circumstances, everything somehow, in a strange sort of way, turned out to be okay. (see Chapter 17, 'The Hidden Benefit Of Tragedy'). That's the sort of happiness we're interested in because it's less dependent on the

random vagaries that life throws at us. It depends more on ourselves than our circumstances. We're after happiness you can do something about, rather than just plain luck.

HAPPY GENES

The second problem with happiness is that we're not all created equal. Some people are born with naturally 'happy genes' and some are born with 'sad genes'. Scientists discovered this when they studied hundreds of identical twins who were separated at birth and brought up in totally different environments. Maybe one was adopted by a family in New York while another lived in Phoenix. When the scientists brought the twins back together twenty years later to study them, they were surprised to find that if one twin had a happy life, then *on average*, the other twin also did. Even if one of the twins was brought up in a wealthy family with kind, caring parents and the other twin was brought up in a deprived neighborhood, *on average* they shared similar amounts of happiness.

This is not to say your environment and upbringing isn't important. *It absolutely is*. What the research is saying is that some people get a head-start with their genes and are more likely to be naturally happy than others. This is because your genes partly determine the levels of various chemicals in your brain like serotonin, which directly affects your happiness (the anti-depressant Prozac works by increasing your serotonin levels). But you can still screw up this head-start by having poor mental Skills or by running bad thoughts through your head. Bad thoughts and experiences can reduce your serotonin levels. Conversely, other people are born with 'sad genes' which means they are much more likely to become depressed.

The general rule is that for people who haven't read this book, happiness is split roughly down the middle. Approximately 50% is due to your genes and 50% is due to your environment. So both are crucial. But even if you have 'sad genes', this shouldn't be a 'show stopper' because this book is all about how you can overcome your nature and your natural limitations. With the right mental Skills and training, you should be able to face your genes and say, like Loretta (see Chapter 12, 'Loretta's Story'), 'Bring it on!'

NO BRAIN – NO PAIN!

Another issue concerning happiness – which is also affected by our genes – is the natural mental appetite of our brains. Our brains aren't all created equal. Some people's brains have a high requirement for stimulation while other people's brains are much more relaxed. In general, the greater your brain's in-built requirement to compute and analyze, the more difficult it's going to be keeping that brain happy. A cat's brain is much simpler than ours and so it's not surprising a cat can be happy spending two-thirds of its life asleep. With its tummy regularly filled and the odd cuddle, most moggies will be pretty happy.

Humans typically need much more than that. In general, the more powerful your brain the more you will require in order to be happy. In some ways this is part of the attraction of sedatives like alcohol or barbiturates. They temporarily turn down the brain's power which means you can be happier just chilling out doing very little. Even boring conversations and dull people become more interesting after a few drinks. We can summarize this state of affairs by saying, 'No Brain – No Pain'. A powerful, active brain is therefore like a double-edged sword: both a blessing because of what it can achieve and a challenge because you have to work to keep it happy.

CHOOSING THE HARDER PATH

Now before I introduce you to Happy Harry, I want to say that sometimes it's okay to choose the path that isn't naturally paved with happiness. Happiness isn't always the highest Goal. You see, some careers and choices in life naturally make it very much harder to be happy than others. Nelson Mandela chose justice over his own personal happiness. No matter how you slice it, being in solitary confinement for 27 years isn't the choice that's going to make happiness come easily to you. But then again, Mandela was made out of the sort of fabric that almost certainly meant he wouldn't have been happy living in a comfortable house while his fellow blacks were still discriminated against. Mandela's nature and his values predisposed him to a more troubled path. Einstein was another person afflicted with a burden which made 'happiness' more difficult to obtain. He worried incessantly about the nature of light and gravity. It drove him to distraction and caused him endless nights of insomnia. The only way to quieten his mind was to play his violin loudly while the rest of mankind enjoyed untroubled sleep. Even when he was out hiking in the mountains with his friends to relax, he just couldn't switch his mind off. He'd repeatedly tell them he just *had* to know what would happen if you rode on the end of a light beam. He just couldn't let it rest.

Philosophers are another breed of people pre-disposed to unhappiness. They also can't leave alone the simple things that most people take for granted. They constantly want to know *what* lies behind our everyday experiences and *why*, when everyone else is happy just enjoying them. It's a dangerous business.

The reasonable man adapts himself to the world;
the unreasonable one persists in trying to adapt the world to himself.
Therefore all progress depends on the unreasonable man.
George Bernard Shaw, *Man and Superman* (1903)

THE WORST CASE SCENARIO

In some ways, I guess I'm the intersection of all the risk factors I've listed above. I was born with naturally 'sad genes'. I had a troubled childhood and I chose to study those risky subjects of philosophy and neuroscience. My brain has a huge appetite for the sorts of things that can drive many people mad. Worse still, after spending most of my life doing maths and physics in the glitz and glamor of Formula 1, I've even ended up working twelve-hours-a-day in a career I don't naturally like. I didn't want to write this book because I find each word a monumental effort; writing isn't something I naturally enjoy doing. Maths and physics I love; words are things I wrestle uncomfortably with. This book wanted *me* to write *it* and not the other way around. And yet ... and yet ... despite all these natural obstacles, my friends will tell you I'm one of the happiest guys they've met. I tend to agree with them. I genuinely think I'm happy these days – but it wasn't always that way. I spent the entire first half of my life genuinely unhappy. It was only as I learned the Skills embedded in this book that I gradually started to become happy and successful. I guess that's part of the reason this book wanted me to write it. You see, there's no point in asking a person who simply inherited a fortune, 'How do you become rich?' You can't just choose to have wealthy parents. And there's little point in asking this question of someone who was in the right place at the right time and got a lucky break. If you truly want to learn how to become wealthy you need to take tips from people who – despite all the bad breaks, bad luck and unfavorable circumstances – still consistently manage to make a fortune. Those are the people you need to listen to. It's against this background that I feel qualified to finally introduce you to Happy Harry and why I think he was so happy.

MEETING THE WORLD'S HAPPIEST PERSON
I told you I met the 'World's Happiest Person' who I nicknamed 'Happy Harry'. Well, I sort of simplified things. It was actually a nine-way tie with nine different 'Happy Harrys' and 'Happy Henriettas'.

They were *all* so happy and all so closely matched that I just couldn't separate them out. But the interesting thing about all nine of them was that they shared something in common. They were all quite different to 'normal' people and stood out starkly when it came to the following seven attributes. They all:

1. Had a clear sense of their Optimal Future which perfectly matched their Intrinsic Drivers (Chapter 14).
2. Had an ability to overcome disappointment (Chapter 17).
3. Had an exocentric view of life (Chapter 17).
4. Lived by the Golden rule (Chapter 27).
5. Loved and were loved by like-minded people (see Chapter 21).

6. Had a variety of interests – Passions – and led a rich, full life (see Chapters 14 and 15).
7. Had an Unshakeable Belief in themselves (Chapter 12).

You can see that each one of these assets is something *The Winner's Bible*™ is aiming to teach you. *You too can be a Happy Harry or a Happy Henrietta.*

Oh, and before I finish this chapter, I'm guessing you'll want to hear a bit more about these Happy Harrys and Happy Henriettas? Let's just say you'll find them scattered throughout the book at various times. For example, one such Happy Henrietta inspired me to spontaneously write the little vignette 'Mangere Matau'. You'll can *easily* see she met criteria 3, 4 and 5 … so keep an eye out for them …

CHAPTER 26
EFFICIENCY

I was originally going to leave this part out because I wanted you to get to my favorite section as quickly as possible. However, I've seen too many people gain power by using the Tools in this book and then rush off half-cocked and burn up all their new-found energy inefficiently (see Chapter 16, 'The Highway of Life'). Even though I've made this section very short, I can't overstate how important it is. It could be the difference between your success and failure.

THE PERCENT THAT LASTS

Take a moment to think of all the Goals and dreams you have pursued. All the effort you've expended in your life thus far. When you do this I don't want you to just read those words and give them casual acknowledgement and say; 'Oh, yes, I've put in a huge effort.' I want you to genuinely think back over last year and weigh up all the emails you've written, phone calls made, dreams hatched and Goals chased. Friends or lovers won and lost. Houses bought and sold. Then repeat that for the year before and the year before that – right back till you were a teenager. Recall all the times you were excited about some future plan or disappointed about something that didn't work out.

That's an absolutely huge amount of effort and energy.

Now look around yourself and see where you've ended up and what you have to show for all that effort. In all probability what you have left accounts for less than 5% of all that effort. The other 95% of your life's endeavors has provided no lasting financial or material benefit. Of course life should *never* be measured solely by your material possessions or your career successes and nothing is ever truly lost. Every one of those experiences, even if they produced nothing materially, has helped you grow and become the person you are today. They have all been part of the rich tapestry of life. But the point remains: if you want to increase your material success you have two options:

1. You can put in more effort.
2. You can increase the percent of your effort which lasts.

It only takes a minute's thought to realize it's vastly easier to double your success rate from 5% to 10% than it is to double your effort from 100% to 200%. You know it would be absolutely impossible to double the effort spent in your life so far. Absolutely impossible. This means you'll most likely make the same progress this year as you did last year. Therefore, the only way you can break out of that future is to drastically ramp up *the percent of your effort that lasts.*

DO YOUR HOMEWORK WELL

One of the most common reasons why we have such a low 'hit rate' is because we get an idea in our minds, get all excited about it and start powering ahead without first doing our homework. We get 70% of the way through a new project before we discover we're missing some key ingredient or we've run out of effort or used up all our resources. When that happens, all your efforts till now have been totally wasted. No matter how elegantly you construct 90% of an airplane, it still won't fly if 10% is missing. That 90% of a plane is little more than a pile of nuts, bolts, dreams and sweat that ultimately adds up to nothing until it's completed. Doing your homework well means you need to research as thoroughly as possible if anyone has done something similar to what you are planning to do. How long did it take? What Skills/resources did they need? What obstacles stood in their way?

Never just look at a project (such as building a plane) and count up the cost of all the components you can see and then estimate how much time and money you think it's going to take. You need to learn from other people's experiences because there will be hundreds of unexpected obstacles, hidden traps, regulations, technical difficulties and so on. Failure to take into account what is already known is illustrated by the fact that 80% of all new newspapers and magazines that are launched go on to fail within a year. The reason why this happens is because readership takes a long time to build up and the newspaper shelves are full with a myriad of glossy covers competing for the buyer's dollar. Advertisers are reluctant to commit until you have a proven sales record. That means you need to have sufficient financial resources to run your newspaper at a loss for at least two years or you'll just end up working your butt off and have nothing to show for it except piles of unsold back issues. If you don't know that rule and resource yourself accordingly you're bound to fail regardless of how energetic and creative you are.

RESOURCES: THE RULE OF TWO
After you've completed all your homework and counted up all the resources you realistically think you need – such as people, money, time and materials – *DOUBLE* your estimate. If you can't come up with twice what you think you need then seriously think about whether you should even start. I'm not going to expand on why I've said this because this isn't a business manual. Let's just say that in my experience, one of the most reliable predictors of success is starting with far more Skill, time, money, quality people and energy than you initially think is necessary.

REASONS WHY NOT TO DO THE PROJECT
Before you start any project you also need to think about all the reasons why you should *not* get involved. Unfortunately our emotional system gets fired up and carried away with all the exciting reasons for doing a project and this overshadows all the concerns about why we shouldn't do it. We're like impulsive teenagers who recklessly take a corner at 80 mph because of the obvious thrill but we don't count the possible cost of crashing into a tree and spending the rest of their lives in a wheelchair. As you think of 'Reasons Why Not To Do The Project', you'll also need to add in the cost of lost opportunities. If you start one project then by definition you'll rule out other projects. Even if this is a good project, there may be others you haven't considered that are even better.

SPECIAL DOCUMENTS ON YOUR PC
There are a number of simple little things you can do which will automatically increase your efficiency. One of the most successful tricks for me was to get rid of 'scraps of paper'. I used to write everything down on paper. Ideas, 'Things To Do', notes, and so on. Scraps of paper are a huge waste of time! I've lost track of how many times I've lost a note or written the same reminder three times without realizing it. What I now do is have a 'Special Documents' file on my PC

desktop, specifically reserved for things I'd normally write down on paper. Here's a few of my favorite documents:

a) Wallet.doc

This document contains a list of all my passwords, bank account numbers, credit card details, website log-ons, telephone codes, airline loyalty numbers and so on. This is clearly an extremely confidential document and because I don't want anyone else to find it, I protect it by saving it under an unsuspecting name like 'Brain Stem Research.doc'. I'm sure no one else would ever bother to look at a file like that even if they did get hold of my PC!

Having this document also means if anything ever happens to me, my family have total access to all my affairs. I've left instructions with my lawyer in a sealed envelope telling my family about this file. Because my Wallet.doc is a 'live' document, it always represents an up-to-date snapshot of my life. I remember how difficult it was to finalize all my father's affairs after he died. He had bank accounts and term investments all over the place and just finding out where they were and how to get access to them in a timely fashion was quite a mission. Even things like setting up his broadband router was a major mission because no one knew the internal password for it. But if Dad had created a Wallet.doc this would have all been so easy.

I'm amazed at how large this document has become over the years and how often I refer to it.

b) FactsLearnt.doc

This is one of my favorite documents. Whenever I learn something new or interesting I write it down in here. But I don't just write things down in any old random order. My document has an order and a hierarchy to it. Section 1 contains all the new words I've learned, in alphabetical order, with their definition underneath. I also use Microsoft Word's built-in indexing system to automatically compile an index of all my words at the front of the document so I can periodically test myself.

Section 2 contains facts I've learned from physics (because I'm interested in these things), Section 3 from philosophy and so on. Again, I'm amazed at how large this document has become and how often I refer to it.

The reason why I have this document is because as we get older we naturally can't absorb information as easily as we could when we were young and our brains were highly plastic. For example, two-to-five-year-olds learn thousands of new words a year while the average adult learns only a handful in the same period. As adults we can still learn huge amounts of new information but we need to be a bit more organized and make a little more effort. Learning new information keeps our brain protected from dementia and makes our lives more interesting. It's a scientific fact that we'll remember far more if we write something down than if we just try to memorize it. Even more important than just writing something down is if we can help out our brain by providing order and structure to our new information.

A

Dictionary Words
1. Acolyte
2. Alethiometer
3. Anathema
4. Aphorism
5. Apotheosis

For my FactsLearnt.doc, I just leave it on my PC desktop in full view and for easy access. Try putting together your own FactsLearnt.doc for a month and see how valuable it is. You may be surprised at how much interesting stuff is stored that might normally have slipped right on by you.

c) Scratch Pad

My Scratch Pad document contains all the random things I need to keep my finger on but which aren't yet important enough to be on my 'To Do' list. Things such as checking out yachts to rent in the Greek Isles for my next holiday. Or website addresses for furniture manufacturers. There's no urgency in checking out the yachts because I'm not planning to go there until next summer, but by the same token, I don't want to leave it till the last minute either as I'll miss out. Same with upgrading my office furniture. That's something which is quietly bubbling away in the background. So this is a good place to save things without cluttering up my actual 'To Do' list.

Another section in my Scratch Pad contains a list of all the things I'm waiting for other people to get back to me on. I call this the 'Pending' section and it's a really good one. I'm always surprised how many things are currently up in the air while I'm waiting for other people. There's nothing on this list I need to do right now but I also can't afford to forget them. Having all these items in my Scratch Pad helps keep my mind uncluttered because I don't have to hold a million things zipping around in my brain. It leaves more space and processing power for being *creative*.

ORGANIZATION

Successful people are almost always more organized than unsuccessful people. The reason we so often get this aspect of our lives wrong is that organization feels – at least *emotionally* – like it's a non-productive process. Logically we know that being organized is going to help us but spending half an hour tidying up the tools on our work bench still feels like wasted time because our projects aren't any further ahead at the end of the tidying up.

Another benefit of organization is that you see all the components of your 'project of life' more clearly. If your files are scattered all over the place or if your list of things to do is written on dozens of different scraps of paper, there is a very good chance you'll overlook something important because it's buried beneath something less important. There is a difference between simply being tidy and being *organized*. For example, you could have all your work nicely filed away in your cabinet and a clear desk every night and yet still be totally disorganized. You might have your taxes filed next to your car registration documents and your insurance policy filed next to unrelated correspondence. Even though everything is tidy, there is no structure or hierarchy to your files and so when you come to find something, you still have to hunt around for them.

A trait of successful people – of Winners – is that their organization has structure and a hierarchy. Let's not forget, 'You.Inc' needs to be run smoothly, just like these organizations.

IMPOSING A HIERARCHY

It's easier to get a strategic view if related items are adjacent to each other in the correct hierarchy. What is important here is not just that things are arranged in piles but that there is a proper hierarchical structure. That's why the hard disk on your computer has a folder system with levels. Each folder describes all the items contained beneath it in the subfolders. You only have to look at the name of the top level folders to know which one you'll go looking inside. If you want to find a letter you wrote in 2008, you can immediately ignore all the other top level folders like Music or Photo or Video and go straight to the Documents folder. You don't have to search through all the thousands of files in the Music and Photo folders.

The more structured your hierarchy, the more quickly you can find anything. Having a proper hierarchy also makes it much easier for you to scan over your project and make sure you haven't overlooked anything. Spending time developing a well thought out hierarchy for your life – 'You.Inc' – or any project will ultimately save you time and simplify your life. That's how my friend, 'The Billionaire', can run 300 companies at the same time. If all he had was a tangled mess of details in his mind he'd never cope. This is also how your brain prefers to work. It loves to establish connections and order rather than store unrelated facts. It's why Mind Maps are so important (see Chapter 18, 'You.Inc').

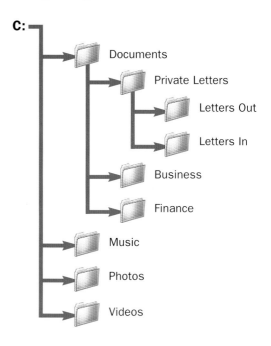

REORGANIZING AND RESTRUCTURING AS YOU GROW

Organization isn't a one-off process. As your life evolves you'll need to continually re-organize your structures so they keep up with the *new and improved* you. After all, the organizational structure that is suitable for running a Mom and Pop corner store isn't suitable for running a supermarket. So from time to time check to see whether your organization has kept up with your progress in life.

In closing this section let's just recap why ensuring you are efficient is so important. Put quite simply, you can't double the amount of effort you've put into all your life so far, but you *can* double your efficiency.

CHAPTER 27
THE 'LIMBIC MASTER'

A BIT OF A DILEMMA

As we move towards the end of *The Winner's Bible*,™ I should tell you about one thing which nearly drove me mad when I was writing this book. For almost a year, I went backwards and forwards in endless discussions with my friends as I tried to make one final decision. On Monday I'd settle on one option but on Tuesday I was equally convinced the other option was the right one. In frustration I even asked complete strangers in the street for their advice. The problem was, I just couldn't choose between two possible titles for this book. As you know from reading 'Gonzales' Happy Day' (see Chapter 11), I always intended to call this book, *The Winner's Bible*.™ But while that is an easy title to understand and everyone automatically 'gets' what it's about, the more I wrote, the more compelling the case became for calling this book *The Limbic Master*. The problem with this alternate title is that it conveys little meaning to the average person in the street. And yet, despite that objection, I really grew to like it because it brings together so many different aspects of this book into a single, unified concept. Indeed, becoming a Limbic Master should be one of the key Goals that each reader of this book should aspire to.

The phrase Limbic Master conveys many things to me. First of all is the idea of *mastery*. While you can put the Tools in this book to use immediately, you will need both time (see Chapter 10, 'Pomegranates') and practice in order to *master* them. The phrase also highlights the key role your Limbic modules play in your brain. In the past, we were too busy being impressed by the logical aspects of our brain and as a result of neglecting our Limbic System, we got ourselves into trouble. I also liked the idea of a Limbic Master conveying a semi-mystical image of an advanced soul. Of course, in this sense the word 'Master' is without gender because I think the phrase 'Limbic Mistress' is open to the wrong sorts of interpretation. So let me draw a number of threads in this book together by painting a gentle image of what a Limbic Master is and how they behave.

> Becoming a Limbic Master should be one of the key Goals that each reader of this book should aspire to.

THE 'WISE PERSON' AND THE 'LIMBIC MASTER'

A young child is naturally self-centered, greedy and ruled by its primitive emotions. However, with experience and training, children gradually develop and learn to become adults of varying levels of proficiency.

A number of ancient texts tell us that the next step in the development of man beyond a normal adult is to become a 'Wise Person'. This is a person whose life is controlled by wisdom and knowledge – essentially a set of rules. At its extreme, some texts encourage us to forsake the world and all its pleasures and to turn off our emotions so we become dispassionate and detached. Unfortunately, while that ancient approach will increase our chances of success and reduce our chances of pain, it also reduces our experience of pleasure.

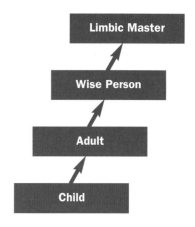

The Limbic Master on the other hand is further evolved. He understands and is guided by knowledge but at the same time is not afraid of his emotional system. He does not seek to turn his emotions off, but instead he masters them. This is achieved by ensuring his Limbic System is correctly aligned with his own unique Optimal Future. After all, when you master a Tool you don't throw it away, you put it to use. In the same way, mastery of your emotions is not about throwing them away, but savoring them correctly.

MOCCASINS AND THE GOLDEN RULE

This contrast between the 'Wise Person' and the 'Limbic Master' is shown by how they interact with other people. The Wise Person is guided by rules. The greatest of all rules is the ancient 'Golden Rule' which says: 'Do unto others as you would have them do to you'. The Limbic Master, however, is guided by a *force* which is even higher than the Golden Rule. The Limbic Master doesn't just follow the Golden Rule – he actually *feels* at a gut level the other person's pain or viewpoint, so deeply, that it genuinely feels as if it was his own. As a result, he acts in a way which is in accordance with the Golden Rule – but which transcends it. He can do this because he has learned how to rewire his own emotional system so that it responds to other people's situations as if their emotions were wired directly into his brain. In the ancient wisdom of the Native American Indian, he has learned how to *walk in the moccasins* of others.

Because the Limbic Master is deeply and genuinely interested in the other person he makes friends easily. Without consciously being aware of it his actions are automatically in line with the sage advice found in Dale Carnegie's best-seller, *How To Win Friends And Influence People*. When he listens to another person the Limbic Master does so in order to understand them, instead of listening so he can work out a clever rejoinder or counter-argument. He is more interested in talking about them than himself. Like any rewiring of the brain, this takes time and practice and cannot be accomplished by simply learning a rule. It is an advanced Skill which requires the same sorts of Tools we have already used in previous sections to rewire our emotions. (see Chapter 9, 'Emotionally Supercharged CDs').

EGOCENTRICITY, SELFISHNESS AND THE LIMBIC MASTER

As I mentioned, a young child is naturally concerned entirely with its own small world. It immediately wants any toy another child is given even if it already has a better one itself. It makes a lot of noise because being the centre of attention allows the child to get its own way. Children are gradually weaned off this selfish and self-centered approach to life as they become socialized. But a surprising number of fully-grown adults continue to display egocentric behavior. For example, they'll see a well-formed queue of cars when two lanes need to merge into one and instead of slotting into the queue, they drive past all the cars and then try to force their way in at the last minute. They clearly think they're more important than anyone else. They'll make a time to meet a friend for coffee but then arrive late. The underlying message to this lack of punctuality is that their time is more important than their friends.

The list of left-over childish traits that continue to affect adults when their selfish core is not mastered is long and varied. Another person's pain or needs are clearly not as great as their own. They eat at fine restaurants on a regular basis without giving more than a cursory thought to the starving in Africa. They see the splinter in their neighbor's eye but cannot see the log in their own eye.

The Limbic Master behaves differently because his primitive egocentricity is replaced with a naturally exocentric view. His emotions are now connected to the wider community so they have become social emotions which make him *want* to act differently.

FORGIVENESS AND THE LIMBIC MASTER

Primitive man responds to his environment in a knee-jerk manner and automatically swings his club in anger when he is wronged. While this reflex reaction had survival value in prehistoric time, it is not suited to modern civilization. The Limbic Master is able to control his natural urge to strike back because he views the situation from a higher plane. Instead of going into confrontation mode the Limbic Master sees through the red mist of anger and observes the Weaknesses in the other person which caused them to wrong him in the first place. Instead of retribution there is understanding and a genuine desire to help. This does not mean the Limbic Master is a spineless wimp – quite the opposite. The Limbic Master insists on fairness and correctness and on boundaries not being crossed. But this is done with the hand of compassion, education and enlightenment, rather than by the arm of force or anger.

When a friend makes a mistake
The mistake is still a mistake
And the friend is still a friend
Israeli Prime Minister Shimon Peres

ROMANCE AND THE LIMBIC MASTER

Like most things in this book, romance operates best when there is the correct balance. If lust is allowed unfettered rein then we risk being blinded and cannot see the true nature of our potential partner. We may start building a relationship based on the sizzling fire of lust but this is something that usually dims to a warm and pleasing flame. If the sizzle is not correctly matched by a connection of the souls then the romance will fade as the fire becomes less intense. But conversely, if there is not enough chemistry then there will be insufficient glue to bind the relationship together in tough times.

What is important is not just the quantity of raw chemistry but rather how it is harnessed by the soul. A Limbic Master is not unduly ruled by physical attraction but is one, who even in the white-hot flare of the initial chemistry, can see past the outer form of the other person to calmly and accurately assess their inner soul. Not as one who sits in judgment counting the other person's faults, but rather as one who rightly divines the appropriateness of the relationship by taking into account his *own* Weaknesses and limitations. For example, while a potential mate may be the life and soul of the party, oozing zing and zoom from every pore, is that person going to be too boisterous to actually live with on a daily basis given your own need for peace and quiet? Is he going to wear you out? Or does he actually complement your introspective nature and provide you with an extra boost? Being able to follow your Optimal Future requires a partner who is suited to accompany you on that particular journey.

The Limbic Master can calmly assess this suitability using both their reason and their emotion. The Limbic Master is able to savor the Passion without being consumed by it. To love and adore their partner without becoming dependent. To do this the Limbic System is given full authority to be aroused and fired up. This is another example of where the Limbic Master experiences more and transcends the pure wisdom and knowledge of the Wise Person. The Limbic Master's emotions soar but are never allowed to run completely unfettered and out of control. This balance is an essential part of the mastery.

THE INTELLECT AND THE LIMBIC MASTER

The primitive man abhors intellectual uncertainty because it is emotionally too uncomfortable for him. He likes everything black and white and as straightforward as possible. When he sees lightning and hears thunder his undeveloped mind needs an explanation. This desire for knowledge is good, but the problem arises when he is not wise enough to know the true explanation. When that happens, the primitive man will invent a god like Zeus who throws thunderbolts in anger from heaven. This satisfies him because his uncertainty is removed. In contrast, the Limbic Master can simultaneously hold in his mind the strong desire for knowledge alongside an admission that he does not yet know the answer. This means he does not need to invent fictions. He can even accept two absolute truths that he cannot yet reconcile, even though with his limited knowledge those two truths appear to him to be in conflict.

When challenged by someone else's belief, the primitive man will hold on to his own particular theory with the white knuckles of fear because he has too much emotion invested in his own framework – whether that is religious or political. In order to reduce his own internal emotional conflict, the primitive man classifies people as either heroes or villains, with few people occupying the middle ground.

The reason the Limbic Master is different is because he sees each person more clearly. He sees not just with his mind, nor just with his emotion, but with both which are aligned like the aerials of a TV for perfect reception.

THE LOTUS AND THE LIMBIC MASTER

Buddhists often use the Lotus flower as a metaphor for the process of achieving enlightenment.

The lotus has its roots in the mud,
Grows up through the deep water,
And rises to the surface.
It blooms into perfect purity
and beauty in the sunlight.
It is like the mind unfolding
to perfect joy and wisdom.

This metaphor also describes the journey necessary to become a Limbic Master. Our brains have their roots buried deep in a dark, prehistoric antiquity where the rule of the jungle shaped our primitive brain modules. The natural result of this history is that our untrained brains are childlike. In order for our lives to blossom into beauty, joy and wisdom, we must help our brains grow through the muddy, confused soup of experience. We are guided in that growth by constantly reaching for the bright sunlight where our emotions and our reason work in harmony. We do not deny our nature or our emotions, but rather we Supercharge them so they become even more powerful. The key difference is that we align our emotions and our reason so they work in harmony. Our *rudders* and our *paddles* are working together so we can sail the good course.

CHAPTER 28
A VERY INTIMATE CONCLUSION
GRANDPA'S COTTAGE

This is easily the most personal chapter in this book. Over the next few pages, I'm going to lay bare the most private and intimate parts of my life. I don't do this because I'm egocentric and think you'll be interested in me as a person and I certainly don't do this because I think my particular life has been that important. In fact, I'd rather keep my private life completely private.

However, after I'd finished writing the first draft of this book it felt as if something vital was still missing. The more I tried to put off writing this chapter, the more it kept insisting on being written. So reluctantly, I'm just going to have to take a deep breath and let you inside my head.

CENTRAL OTAGO

Without doubt the most powerful image of my entire life is that of my grandpa's small, white holiday cottage. This is the same Grandpa you've already met in Chapter 22 ('Grandpa's Little Stories'). Grandpa's cottage was a simple affair, perched on the river banks of the Clutha River in a tiny settlement consisting of only nine houses. This cluster of homes was optimistically called Albert Town and was

Grandpa in front of his cottage looking over the Clutha River.

reached by only one unformed road that wasn't even important enough to have a name. Albert Town is located in a remote part of Central Otago in the South Island of New Zealand – not far from the spectacular scenery where *The Lord of the Rings* was filmed.

When I was nine-years-old I spent an entire five-week summer school holiday living with Granny and Grandpa in their cottage on the banks of the Clutha. That experience affected me so deeply that I was never the same person again. Ultimately it made me a far better person, yet it took me another forty years before I realized exactly how that holiday had shaped my life.

The Clutha River itself is a fast-flowing river of deep, pristine water. It is the cold and sparkling result of snow which has melted and run off The Remarkables – mountains which earned their name because they truly are remarkable. The water from the Clutha is so pure that it's pumped up into tanks behind each house and used for drinking water without any filtering whatsoever. Over the years, I've traveled to pretty much every corner of the world, but I have to say, the scenery in Central Otago is without doubt the most spectacular I've ever seen. People jokingly say God was practising when he made the rest of the world, and it was only after he'd finally perfected his Skills that he finished with a flourish by creating Central Otago. The image above is a photo taken from the small living room of Grandpa's cottage. It was taken when I was nine and shows Grandpa looking out over the Clutha from the edge of the river bank. These two images, the cottage and the river, are the ones which are so powerfully burnt in my psyche. Before I can explain their significance to me – and what it means for you – I need to take one step back and first tell you a little bit about my father and my own childhood growing up in Auckland.

MY FATHER

Grandpa, or Sir Trevor Henry, was my mother's father and, as you now know, was New Zealand's most distinguished judge. This meant my mum was brought up in a life of relative privilege and high society (at least for New Zealand at the time). My father, on the other hand, was the oldest child in a rather poor family with five children. Their food was still cooked over a coal range that was laboriously stoked up each morning even though most houses in New Zealand had switched to electric stoves decades before. This coal range was the lifeblood of the house as it provided heat for cooking, hot water and warmth for the house in winter. Despite the poverty, the house was well run and there was usually enough money to scrape by.

In my mind, I can imagine my father waking up one day in that household and deciding he wanted to 'make something' of himself and not live the rest of his life in poverty. Dad wasn't a naturally gifted academic – he was a hard grafter. He worked incredibly hard at school, and against all odds, qualified for entry into medical school.

In those days, most medical students came from wealthy families who could afford the luxury of seven years at university and all that expensive medical equipment. Instead of arriving with mountains of suitcases like the other students did, Dad arrived with little more than the clothes on his back. His shoes had holes in them and leaked during the cold winter months because he couldn't afford a new pair. In order to feed and house himself Dad would study all day and half the night with the rest of his peers, and then when everyone else was exhausted, he'd start work in a bakery on the midnight shift. It was only after the bread had risen in the early hours of the morning that Dad finally climbed into his bed for a few hours rest before once again

heading back to university. Dad succeeded because of his burning drive and sheer hard graft (see *The Winner's Bible For Elite Sport* and 'The Case of the Missing World Champions').

Dad did everything he could to fit in with his peers and part of this involved going to the monthly church dances which were so popular in those days. It was at one of these dances that he met my mum. He immediately set his heart on winning her, another seemingly impossible task because she was easily the most beautiful woman there. Mum had her choice of all the sophisticated, wealthy, dashing, young doctors and lawyers. But Dad was nothing if not eternally optimistic and willing to do whatever it took. He believed in himself even if the cold hard facts were against him. Of course, he won Mum's hand otherwise I wouldn't be writing this story. Dad then graduated and set up practice in Auckland. But this was no ordinary surgery. Because of Dad's drive and ambition, it soon became the busiest one-man practice in all of New Zealand.

Dad was one of the most driven men I've ever met. Let me give you just the tiniest window into what I mean when I say 'driven'. Years ago, long before it was accepted practice in Western medicine, Dad heard about a new procedure being performed in China called 'vasectomy'. So he flew halfway around the world to China to learn how to do it. This was long before China had opened its borders to foreigners and so I have no idea how he managed the logistics of meeting the right people, let alone overcoming the language barrier. On returning to New Zealand, Dad quickly added an operating theatre to his surgery and purchased all the latest surgical and sterilizing equipment. He had, in effect, set up his own mini-hospital to run alongside his general practice. This was a big risk for a lone GP – especially considering no one else was doing vasectomies in New Zealand at the time. After a few months of operations Dad decided he wasn't happy with the performance of his Philips Autoclave (sterilizing unit), so in typical Dad-fashion, he decided he'd build his own. He could make a better product than Philips. Why not? First he researched how these machines worked by visiting libraries (long before the internet made such things easy) and then he enrolled in a night class to learn welding. Before long the big stainless steel chambers he needed were welded up and vacuum tight. Then Dad designed the electronics and wired up all the pumps, heaters and vacuum motors. This 'home-made' sterilizing unit performed faultlessly for the next thirty years. Indeed, Dad performed so many vasectomies over the following years that other GPs called him, 'Spackerman the Knackerman'.

Let me give you some other examples of Dad's drive. He was a passionate, fundamental Christian, but after attending the local Baptist church for a few years he decided it wasn't being run correctly. The only solution was to start his own church. He became the minister preaching every Sunday as well as taking *Bible* classes midweek – all while being New Zealand's busiest doctor. But this was just the tip of the iceberg. Dad started a ministry recording and distributing evangelical tapes and films. He formed his own international correspondence school for Christians and wrote all the material and marked all the papers himself. Then one Saturday night the church had a Square Dance for fun. Dad liked it so much he started his own Square Dance club. It was a huge success because of Dad's enthusiasm. Hundreds of people would turn up each week and Dad would do the 'calling' of all the dance moves. Dad spent countless hours each night practicing his 'calling' and organizing the club.

I could go on and tell you about fifteen other major enterprises that Dad was involved in (such as running his own film developing studio) but the details aren't important. All you need to know is that Dad was driven with a capital D. And why? Because he was determined to make a success out of himself and not lead a life of mediocrity.

Unfortunately, his best intentions had a hugely negative impact on me.

MY CHILDHOOD

Being the only boy in our family it was not surprising that Dad wanted me to be successful. And if hard work and discipline had made him successful, then twice as much hard work and twice as much discipline would make *me* even more successful. So our house was run like a military operation and Dad ruled it with an iron fist. Children were to be seen and not heard – and preferably not even seen. Being a naturally sensitive boy, I was constantly anxious in case my manners weren't perfect or I'd done something wrong during the day. Meals were timed to the minute, and were for me, frightening events. We ate dinner every night at 5:30. Not 5:40, not 5:20, but 5:30. We had to sit up straight, no elbows on the table and our knives and forks were to be returned to the plate at the correct angle while we chewed each mouthful of food. I couldn't wait till meals were over so I could retreat to the safety of my bedroom, which was located downstairs beneath the house, all on my own, away from my parents and three sisters.

When it came to my 'progress'- I was *never* good enough. If I came top of my class by thirty points, well, it just wasn't good enough. A minimum of fifty points would have *almost* been acceptable, but thirty points was clearly a catastrophic failure. On rare occasions, say once or twice a year, we'd do 'family' things like go to a restaurant or a movie. These were the most stressful times of all. We were in public and no matter how hard we tried we always managed to do something wrong and get a blistering telling-off. What should have been a good time turned into one of extreme unpleasantness for me.

I used to hate coming home from school each day because our house always evoked anxiety in me. I never had any close friends because I'd unconsciously learned that all the boys in my neighborhood 'weren't acceptable'. It's not that I wasn't *allowed* to play with them, but rather, I'd been subtly *conditioned* by my parents' words to find them not good enough. So I spent hours downstairs alone – reading and thinking and quite often being sad. I was incredibly lonely and I never felt I was good enough. Not feeling good enough is like a cancer that eats into your soul. Slowly but surely it poisons your whole system and your view of life. This problem of 'not doing well enough' culminated in one memorable event. Many years later, after I'd won the *Senior Prize In Applied Mathematics* at Auckland University, I excitedly zoomed over to tell Dad. *Finally* I thought I'd done something good enough for him. On hearing my news, Dad simply said in a voice without emotion, 'That's good,' and promptly carried on with what he was doing.

Many years later Grandpa told me he knew what I was going through as a child and that his heart used to bleed for me. Like all good stories this one has a twist in the tail. Something quite extraordinary happened to my dad as he grew older. He became a truly wonderful, wise and warm man. He was kind, positive, enthusiastic and intensely proud of me. He became one of my best friends. We ended up sharing genuine camaraderie, private moments and love. But I'm getting ahead of myself, we'll return to that 'other' Dad in a moment. Right now, I need to take you back to Grandpa's Cottage.

ALBERT TOWN HOLIDAY

In the southern hemisphere, Christmas falls in the middle of summer so we combine Christmas, New Year and our annual vacations all into one big holiday. For school kids this means a break of six whole weeks. Yippeee! Most of this time is spent at the beach or on the lake because we 'Kiwis' love our water sports.

As I mentioned, when I was nine I was sent on my own from Auckland to join Granny and Grandpa for five weeks in Albert Town. Back in those days this took an entire day of flying in a little DC-3. It seemed like we'd only been airborne for a few minutes before we were forced to land on another little grass runway for yet more fuel. And when I say 'runway', that's a bit of an exaggeration because this was little more than a flat(ish) paddock in the middle of some farm. It was a

genuine adventure. Today the whole journey can be accomplished by jet in a two-hour direct flight – convenient for certain, but doing it the modern way feels sterile compared to the adventure of the old days.

Grandpa met me at the airport when I arrived in Queenstown. His voice, manner and even his hands were soft as he helped me into his Humber Super Snipe. And so began the happiest time of my life. You see, in those nine houses on the banks of the Clutha River were fifteen children of a similar age to me. Each day was a time of unbridled fun, adventure and excitement. We laughed, we played, we swam, we ate, we rode bikes and invented all sorts of games. Some nights we'd camp out together in tents while other days we'd all snuggle up on the floor in masses of blankets and listen to stories. Not once in five weeks were we told off.

Each morning Grandpa would get up at around 5 o' clock, go down to the river and catch two large Rainbow trout for breakfast. He never, ever failed to arrive back in time with these two magnificent trout. Meanwhile, Granny would have picked a huge bowl of wild raspberries and set them on the table for our first course. We ate them lightly frosted with coarse castor sugar.

It never rained in the entire five weeks I was there. The weather was hot but pleasantly dry. As the weeks passed the grass became dry and some of the small flowers began to give off a special, sweet smell (over the years, I'd sometimes come across that smell quite by accident in some remote part of the world, and when I did, it immediately transported me back to Albert Town).

No amount of words can tell you how happy I was down in Albert Town. It was simply magic! I had this indescribable warm feeling inside me that I'd never had before. It was so vivid, I swear this feeling had a *flavor* to it. And I could smell it with my inner soul. That's not a metaphor, I really could smell it.

But like all good things, this holiday had to end. We packed up my bags and Grandpa loaded them back into the trunk of the Super Snipe. I went around to the passenger's door, and as I put my fingers around the door handle, I was struck by an overwhelming feeling. I had absolutely no idea what it was. I said to Grandpa, 'I don't know what's wrong but I feel very strange. It's like I feel sick but I'm not sick. Maybe I've eaten something.' I think Grandpa knew what it was but he didn't let on. He just said to me in a calm soothing voice, 'Hop up in the front beside me, I'm sure the journey will help settle your stomach a little.' In those days there was no such thing as power steering and the Super Snipe was the biggest car around. So it required a big steering wheel in order for the driver to have enough leverage. Grandpa was a big man and of course I was only a small boy. So I sat there on the nice, leather seats feeling very small. Grandpa talked about interesting things on the two-hour ride to the plane to keep my mind busy. He could easily do this because he was one of the smartest people I've ever met. Without diverting too much from the story, I'd like to indulge in one short paragraph just to refresh your memory as to exactly how interesting my Grandpa really was.

Just before Grandpa turned 100-years-old, he was at my place on one of our usual Tuesday afternoons together. As we were sitting by the pool talking, a kingfisher landed and started drinking. I told Grandpa they were my favorite bird. I liked them for a number of reasons. They sat upright, rather than horizontal like most birds. They flew incredibly fast, and of course, their colors are a stunning teal blue. But most of all, I always seemed to have a fabulous day whenever a kingfisher landed in my back garden. Grandpa replied by telling me about the origin and lineage of the kingfisher and the various birds it was related to. Not to show off, of course, but because he thought I'd be interested in learning about my favorite bird. Later that night after I'd dropped Grandpa back at his home I got a phone call from him. He said he'd been reading through his *Encyclopedia Britannica* again and he discovered he'd forgotten to tell me a small detail about the kingfisher. He was most apologetic for his omission and finished by saying, 'I found it a bit hard to read because I've worn that volume out and all the pages are coming apart.' Now how many other people in the world have worn out an entire set of *Encyclopedia Britannica* by reading them? Probably none. But Grandpa used to sit and read them for hours – even into his late nineties – and absorb each article with a boyish fascination at the richness of the world. But anyway, I digress, it's time to go back to Albert Town.

With Grandpa for company, the trip to the airport was intensely interesting. But as soon as I left him to board the plane that same old feeling came back again. It felt like a black cloud had formed in my stomach. That happy feeling I could taste and smell only a few hours ago was now replaced with an unbearable sadness which smelt very strange. If life was sad before, it was thirty times worse now! Before I hadn't known what I was missing out on – but now I did.

Once back at home, I suppose I never really got over that sadness. Rather than fading, my inner thoughts fanned the loneliness for months on end until the only way I could cope was to let all my emotions slowly die inside me. It was only then, when I stopped *feeling*, that the pain began to fade and I could gradually get on with life. The problem was, this method of coping meant I became even more alone and independent. I became bored with other people very quickly and even when I laughed and appeared to be enjoying their company, I was somehow still rather sad inside. So I spent hours alone lost in maths and physics because it seemed so pure and precise and it never judged me. At ten I 'invented' the supercharger without knowing it had already been invented; at eleven, I derived the formula for centripetal acceleration without reference to any texts.

To make matters worse, I'd already lost my innocence at eight years of age in one frightening moment. That moment had been brushed under the carpet while I was in Albert Town but now it came back to haunt me with a vengeance. What happened was I'd stared into a mirror. The physical face in the mirror looked back at me and I looked back at it. For a moment, I spiraled down into an endless feedback loop of various 'Kerrys', wondering how this physical thing called 'Kerry' could produce the emotions and feelings I was experiencing. It didn't make sense and I was filled with a horrible feeling it was all just a charade (I've never looked deeply into a mirror ever since; a quick glance to brush my hair maybe, but I always look away before it gets too serious). There, as an eight-year-old, I began to wonder desperately about the 'meaning of life'. What really worried me wasn't what would happen to me after I died, but rather what 'I' was *before* I was born. This seemed far too mind-boggling to comprehend. I could accept the concept of either Heaven or a gentle fade into non-existence after I died, but how could 'me' never have existed and how could 'I' be created out of nothing?

With time I learned to accept these feelings as being part of my fate and I gradually got on with life. I fell in love with some truly wonderful women, and in turn, I was loved by them. On the outside I was a happy, out-going, intelligent and highly motivated guy functioning at a high level. But something was still missing. I wondered if everyone else felt as hollow as I did inside, or was I just cursed by an overactive mind which caused me so much pain?

GRANDPA'S COTTAGE REVISITED

Over the following years Grandpa's little, white holiday cottage began to take on mythical proportions in my mind. It seemed like a fairy tale and a dream all rolled into one. I began to wonder if my experiences actually ever happened or whether they were a wonderful fantasy I'd concocted in my mind. Because I'd never been back there since, I had no way of knowing.

That is until a few weeks before completing this book, when on the spur of the moment I decided to take a long weekend holiday down in Queenstown. Within two hours of leaving Auckland I'd picked up my rental car and was driving to a luxury lakeside apartment. The next morning at 5 o'clock I went hot air ballooning. It was truly spectacular. We climbed to a staggering 8,000 ft and there, far away in the distance, I could just make out Lake Wanaka. What was interesting about Lake Wanaka is that it is the final resting place of the Clutha River after it has flowed past Grandpa's old cottage. It seemed to beckon me. When we were safely back on the ground and drinking a celebratory glass of

breakfast champagne, I asked our pilot about Albert Town. He said it had now become a bustling new development consisting of thousands of houses which all looked like they'd been stamped from the same mould. My heart sank. In my mind I still had the image of Grandpa's white cottage nestled among eight other houses on an empty, gravel road. But I was so close I decided I ought to make the two-hour twisty drive over the gnarly ranges anyway.

I didn't have a map but I knew exactly where Grandpa's old road was because it was right beside the river. It left the main road at a right angle, just before the bridge which crosses the Clutha River. As I turned off the main road I was saddened to see Grandpa's road appeared to now be a wide tarmac affair that clearly fed a substantial town. There was a large block of shops on the corner of Grandpa's road and the main road. So I drove along about 300 metres and then, miracle of miracles, the road forked in two! Left went down towards the town and away from the river but to the right was a smaller road heading up to where Grandpa's cottage used to be. I took the road to the right and instantly the town was left behind, out of view.

I crept gingerly along the road and there, suddenly, was a tiny little clutch of houses exactly where the original nine had stood. You could only see one house at a time because each was shielded from the next by huge hedges that grew at least thirty-feet-high. The first three houses had been replaced with massive new homes that I didn't recognize, but as I drew alongside the fourth driveway, *there was Grandpa's little cottage* … completely unchanged. It had been stuck in a time warp. It was exactly − and I mean *exactly* − how I remembered it all those years

43 Years Later – Exactly as I remembered it

ago. In fact the photo of Grandpa's cottage at the start of this chapter is actually a photo I took on this last visit, not from 43 years ago.

I parked my car outside and started to walk down 'Grandpa's driveway'. No sooner had I taken fifteen steps when another car pulled in. A smiling lady got out and asked if she could help me. I explained the long history. She said, 'Oh my gosh, come on in. It's now owned by Jo and I'm sure she won't mind me showing you over the place. I have some spare keys.' I hesitated to go into someone's house without their permission but she grabbed me by my arm and dragged me in.

It was absolutely amazing. *Nothing* had changed. The kitchen was exactly as I remembered it. Even the same old clock was in the same place. For some reason known only to Jo, she had decided to keep the cottage exactly as it was forty years ago. It was as if I was walking into a dream. It hardly seemed real. I went outside and looked over the river and my 'tour guide' took my photo standing where I had myself taken a picture all those years ago.

In a moment of reflection, I was truly, *deeply* happy and I'd learned tons of lessons along the way. But there's another interesting part of this story. My deep happiness was only a relatively recent phenomenon. I only started my journey towards contentment the day I sat down with Gonzales and that blank piece of paper which became the very first *Winner's Bible*. It was an accident. I'd set out to develop some new Tools to help Gonzales but in the end they helped me as well. Until that time I'd been forced to accept my situation as it was, because despite reading hundreds (if not thousands) of books on philosophy and self-improvement, nothing had worked. So I'd just gotten on with life for nearly four decades and accepted my situation. But after seeing the amazing transformation in Gonzales and thereafter so many other athletes when they'd used the Tools in this book, I began to try them on myself. The process of re-assembling my life had begun.

MY 'SECOND DAD'

As I mentioned before, I felt like I had two Dads: the one I've already told you about and another truly wonderful, positive, kind, loving father who would do anything in the world for me. This 'second Dad' only began living five days after he nearly died of a heart attack.

Even Dad's heart attack was a remarkable story. He was in his mid-sixties, in the middle of surgery and had just shown a patient out of his consulting rooms when he was floored by a massive heart attack. He collapsed alone in his consulting room while all the nurses and patients were outside, totally unaware of the drama unfolding inside. When Dad regained consciousness a few minutes later he knew he'd had a heart attack, but was stubbornly determined to see the day out. He hadn't missed a single day of surgery in over forty years and he wasn't about to let his patients down now! He struggled to his feet and saw another eighteen patients before finally going across the road to the diagnostic lab to get a blood test to see how bad the heart attack was. Then he drove for an hour back home to his farm before collapsing in bed again (I guess I forgot to tell you he ran a small 10-acre farm with 100 sheep). He told Mum he had a really bad virus but would be fine by the morning. You see, he didn't want to disappoint her because the next day they were due to go on a week's holiday up north and Mum was really looking forward to it. Dad put on a brave face in the morning and convinced Mum he was okay to go on holiday. However, an hour into the journey, Dad finally realized he might be about to die and owned up to Mum. She promptly turned the car around and headed straight for the hospital emergency room. The surgeons didn't think Dad would last the night. His arteries were 95% occluded. But Dad was nothing if not a tough old rooster and after a quadruple bypass he lived for another thirteen years before dying instantly in the middle of yet another electronic project.

For those last thirteen years I had the best Dad the world has ever known. I really mean that. He was just marvelous. From the moment Dad recovered he was a different person. Full of smiles, always looking on the bright side of life and happy for every single minute he was alive. He acquired an impish, almost mischievous demeanor as you can see in the photo of him standing beside the sign saying, 'Authentic Fossil' (he thought it was a perfect description of himself and laughed like a child as he ran up beside it). He was fun to be around. In the last two pictures of Dad you can see he's smiling – he did a lot of that after his heart attack. But if you look back at the earlier pictures, there wasn't a smile to be seen.

I've long since realized my first Dad *always* did his very best to help me have a great life. He may have got it all wrong, but he honestly, honestly always meant well. He was simply a product of his own unfortunate upbringing.

I miss you Dad – like the mountains in Central Otago – you were truly 'remarkable'.

I've realized a few other things as well. Those childhood experiences helped make me the successful person I am today. I wouldn't have been able to achieve one-fifth of the things I've accomplished in my life without them. As I stood beside the Clutha River a few weeks ago, I looked back and could honestly say I was thankful for each and every experience in my life. Even my greatest failures, hurts and disasters have somehow – against all the odds – turned out to be a blessing. I never imagined that would be possible. I've also learned how unbelievably powerful our emotions are. Unless we align them correctly they can destroy our happiness.

As I stood there outside Grandpa's cottage 43 years later, a smile spread across my face, and I realized, *I needn't have been hollow inside for so long; life has worked out okay after all these years …*

THE END

FORTHCOMING *WINNER'S BIBLE* BOOKS

THE *WINNER'S BIBLE* FOR SOCIETY

Why 'Society' Is Important For Winners

One of the most important things that determine the quality of your life is the society you live in. No matter how good your Winning Mind is, if you live in Darfur, then on average you will have less opportunity of leading a fulfilling life than someone born in Norway. In other words, it's hard to be a Winner in a losing society.

What is key to the success of any society is how it is structured and organized. When we look back over history, we are graphically reminded how true this statement is. Civilizations like the Roman Empire were able to flourish because of the superiority of their structure. East and West Germany provides a more contemporary example.

It's hard to be a winner in a losing society.

Our Sub-Optimal Society

The Winner's Bible For Society will show that how we currently organize and run our societies is simply no longer suitable for modern life. No amount of adding more rules or tinkering with the existing rules can possibly give us the optimal result. We need a radical overhaul.

We can illustrate this need for change by considering how aircraft have developed over the last 100 years. When the Wright brothers flew the first plane in history, their engine could only produce twelve horsepower. This measly output meant they needed to have very light wings with a large surface area to provide sufficient lift at the plane's 30 km/h top speed. Light canvas fabric wrapped over slender beech wood frames was the perfect solution. But this design and construction would have been totally hopeless if the Wright brothers had strapped a modern 75,000 horsepower F-16 jet engine onto the frame. If they'd done that, the wings would have been torn clean off the fuselage as soon as they'd opened up the throttle and reached any significant speed. What was perfect for 30 km/h clearly wasn't going to work at 1,300 km/h. And the exact opposite situation is also true. If you put the Wright brothers' engine in a modern aluminum aircraft frame, it would never take off because the aluminum fuselage is too heavy and the wings are far too small for the power of the craft. So the wings and the engine need to be perfectly matched.

The Winner's Bible For Society analyzes our society from a completely new perspective. When we do this, we not only see why society *has* been so incredibly successful up until now, but we also discover how and why we've recently outgrown the structures which are holding our society together. As a result of using old-fashioned systems, we're all leading sub-optimal lives. We're all working harder and having less fun, peace, prosperity and happiness than we should.

> How we currently organize and run our societies is simply no longer suitable for modern life.

It is time to upgrade society's 'engine' and bring it into the 21st Century. *The Winner's Bible For Society* provides a comprehensive and completely fresh approach to realistically re-engineering society for the benefit of everyone. It is written in the same clear and engaging style as the original *Winner's Bible* and contains numerous stories to illustrate each point.

THE WINNER'S BIBLE
OF PHILOSOPHY

The Ant And The Ferrari

Imagine a close up shot of an ant walking on a shiny, red surface. You see the ant's antennae waving around, sensing its environment and its compound eyes looking for food and threats. You notice its legs struggling for grip because the surface on which it walks is so highly polished.

Now allow your mind to slowly zoom out so the ant becomes smaller and smaller, until it is just a spec on an endless flat plane of incandescent red. On this scale there is nothing for the ant to see but a shiny emptiness stretching out like a desert without end. The ant has become insignificant. As you let your field of view widen even further, you see that the shiny flat surface on which the ant walks actually starts to curve and that the curve forms a shape you recognize. It is the bonnet of a Ferrari.

This image reminds us that there are many things the ant will never understand, no matter how hard it tries. Its view of the world is so limited that it has no idea of what lies beneath the bonnet or that there is even a world beneath the bonnet. Its senses simply aren't powerful enough to see the overall picture. But even if we could somehow show the ant the complex electronics and hydraulics beneath the bonnet, it would never understand how they work and interact because its brain is just too small.

It's obvious from our bigger and smarter viewpoint that the ant only comprehends a tiny fraction of the Universe and how it works. But are our brains equally limited? Maybe we'll never know more than 1% of how the Universe works, no matter how much science we do, because our brains are also too small. After all, it would be more than a coincidence if our brains were exactly the right size to understand everything when every other animal knows less than 1% of what is going on. *Maybe we are also just like ants crawling across the bonnet of the Universe, blissfully unaware of how the vast majority of it really works?*

Seeing ourselves from this viewpoint raises many questions:
- Do we have any real hope of knowing anything for certain or is our so-called 'knowledge' just a vain mirage, a faint reflection of the real world?
- Is there even any such thing as 'truth' at all?
- Is 'truth' just a relative term?
- Do we have an Optimal Future or is life just a random series of events that we must deal with as best we can?
- What is the meaning of life?
- Can we ever know for sure?

These are vital questions because they concern the rules under which we all live and, ultimately, all die. They aren't just academic questions; they are the most important questions you will ever face in your life because if you don't know the rules by which the 'Game of Life' is played, then you are as doomed as that gambler who sits down at the poker table without first learning the rules of that game. Any gambler that foolish will always lose everything he has, no matter how many chips he starts with, no matter how hard he tries and no matter how clever he is. It is the same with your life. And it's no good trying to ignore these questions or paper over them by being so busy you don't have to think about them. Hoping it will all just somehow work out for the best simply means you are living according to a random set of rules that you haven't chosen or understood. You're gambling without learning the game.

The Winner's Bible Of Philosophy is about discovering the rules that the Universe actually runs on. It is about what we can know and what we can't know. It is about truth and the limits of truth. This process of finding truth, despite our ant–like limitations, is called philosophy. You'll discover it turns out to be far more exciting and more unexpected than you could *ever* have imagined in a million years.

'Doing Philosophy' reminds me of that great wood carving by Camille Flammarion, which shows a peasant farmer lying in a country field. Somehow the peasant has managed to poke his head out behind the superficial fabric of everyday life and see all the hidden 'cogs and wheels' which drive the Universe.

The Winner's Bible Of Philosophy will give your life a richness and complexity that it never had before. Life will suddenly gain an extra spicy edge, laced with even more purpose and meaning.

The Winner's Bible Of Philosophy is also written in the same clear and engaging style as the original *Winner's Bible* and contains numerous stories to illustrate each point.

THE WINNER'S BIBLE FOR ELITE SPORT

The Mystery Of Missing World Champions

You might think world champions are those people who were lucky enough to be born with the greatest natural talent. But if you think this, you're completely wrong! The facts tell us a completely different story. A story that dispels a number of myths and reveals how champions are actually *made*.

We can get a good idea of how important natural talent is by looking back over the last sixty years of Wimbledon tennis. Wimbledon is an excellent place to look because each year it has championships for men, women, boys and girls. The Wimbledon Boys and Girls Championships are for the world's best players under sixteen years of age. What is really noteworthy is that only four Wimbledon Boys Champions in the last sixty years have ever gone on to win the Men's title in their career (Federer, Borg, Edberg, Cash) and only three Girls Champions have developed into Women's Champions (Mauresmo, Hingis, Haydon). This is an important statistic because you'd think if you were good enough to be the best in the world at sixteen, then you'd have enough talent to go on and win Wimbledon at some later stage. But the facts speak for themselves. Very few actually do. What is even more surprising is how many Boys and Girls World Champions ended up going absolutely nowhere at all. Not only didn't they win Wimbledon, but they didn't even go on to have a mediocre professional career. Champions at sixteen only to fade and ultimately produce nothing of significance. If you take a look over the list of Boys and Girls Champions, you'll probably see a lot of names you've never heard before.

This phenomenon isn't restricted to tennis. The list of World Karting Champions – which is traditionally seen as the breeding ground for Formula 1 – tells a similar story. Two or three well-known names alongside a long list of people that no one has ever heard of.

Clearly some talented youngsters like Federer and Mauresmo or Ayrton Senna do go on to win the ultimate prize, but early form and natural talent isn't enough. Conversely, if you look at those who do become world champions in any sport, you might be surprised to find how many of them struggled early on in their careers. The young Martina Navratilova was slow, overweight and lacking in technique when she first came to America. But she went on to be the greatest ever Wimbledon Champion, winning nine singles events, seven doubles and four mixed doubles titles. The same story is repeated in business and even academia — a place where you'd think natural brains would supercede absolutely everything. But history tells us Einstein displayed such poor academic ability when he was young that all his teachers thought *he shouldn't even be allowed to enter university*. No one expected him to pass his exams, let alone become the greatest scientist the world has ever known.

So what's going on? What is it that makes world champions? In this book, I will take you far beyond the usual approach used by sports psychologists or performance consultants. In *The Winner's Bible For Elite Sport*, I'll reveal the revolutionary techniques I use so successfully to take even the world's best performers up another notch. These are techniques that, until now, only the top professionals could afford to pay for.

Every step of the journey is illustrated with real life examples and memorable stories.

Visit www.winnersbible.com and subscribe to our newsletter to receive regular updates and notification of new title releases.

PERSONAL WINNER'S BIBLE

On www.winnersbible.com you will find a document template with the most common sections for your *Personal Winner's Bible*.

Below is a list of the main headings:
- You.Inc
- Photos of Family/Friends
- Photos of Material Goals
- My Career Goals
- My Personal Development Goals
- My Heroes and Mentors
- My Strengths and Weaknesses
- An Unshakeable Belief in Myself
- Carpe Diem
- My Wheel of Life
- My Happy Section
- My Intrinsic Drivers
- Poems

TESTIMONIALS

'Well done on writing the best ever book on how to become a Winner! The whole time you kept me spellbound with all the interesting stories and fascinating explanations. I couldn't put the book down. I read it like a mystery novel unlocking all the secrets of my own universe. I came back to it time and again as I worked on improving myself.

As a result of reading your book I am now the 'souped up Ferg', while still retaining the older classic chassis. Unlike other books, you don't just tell us what Winners should do – you first show us what goes on inside our brain and then how we can supercharge it to become who and what we want to be.'

Ian Ferguson
Winner of four Olympic Gold Medals, Hall of Fame, Sportsman of the Year

'I wish Kerry Spackman had produced *The Winner's Bible*™ before I started to compete in world championships ... and only gave it to me!! With that sort of extra help I reckon I could have won a few more world titles. Everybody is looking for the winning edge, whether in sport, business or any other walk of life. That is how it has always been. But more emphasis has been placed on this type of preparation and organization in recent years.

Take it from a multi-world champion – every parent should buy *The Winner's Bible*™, study it carefully and then give it to their children if they want them to be successful and happy. It may well be the best thing they ever do for their kids. *The Winner's Bible*™ certainly will be a huge part of my worldwide training schools in the future. I found it compulsive reading; when I picked up the book I could not put it down until I read it from cover to cover'

Ivan Mauger OBE MBE
Fifteen times World Motorcycle Champion, Twice Sportsman of the Year, Hall of Fame

Winning is more than beating one's gremlins and the opponent, just as coaching is more than an expert telling someone what to do and not to do. In *The Winner's Bible*™, Dr Kerry Spackman walks us through the neuroscience of both in a clear and accessible way that is well illustrated both visually and by many examples, and through his own very personal experiences. The book is inspirational, fascinating and informative, and I believe will create far more Winners in the broadest sense of the term in these times of opportunity, and uncertainty. And this is only the first of several volumes ... I can't wait.

Sir John Whitmore
Author of Coaching for Performance *– the International Best-seller in seventeen languages, Winner of the President's Award, 'Number 1 Business Coach' – The Independent Newspaper, Champion Race Driver, Founder and Executive Chairman of Performance Consultants*

'*The Winner's Bible*™ fills the void between the theoretical and the applied. It empowers and equips its readers not only with the secrets to success, but the processes as well. The information is powerful, it's accessible and, if you commit to the concepts Dr Spackman espouses, you will become a Winner.'

Hugh McCutcheon MS, MBA
2008 United States Olympic Committee – Coach of the Year, Head Coach USA Women's Volleyball Team, Former Head Coach USA Men's Volleyball Team, 2008 Olympic Champions, 2008 World League Champions